MW01120384

Iraq's Modern Arabic Literature

A Guide to English Translations since 1950

Salih J. Altoma

THE SCARECROW PRESS, INC.
Lanham • Toronto • Plymouth, UK
2010

Published by Scarecrow Press, Inc.
A wholly owned subsidiary of The Rowman & Littlefield Publishing Group, Inc.
4501 Forbes Boulevard, Suite 200, Lanham, Maryland 20706
http://www.scarecrowpress.com

Estover Road, Plymouth PL6 7PY, United Kingdom

British Library Cataloguing in Publication Information Available

Library of Congress Cataloging-in-Publication Data

Altoma, Salih J.
  Iraq's modern Arabic literature : a guide to English translations since 1950 /
Salih J. Altoma.
    p. cm.
  Includes bibliographical references and index.
  ISBN 978-0-8108-7705-4 (cloth : alk. paper) — ISBN 978-0-8108-7706-1
(ebook)
  1. Arabic literature—Iraq—Translations into English—Bibliography. 2. Arabic
literature—20th century—Translations into English—Bibliography. 3. Arabic
literature—Iraq—History and criticism—Bibliography. 4. Arabic literature—20th
century—History and criticism—Bibliography. 5. Authors, Arab—Iraq—Bio-
bibliography. I. Title.
  Z3014.L56.A46 2010
  [PJ8043.5.E5]
  892.7'0995670904—dc22
                                                                      2010010840

∞™ The paper used in this publication meets the minimum requirements of
American National Standard for Information Sciences—Permanence of Paper for
Printed Library Materials, ANSI/NISO Z39.48-1992.

Printed in the United States of America

To all Iraqi poets, writers and artists
who seek
Iraq's rebirth
A nation united in peace
A homeland sovereign, indivisible, and free from the blight
of tyranny, occupation,
sectarianism, ethnic fanaticism, and tribal loyalties.
SJA

Iraq, as was known, will never come back
And the larks will never sing
So go on – if you wish – for a long time
Beseech – if you wish – all the angels
All the demons of this universe
Beseech the bulls of Assyria,
A soaring Phoenix,
Beseech them all
And, through the smoke of nightmares,
Wait for the censer's miracle
From "Vision" by the Iraqi poet

—Sa'di Yusuf

. . . I have come to belong to a "movable" Iraqi homeland consisting of friends, values, memories, books, recordings, e-mail addresses, and scents.

—Inaam Kachachi, Iraqi woman novelist,
author of *If I Forget You, Baghdad.*

. . . a thorough reading of the contributions to this issue may well allow us to conclude that Iraqi society, in all its fabled diversity, is far more durable and resilient than is realized . . .

—Hala Fattah, noted Iraqi Historian

Contents

Contents

Acknowledgments

An earlier version of this book was published as an article in the *Journal of Arabic Literature* Volume 34, Issue 1 (2004): 88–138. I wish to thank Koninklijke Brill N.V. for granting me permission to incorporate the article in this revised and expanded work on Iraq's Arabic literature in English translation.

My thanks are due to the staff of the Interlibrary Loan Department of Indiana University Libraries who have never failed me in my efforts to consult innumerable sources not held by Indiana University Libraries and to both the reference librarians and Dr. Akram Khabibullaev, the Middle Eastern and Islamic Studies librarian, at Indiana University for their assistance and guidance, which they have extended to me in matters related to this work and other ongoing research projects.

To professor Nazif Shahrani, the chairman of the Department of Near Eastern Languages and Cultures, I wish to express my appreciation for his support and keen interest in my work over the years. I am indebted to Reef Altoma-Larsson, Rebecca Dyer, Hatif Janabi, David Keppel, and Breon Mitchell for reading parts of the work and offering helpful comments or information.

Thanks are due to Elijah Reynolds for his technical help in preparing the final version of the bibliography. I am most grateful to Martin Dillon, the senior consulting acquisition editor at Scarecrow Press, for his positive interest in this guide, his thorough review of the manuscript, and the constructive suggestions he has made.

Last but not least my gratitude goes to my wife Amal who has always understood and tolerated my seemingly excessive or sole preoccupation in recent years with Iraq's literature. None but I assume responsibility for any shortcoming in this endeavor.

Transliteration

Spellings as they appear in the original publications have often been followed with minor modifications in selected names (e.g., Sadiq Assaieg > Sadiq al-Sayigh; Saadi Youssef, Saadi Yousef, Sa'di Yousuf > Sa'di Yusuf; or al-Tikerli, Tekerli > Takarli). All names are listed in alphabetical order under different sections of the book including names that begin with the article /al/ (e.g., al-Haydari, Buland > Haydari, Buland al-). No diacriticals have been used to represent certain Arabic consonants or long vowels (e.g., Arabic names such as Sāmī Mahdī and Ṣalāḥ Niyāzī are listed as Sami Mahdi and Salah Niyazi, without their diacritical marks).

Introduction

Iraq's seemingly endless tragic ordeal has dominated the news in recent years particularly following the 2003 American invasion. This is not surprising given the fact that Iraq for many years has been the victim of a most vicious tyranny, senseless wars (Iraq–Iran, 1980–1988; Iraq–Kuwait, 1990; the 1991 Gulf War; and the latest American invasion of 2003), and indiscriminate economic sanctions lasting for more than thirteen years. It is therefore natural for Iraq to become an inexhaustible source of multifarious studies both academic and nonacademic focusing most often on war-related issues: violence, religious or ethnic conflicts, oil, depleted uranium, and other topics, which are undoubtedly significant. Furthermore, Iraq has served and will likely continue to serve as a subject for an increasing number of American literary works in poetry, fiction, drama, and other genres. What seems absent, however, or marginally represented are Iraq's humanistic contributions to Arabic literature and arts since the 1950s in spite of the fact that Iraqi writers, poets, novelists, and others have persisted in their creative efforts in recent years—even under the harsh conditions within Iraq or in their respective diasporas in Arab and Western countries. As is widely known, hundreds if not thousands of Iraqi writers, artists, and other intellectuals have been uprooted and are now living in exile in various Western countries, such as Australia, Britain, Canada, Denmark, France, Germany, Italy, Netherlands, New Zealand, Norway, Poland, Russia, Spain, Sweden, and the United States.

It is with the nearly invisible status of Iraq's modern literature in mind that this bibliography has been prepared as a guide to the growing corpus of Iraqi literature published in English translations since the

1950s. The bibliography lists translations that appeared as books or in other print and non-print publications in various Arab- and English-speaking countries: Australia, Canada, New Zealand, the United Kingdom, and the United States. It seeks also to identify relevant studies and other secondary sources including selected reviews that cover Iraqi literature and writers. A special effort has been made to represent the perspectives of writers who are not Arabists or specialists in the field of Arabic literature to indicate the growing interest in Iraqi literature among general readers.

As noted earlier, the bibliography's scope is limited to Iraq's Arabic literature. Iraqi literature written in other languages, such as Kurdish, Turkmen, Hebrew, and others is not included in this survey.

Iraqi Jewish writers who were noted for their literary efforts during the pre-1950 period are cited only if their translated works were originally written in Arabic and published before their departure from Iraq (e.g., Ya'qub Balbul and Anwar Sha'ul). Their writings are often recognized as an integral part of Iraq's Arabic literature. The 1988 anthology of *Iraqi Short Stories*,[1] a government-sponsored publication, refers, for example, to "the sincere earnest efforts made by writers of that period [the 1930s], namely Mahmoud Ahmed Al-Sayyid, Anwar Sha'ul, Dhu-Noun Ayyoub, Abdul-Haq Fadhil, Yousif Matti, Shalmon [Shalom] Darweesh and others." (p. 10). In addition, recent anthologies of Iraqi poetry and fiction in English translation have also included selected works by Iraqi Jewish writers, such as Ronny Someck,[2] Samir Naqqash, and Shmuel Moreh.[3] Additionally, Iraqi Jewish writings and contributions to Arabic literature have received wider attention in a growing corpus of literary studies, especially since 2003.[4]

Other works written by Iraqi writers in Western languages (English, French, German, Swedish, and others) or their translations into English were also excluded with a few exceptions. Such works undoubtedly deserve to be covered in a separate study as an extension of Iraqi literature, not only because of their literary quality or their focus on Iraqi concerns, but also because of their relevance to the broad theme of exile and more specifically to the experience of Iraqi communities or refugees living in different Western diasporas.[5]

As the various parts of the bibliography suggest, both English literary translations and critical studies have focused on the significant contribution that Iraqi poets have made, especially since the 1950s, to contemporary Arabic poetry. This is particularly evident in the numerous entries covering poets such as Badr Shakir al-Sayyab (1926–1964), Nazik al-Mala'ikah (1923–2007), 'Abd al-Wahhab al-Bayati (1926–1999), Buland al-Haydari (1926–1996), Sa'di Yusuf (b.1934), Lami'ah Abbas Amarah (1929–), Fadhil al-Azzawi (1940–), Sargon Boulus (1944–2007), and Yusuf al-Sayigh (1930–2005). Additional relevant entries can be found in the first section under Selected Studies (e.g., Abbas 2003; Altoma 1997, 1999; Azouqa 1999, 2001, 2008; Boullata 1970, 1971; Chalala 2005; DeYoung 1998; Huri 2006; Rosenthal 1997, 2000; Smoor 1990).

On the other hand, traditional or neo-classical poets who are noted for their contributions specifically during the first half of the 20th century are either overlooked or marginally represented in both translations and studies. Note for example the entries under Muhammad Mahdi al-Basir (1895–1974), Muhammad Mahdi al-Jawahiri (1899?–1997), Ahmad al-Safi al-Najafi (1897–1977), Ma'ruf al-Rusafi (1875–1945), Muhammad Rida al-Shabibi (1889–1965), and Jamil Sidqi al-Zahawi (1863–1936). They are represented by only a few fragments of their rich poetic legacy just as they are treated in a small number of entries under the first section of this bibliography (examples: Badawi 1975, 1993; Hamarneh 1972–1973; Jubran 1992–1994; Khoury 2001, 2002; Khulusi 1949; 50, 1977; Masliyah 1976, 1996; Musawi 2006; Tramontini 2002–2003). There is no doubt that the current literary taste, in targeted Western languages, is not receptive to such traditional poetry for a number of reasons, including its topical orientation and reliance on rhetorical devices and allusions or usages spanning more than fourteen hundred years of Arabic poetry. It is relevant to cite here comments made by Denys Johnson-Davies with regard to the translation of pre-1950s poets. In reviewing Salma Jayyusi's *Modern Arabic Poetry*, Johnson-Davies questioned the wisdom and rationale for including in her anthology such historically important poets as Shawqi and Hafiz Ibrahim. He seems to suggest that such poets are not "capable of being read with pleasure in translation" largely because of their reliance on rhetoric. Quoting Jayyusi's own words, he adds that such poetry "loses much of its heat and punch when denuded of its rhetoric in translation."[6]

Three other observations should be made with reference to the translated corpus of Iraqi poetry.

First, many of the poems published in the last three decades revolve in one or another respect around exile, resistance to the former Iraqi regime and war-related themes. The latter reflect a pronounced opposition shared by poets of different orientations to the 1991 Gulf War and the 2003 American invasion and occupation of Iraq. As was noted earlier (Altoma 1997) such an opposition is not limited to state-sponsored or pro-Saddam Hussein poets or extremist groups hostile to the United States; it is featured as well in the poetry or fiction of other writers opposed to the former Baathist regime. Note, for example, Abd al-Razzaq Abd al-Wahid, Bushra al-Bustani, Sami Mahdi, and Hamid Sa'id, who can be viewed as sympathetic to the former regime in contrast to other writers and poets in exile, such as Lami'ah Abbas Amarah, Sinan Antoon, Fadhil al-Azzawi, Sargon Boulus, Jamal Juma, Dunya Mikhail, Salah Niyazi, and Sa'di Yusuf. Perhaps it would be useful to illustrate this shared opposition to the American action in Iraq by referring to three poems: "Andalusian Songs for the Wounds of Iraq" by al-Bustani, an Arab nationalist; "Mr. America" by Sargon Boulus, an apolitical Assyrian poet, both were written in response to the 2003 American invasion; and "America America" by Sa'di Yusuf, known for his anti-Baathist orientation.[7]

Works of fiction or drama dealing with the latest war were, as expected, slow in emerging and began to appear first, according to the Iraqi novelist Shakir al-Anbari, in the daily newspapers (Muhanna). Thus, only a few works of fiction are listed in the bibliography, two of which are written by Iraqi women living in exile, Iqbal Qazwini (Germany) and Haifa Zangana (United Kingdom). Both writers stand out for their unreserved opposition to the war in spite of their anti-Baath orientation. There are other works of fiction (short stories and novels) published in Arabic including two by women writers. The first, published in Damascus 2008, is a collection of short stories by Kulshan al-Bayati entitled *hadhayan al-ihtilal* (Ravings under the Occupation). According to L. L. Wynn's translation of the book's back cover "*Ravings Under Occupation* is a literary work that brings together a collection of people both aware and unaware. They rave under the effect of occupation: ravings of the Iraqi resistance fighter who fights the occupation to the teeth; ravings of the lowliest agent who despises himself; ravings of those who were murdered mistakenly; ravings of women mourning the loss of their children and husbands; ravings of a poet who lost his verse. . . ."[8] The second is a more recent novel (2009), *al-Hafidah al-amrikiyyah* (The American Grand-Daughter), by Inaam Kachachi, which narrates the experience of a fictional Iraqi–American girl torn between two powerful bonds while serving with the invading American army in Iraq.[9]

Second, the number of women poets, notable as it is, is still small. Only about twenty women poets are listed including Amarah (1929–), Bushra al-Bustani (1950–), Zuhur Dixon (1933–), Amal al-Jubouri (1965–), Atika al-Khazraji (1924–1996), Nazik al-Mala'ikah (1923–2007), Dunya Mikhail (1965–), and May Muzaffar (1940–). Other poets, such as Maqbulah al-Hilli (1929–1974), Hayat Jasim Muhammad (1936–), and Amal al-Zahawi (1946–), are missing. There is also a noticeable absence of separate anthologies or collections devoted to individual women poets, with the exception of Dunya Mikhail. This is particularly evident in the case of al-Mala'ikah, perhaps the most important Arab woman poet who is revered for her pioneering poetic and theoretical contributions. However, al-Mala'ikah's place in modern Arabic literature has been the focus of numerous studies, as indicated in the first section of the bibliography. Note, for example, Altoma 1997, Asfour 2000, Badawi 1975, Furaih 2005, Ghazoul 2002, Husni 2007, Melek 1999, Moreh 1968, Rejwan 1966, Steven 2007/2008, and Suleiman 1995, 2005.

Third, much, if not most, of the writings surveyed in this bibliography is the product of Iraqi writers (poets, novelists, playwrights, and other writers) who have been forced to live in exile as a result of the war or repressive and violent conditions that have marked Iraq's recent history, particularly during the last three decades. It will suffice in this context to cite only a few obvious factors: Saddam Husayn's tyrannical rule (1979–2003), the Iraq–Iran war (1980–1988), Iraq's invasion of Kuwait (1990), the first Gulf War (1991), the unprecedented embargo that lasted more than twelve years, the disastrous American invasion and occupation of Iraq (2003–) and its equally disastrous consequences including, among others, the plight of millions of Iraqi refugees.

What is profoundly remarkable about the wide and painful dispersion of Iraqi writers in Western countries is the fact that they (and poets in particular) have managed, against all odds and obstacles, to pursue their creative efforts with undiminished resourcefulness. In one way or another, they have managed to engender a climate favorable to their creative works, and drawn the attention of literary and artistic communities within their host countries, in a few cases, even receiving awards in recognition of their contributions. A quick review of entries under the names of selected poets and novelists will reveal the wide circulation of their translated works in journals, electronic media, in individual collections of their poetry, and in world literature anthologies.[10] Reference can be made in this context to Fadhil al-Azzawi (Germany), Sargon Boulus (USA/Germany), Basim Furat (New Zealand, Japan), Hatif Janabi (Poland), Jamal Juma (Denmark), Aliya Mamdouh (France), Dunya Mikhail (USA), and Buland al-Haydari, Salah Niyazi, Sa'di Yusuf, and Haifa Zangana, who lived or have been living in the United Kingdom[11].

In contrast to poetry's expected prominent representation, other genres (drama, the novel, and the short story) are still marginally represented in spite of the emergence of an increasing number of fiction writers and playwrights. The bibliography lists only a few plays by Yusuf al- 'Ani (b. 1927) and al-Asadi's two short plays *Forget Hamlet/Insu Hamlit* (2006) and *Baghdadi Bath* (2008) and several articles that deal with or refer to Iraqi dramatists, e.g., Ghazoul (1998); Litvin (2007); Machut-Mendecka 1999, 2000); Moosa (1981); Rakha (1999) and Yousif (1997, 2007). It also includes about twelve novels mostly published in recent years (2003 and thereafter) by such writers as al-Azzawi, Khedairi, Khudayyir, Mamdouh, Iqbal Qazwini, al-Ramli, Shimon, and al-Takarli. There is an obvious gap in the representation of important novelists including Ali Badr (1964–), Gha'ib Tu'mah Farman (1927–1990), Shakir Khusbak (1930–) 'Abd al-Rahman al-Rubay'i (b.1930) Abd al-Khaliq al-Rikabi, and Mahdi Isa al-Saqr (1927–2006).

The short story has nevertheless received greater attention during the past few years with a steadily increasing number of translations published in journals as well as anthologies. Special reference should be made to Jayyusi's *Modern Arabic Fiction: An Anthology* (2005), which includes eighteen works by Iraqi authors representing different generations; Johnson-Davies's *The Anchor Book of Modern Arabic Fiction* (2006), which contains six short stories by Iraqi authors; and Shakir Mustafa's *Contemporary Iraqi Fiction: An Anthology* (2008) noted for its unique and pioneering attempt to present sixteen authors (men and women) from different ethnic and religious backgrounds. This is in addition to two earlier collections of short stories by Daisy al-Amir (1994) and Buthaynah al-Nasiri (2002). What is conspicuous is the absence of individual collections of short stories highlighting the achievement of other famed authors, such as Abd al-Malik Nuri, Mahdi Isa al-Saqr, Muhammad Khudayyir, and 'Abd al-Rahman al-Rubay'i.

The representation of women short-story writers and novelists is still limited to a small number, such as Daisy al-Amir, Lutfiyah al-Dulaymi, Betool Khedairi, Samira al-Mana, Aliya Mamdouh, Buthaynah al-Nasiri, Iqbal Qazwini, and Haifa Zangana. Others, including Maysalun Hadi, Hadiyyah Husayn, May Muzaffar, Suhaylah Dawud Salman, and Aliya Talib, have received scant attention or are unevenly represented. Salman (b.1937), noted for her prolific writings (at least four collections of short stories and two novels), is represented by only one story in an anthology published in Iraq in 1988. Aminah Haydar al-Sadr "Bint al-Huda," who was executed in 1980 because of her commitment to the Islamic Shi'ite movement in Iraq, has been largely ignored in the West. The only exception perhaps is Wiley's essay "Alima Bint al-Huda, Women's Advocate," which outlines briefly Bint al-Huda's use of fiction to advance her vision of Islamic life. According to Wiley "fearing that a strict academic approach would not attract enough readers and constrained by Iraq's authoritarian Baathist regimes (1963 and 1968–), she [Bint al-Huda] saw fiction as the way to make her message safe and appealing" (155). The same observation applies to other women writers who are not included such as Kulshan al-Bayati, Safirah Jamil Hafiz, Hayat Jasim Muhammad, and Duna Talib. Needless to say Iraqi women writers deserve a broader coverage or recognition in view of their historical role in Iraq's cultural and literary life since the early 1920s.[12] It is relevant to note in this context that the recently published guide *Arab Women Writers* (2008) identifies more than eighty women writers known to have published books in different genres: poetry, short stories, novels, plays, and memoirs. Other earlier sources cite more numerous women writers who contributed to fiction and poetry.[13]

Other general observations should be added with regard to the items listed in the bibliography.

First, the spellings used by most authors for their names are problematic in view of the fact that they do not adhere to the standard academic norm. Spellings as they appear in the original publications have often been followed with minor changes in selected names. There are, however, exceptions that require cross references in relation to multiple transliterations or spellings for leading authors for example, Saadi Youssef, Saadi Yousef, Sa'di Yousuf (=Sa'di Yusuf) or al-Tikerli, Tekerli (= Takarli). All names are listed without diacritical points. However, the transliterations by which Iraqi writers are known or which they have chosen continue to cause problems for a consistent bibliographical listing.

Second, an attempt was made to add biographical dates if they were found in reliable sources. The date is given in a parenthesis after the author's name: for example, Basir, Muhammad Mahdi (1895–1974); Mala'ikah, Nazik (1923–2007); Yusuf, Sa'di (1934–).

Third, a large number of items were chosen from Iraqi state-sponsored publications in English such as *Baghdad Observer, Iraq, New Iraq, Iraq Today, Ur, Gilgamesh*, and other publications. In view of recent events in Iraq's history, and the fact that many of such publications are not available or accessible, the present coverage should be viewed as a limited or preliminary representation. Iraqi initiatives in the area of literary translation merit a more comprehensive survey and critical assessment with regard to the purpose of such translation and the criteria followed in translating specific Iraqi writers. Reference should be made to several works that were published in Iraq during the Baathist regime, such as *Battlefront Short Stories, Iraqi Short Stories, Ten Iraqi Soldier Poets, Modern Iraqi Poetry*, and the collections of poems by Abd al-Razzaq Abd al-Wahid, Ja'far al-Allaq, Yasin Taha Hafiz, Sami Mahdi, and Hamid Sa'id.

Fourth, poetry, as stated earlier, understandably occupies a greater part of the bibliography. This preponderance is largely due not only to poetry's historical place in Iraq as the principal genre, but also to the fact that many Iraqi poets have been living in exile in European and other Western countries. As a result, Iraqi poetry's most recent phase, which has taken shape during the last two or three decades, assumes greater visibility in this bibliography. In other words, the bibliography should not be viewed as being representative of modern Iraqi poetry or Iraqi literature as a whole, whether in terms of the various stages, different schools, trends, or ideological currents relevant to the history and development of Iraq's modern Arabic literature.

Fifth, the bibliography indicates that native speakers of Arabic still exercise a dominant role as translators. But it also indicates that an increasing number of native speakers of English have become actively involved in translating Iraqi literature in recent years. Whether working independently, or in collaboration with Arabic-speaking partners, translators such as Catherine Cobham, Tony Curtis, Desmond O' Grady, Denys Johnson-Davies, Christopher Middleton, William M. Hutchins, and Peter Theroux, to cite a few, have contributed toward ensuring a wider circulation and reception of Iraqi literature and of Arabic literature more generally. The bibliography, in addition, reflects the significant role of the London-based journal *Banipal* in promoting the translation of Iraqi literature. *Banipal* was founded in 1998 by Margaret Obank and Samuel Shimon as "Magazine of Modern Arab Literature." Since then, it has proven to be more effective, than any other American or British journal, in translating a large number of Arab writers from various Arab countries.[14] As far as Iraqi writers are concerned, a cursory review of the bibliography will reveal scores of entries covering their works that represent different genres and diverse orientations or trends, though they focus primarily on the post-1950 generation of Iraqi writers.[15] Three other journals that have also published a considerable number of relevant writings and translations are *Al-Jadid*, a quarterly review of Arab Culture and Arts, Los Angeles; the *Journal of Arabic Literature*, Leiden, Netherlands; and *Edebiyât*. The latter was first published by the University of Pennsylvania's Middle East Center and in 2004 it merged with the journal *Middle Eastern Literatures*.

Finally, the bibliography itself surveys in two parts translations and relevant studies published, as indicated earlier, during the last sixty years (1950–2008).

The first part is devoted to studies, author interviews, book reviews, and other writings that cover a wide range of social and political themes, literary trends or movements, the impact of recent wars, scores of leading poets, novelists, and playwrights, and the current state of Iraqi literature in Western exile. Although all items are listed with full bibliographical information, an attempt was made to provide in many instances brief annotations within brackets at the end of their entries. Note, for example, the following items:

Allen, Roger. *Modern Arabic Literature*. New York: Ungar 1987 [Includes translations of Arabic reviews dealing with Yusuf al-Ani (42–45); Dhu al-Nun Ayyub (65–68); Abd al-Wahhab al-Bayati (78–84) . . .].

Juma, Jamal. "Best of Times, Worst of Times." *Times Online* May 6, 2007. [Juma's note regarding his poem "A Handshake in the Dark," which Michael Nyman, the British composer, used for his choral piece under the same title. . . ."].

Khulusi, Safa. "Contemporary Poetesses of Iraq." *The Islamic Review* (June 1950): 40–45. [Covers briefly Rabab al-Kazimi, Umm Nizar al-Mala'ika (Nazik's mother) and Nazik al-Mala'ika, Fatina al-Na'ib, and Lami'a Abbas Amarah].

It is important to remember that this section was prepared not with the intention of representing solely academic or scholarly studies, but also for the purpose of providing a broad historical record of writings relevant to modern Iraqi literature as published by numerous authors of different nationalities as well as in many Arab, American, European, and other international sources.

The second part covers English translations of different genres of Iraqi literature under four headings: Autobiographical Essays, Drama, Fiction, and Poetry.

As stated earlier, poetry occupies the largest space in view of its historical dominance as the primary genre in Iraq in modern and pre-modern periods. The items listed under both "fiction" and "poetry" are divided into two categories: one covers books (novels, short story collections, poetry anthologies) and the second lists mostly items published in journals and other sources. This broad coverage is reflected also to a large extent in the numerous publications listed under Abbreviations.

The guide concludes with two appendixes:

Appendix 1. Iraqi Writers and Poets in Western Countries.
Appendix 2. Iraqi Women Writers Represented in the Bibliography.

NOTES

1. *Iraqi Short Stories: An Anthology*. Ed. Yassen Taha Hafidh and Lutfiyah al-Dulaymi. Baghdad: Dar al-Ma'mun for Translation, 1988.

2. *Iraqi Poetry Today*. Ed. Saadi Simawe [No. 19 Modern Poetry in Translation]. London: King's College, 2003. 233–236.

3. Shakir Mustafa, ed. and trans. *Contemporary Iraqi Fiction*. Syracuse, NY: Syracuse University Press, 2008.

4. For a discussion of the place of Iraqi Jewish writers in modern Arabic literature see the bibliography under the following names: Ammiel Alca-

lay(1996), Orit Bashkin (2006), Nancy E. Berg (1996, 2005), Lital Levy (2003, 2006, 2008), Emile Marmorstein (1959, 1964), Sami Michael (1984), Shmuel Moreh (1981), Mikhlif Hamad Mudhi (1988), Nissim Rejwan (2004), Tova Murad Sadka (2008), Ella Shohat (2005), Reuven Snir for his informative articles written and published between 1991 and 2007, and Sasson Somekh (1989, 2007, 2008).

5. Reference should be made in this context to two widely read works written in English: *Baghdad Diaries* by Nuha al-Radi, an outstanding artist, (1941–2004) and *Baghdad Burning* by "Riverbend" a pseudonym for a young woman writer. Both stand out (and they are cited) as works of urbicide in view of their first hand and detailed account of the massive urban destruction wrought on Baghdad during the 1991 Gulf War and the 2003 war. Note Eduardo Mendieta's reference to al-Radi's work in "The Literature of Urbicide: Friedrich, Nossack, Sebald, and Vonnegut." *Theory and Event* 10.2 (2007):n.pag.

6. See Johnson-Davies's review published in *Third World Quarterly* 10 (1988): 1372–1374.

7. "America America" is one of the widely discussed poems in the United States. See volume 29 of *Poetry for Students* (Detroit: Gale, 2009): 1–21. For a recent concise article on the Iraqis' anti-American views, see Ibrahim al-Marashi and Abdul Hadi al-Khalili "Iraqis' Bleak Views of the United States." *What They Think of Us.* Ed. David Farber. Princeton: Princeton University Press, 2007. 1–26.

8. Wynn, L. L. "Iraqi Resistance Literature." *Khaldoun.* http://khaldoun. wordpress.com/2008/09/12/iraqi-resistance-literature/.

9. See Inaam Kachachi. "The American Granddaughter." Interview, by Antoine Jouki. *The National*, UAE. 16 March 2009. http://www.thenational .ae/article/20090316/ART/.../1093. The novel is scheduled to appear in French in September 2009 under the title *Si je t'oublie Bagdad* (If I Forget You, Baghdad). For excerpts of this novel in English translation, see under Fiction section Kachachi's entry.

10. Among such anthologies are *The Actor's Book of Monologues for Women from Non-Dramatic Sources*. Ed. Stefan Rudnicki. New York: Penguin Books, 1991; *The Art of Growing Older: Writers on Living and Aging*. Ed. Wayne Boothe. Chicago: University of Chicago Press, 1992; *Global Voices: Contemporary Literature from the Non-Western World*. Ed. Arthur W. Biddle et al. Englewood Cliffs, NJ: Prentice Hall, 1995; *Poems for the Millennium*. Ed. Jerome Rothenberg and Pierre Joris. Berkeley: University of California Press, 1998; *Divine Inspiration: The Life of Jesus in World Poetry*. Ed. Robert Atwan et al. New York: Oxford University Press, 1998; *Surrealist Women: An International Anthology*. Ed. Penelope Rosement. Austin: University of Texas Press, 1998; *Poets against the War*. Ed. Sam Hamill. New York: Thunder's Mouth Press/Nation Books, 2003; *Women on War: An International Anthology of Writings from Antiquity to the Present*. Ed. Daniela Gioseffi. New York: The Feminist Press at the

City University of New York, 2003; *World Words: An Anthology of International Writers in New Zealand*. Ed. T. M. Schaeffer. Wellington, NZ: Writers International, 2006; *Literature from the "Axis of Evil": Writings from Iran, Iraq, North Korea, and Other Enemy Nations*. Ed. editors of *Words without Borders*. New York: The New Press, 2006 and *Birthed from Scorched Hearts: Women Respond to War*. Ed. Marijo Moore. Golden, CO: Fulcrum Publishing, 2008.

11. For more information on the dispersion of Iraqi writers in Western countries see appendix 1.

12. For some of the references regarding the early phase of Iraqi women's literary activities see Ferial Ghazoul's essay "Iraq." *Arab Women Writers: A Critical Reference Guide 1873–1999*. Ed. Radwa Ashour, Ferial Ghazoul, and Hasna Reda-Mekdashi. Trans. Mandy McClure. Cairo: The American University in Cairo Press, 2008. 178–203. Note, for example, her reference to the fact that "more than twenty women recited their poetry during the 1920 uprising against the English occupation." (180).

13. See for instance Nazik al-Aʻraji "Qissat al-katibah al-ʻiraqiyyah." *al-Adab* 42. 11–12 (Nov.–Dec. 1994): 74–85, which identifies more than forty women fiction writers who published their works between 1937 and 1989; Jawad Abd al-Kazim Muhsin. *Muʻjam al-adibat wa al-kawatib al-ʻiraqiyyat fi al asr al-hadith*. Vol. I. Hillah, Iraq: Maktabat al-Sadiq, 2004.

14. See *Banipal*'s Global Index. http://www.banipal.co.uk/contributors/issueIndex.php.

15. For more detail, see the author's review essay "Translating Iraq's Contemporary Arabic Literature: Ten Years of *Banipal*'s Record 1998–2008" *International Journal of Contemporary Iraqi Studies* 3.3 (2009): 307–19.

Abbreviations

A	Arberry, A. J. *Arabic Poetry: A Primer for Students*. Cambridge: Cambridge University Press, 1965.
AB	*The Anchor Book of Modern Arabic Fiction*. Ed. Denys Johnson-Davies. New York: Anchor Books, 2006 [Includes stories by six Iraqi authors: Daisy al-Amir, Betool Khedairi, Muhammad Khudayyir, Alia Mamdouh, Buthaynah al-Nasiri, Fu'ad al-Takarli].
AGH	Accad, Evelyne, and Rose Ghurayyib. *Contemporary Arab Women Writers and Poets*. Beirut: Beirut University College, Institute for Arab Women's Studies in the Arab World, 1985.
AK	Khouri, Mounah A., and Hamid Algar, trans. *An Anthology of Modern Arabic Poetry*. Berkeley and Los Angeles: University of California Press, 1974.
AM	Arberry, Arthur J., trans. *Modern Arabic Poetry: An Anthology with English Verse Translations*. London: Taylor's Foreign Press, 1950.
AP	*Arab Perspectives*. Washington, DC.
API	Lu'lu'ah, Abdul-Wahid. Introduction. *Arabic Poetry in Iraq*. Trans. Lulua. Kuwait: The Foundation of Abddulaziz Saud al-Babtain's Prize for Poetic Creativity, 2004. [Bilingual. Includes selected poems of thirty Iraqi poets born between 1863 and 1954].
AW	*The Arab World*. New York, NY.
AWW	*When the Words Burn: An Anthology of Modern Arabic Poetry 1945–1987*. Trans. and ed. John Mikhail Asfour. Dunvegan, Ontario: Cormorant Books, 1988.

BA   *Books Abroad.* Norman, Oklahoma: University of Oklahoma
BHM   Ben Bennani, trans. *Bread, Hashish and Moon: Four Mod-*
          ern Arab Poets. Greensboro: Unicorn Press, 1982.
BI   *Blood into Ink: South Asian and Middle Eastern Women*
          Write War. Eds. Miriam Cooke and Roshni Rustomji-Kerns.
          Boulder: Westview Press, 1994.
BM   Boullata, Issa J., trans. *Modern Arab Poets: 1950–1975.*
          Washington, DC: Three Continents Press, 1976.
BO   *Baghdad Observer.* Baghdad, Iraq.
BR   *The Bend in the Road: Refugees Writing.* Ed. Jennifer
          Langer. Nottingham, UK: Five Leaves, 1997.
BS   *Battlefront Stories from Iraq.* Trans. A. W. Lu'lu'a. Baghdad:
          Dar al-Ma'mun for Translation and Publishing, 1982 [In-
          cludes a novella by Adil Abd al-Jabbar (pp. 7–90) and seven
          other short stories by Khudayyir Abd al-Amir, Latif Nasir
          Hasan, Ali Khayyun, Abd al-Sattar Nasir, Abd al-Khaliq al-
          Rikabi, Adnan al-Rubay'i, and Muhsin al-Thuwadi].
CE   Berque, Jacques. *Cultural Expression in Arab Society Today.*
          Trans. Robert Stookey. Austin: University of Texas Press,
          1978.
CGC   Donohue, John, and Leslie Tramontini, eds. *Crosshatching*
          in Global Culture: A Dictionary of Modern Arab Writers:
          An Updated English Version of R. R. Campbell's "Contem-
          porary Arab Writers." 2 vols. Beirut: Orient-Institut, 2004.
FF   *Flowers of Flame: Unheard Voices of Iraq.* Ed. Sadek Mo-
          hammed, et al. East Lansing, Michigan State University
          Press, 2008.
FH   *Feathers and the Horizon: A Selection of Modern Poetry*
          from across the Arab World. Trans. Anne Fairbairn and
          Ghazi al-Gosaibi. Canberra: Leros Press, 1989.
FK   *An Anthology of Middle Eastern Literature from the Twenti-*
          eth Century. Ed. George C. Fry and James R. King. Spring-
          field, Ohio: 1974 [A 295-page mimeographed anthology,
          funded in part by the Department of Education and Witten-
          burg University. Translations cited below are by James R.
          King. According to King, "some are from Arabic via French,
          and others are directly from Arabic"].
FW   Fernea, Elizabeth W., ed. *Women and the Family in the*
          Middle East: New Voices of Change. Austin: University of
          Texas, 1985.

GAP *The Gateway to Modern Arabic Poetry.* Ed. Abdul Settar Al-Assady. Bucharest, Romania: Art-Gate Foundation, 2008. [Includes about 190 poems by poets from Iraq and other Arab countries].

HN Hamalian, Leo, and D. John Yohannan, eds. *New Writing from the Middle East.* New York: Frederick Unger, 1978.

IJMES *International Journal of Middle East Studies.*

IP "The Poetry of Iraq." Ed. Sadek R. Mohammed, Sohéil Najm, Haider Al-Kabi. *Atlanta Review* 13.2 (Spring/Summer 2007): 20–89.

IPT *Iraqi Poetry Today.* Ed. Saadi Simawe. [No. 19 *Modern Poetry in Translation*] London: King's College, 2003.

ISS *Iraqi Short Stories: An Anthology.* Ed. Yassen Taha Hafidh and Lutfiyah al-Dulaymi. Baghdad: Dar al-Ma'mun for Translation, 1988 [Includes thirty-eight short stories representing different generations of pre- and post-1950s writers].

JAL *Journal of Arabic Literature.* Leiden, The Netherlands.

JAOS *Journal of the American Oriental Society.* New Haven.

JM Jayyusi, Salma Khadra, ed. *Modern Arabic Poetry: An Anthology.* New York: Columbia University Press, 1987.

JMAF *Modern Arabic Fiction: An Anthology.* Ed. Salma Khadra Jayyusi. New York: Columbia University Press, 2005 [Includes selected works by eighteen Iraqi novelists and short-story writers: 'Abd al-Ilah, 'Abd al-Qadir, Dhu'l-Nun Ayyub, Lutfiyah al-Dulaymi, Gha'ib Tu'mah Farman, Ja'far al-Khalili, Burhan al-Khatib, Muhammad Khudayyir, Shakir Khusbak, Musa Kuraydi, Alia Mamdouh, Samirah al-Mana, May Muzaffa, Abd al-Malik Nuri, Abd al-Rahman al-Rubay'i, Salimah Salih, Mahdi Isa al-Saqr, Fu'ad al-Takarli].

JRAS *Journal of the Royal Asiatic Society,* London.

KM Khaled Mattawa.

L *Lotus (Afro-Asian Writings).* Cairo, Egypt.

LFAN *Language for a New Century: Contemporary Poetry from the Middle East, Asia, and Beyond.* Ed. Tina Chang, Nathalie Handal, and Ravi Shankar. New York: W. W. Norton & Co., 2008.

MA *Mundus Artium.* Athens, Ohio.

MAP Megalli, Shafik, trans. *Arab Poetry of Resistance: An Anthology.* Cairo: Al-Ahram Press, 1970.

MAS   *Modern Arab Stories.* London: UR/Iraqi Cultural Centre,
           1980 [No specific translator is cited for each story but refer-
           ence is made to the fact that all stories were translated by
           Denys Johnson-Davies, John Fletcher, Ali M. Cassidy [sic]
           Cassimy, W. McClung Frazier, Farida Abu-Haidar, and
           Rabah Munir Shaikh al-Ard. It includes twelve short stories,
           seven of which are by Iraqi writers: Daisy al-Amir, Dhu
           al-Nun Ayyub, Saad al-Bazzaz, Muhammad al-Khudayyir,
           Samira al-Mana, [Mani`], Abd Allah Niyazi, and Abd al-
           Malik Nuri].
MC   *Contemporary Iraqi Fiction: An Anthology.* Ed. and
           trans. Shakir Mustafa. Syracuse, NY: Syracuse University
           Press, 2008 [Includes selections from the works of sixteen
           authors: Ibtisam Abdullah, Ibrahim Ahmad, Lutfiyah al-
           Dulaimi, Maysalun Hadi, Muhammad Khudayyir, Samira
           al-Mana-Nasrat Mardan-Shmuel Moreh-Samir Naqqash-
           Abdul Sattar Nasir, Jalil al-Qaisi, Abdul Rahman Majeed
           al-Rubaie, Mahmoud Saeed, Salima Salih, Mahdi Isa al-
           Saqr, Samuel Shimon].
MEF   *Middle East Forum.* Beirut, Lebanon.
MIP   *Modern Iraqi Poetry.* Ed. Yasin Taha Hafiz; Trans. Abdul
           Wahid Lu'lu'ah. Baghdad: Dar al-Ma'mun, 1989 [Selected
           poems by 30 poets].
MISS   *Modern Iraqi Short Stories.* Trans. Ali M. Cassimy [al-
           Kasimi] and W. McClung Frazier. Baghdad: Ministry of
           Information, 1971 [Includes eleven short stories by Daisy
           al-Amir, Dhu al-Nun Ayyub, Gha'ib Tu'mah Farman, Abd
           al-Majid Lutfi, Ja'far al-Khalili, Shakir Khusbak, Salah al-
           Din al-Nahi, Abd Allah Niyazi, Abd al-Malik Nuri, Mahmud
           al-Sayyid, and Fu'ad Takarli].
MMAP   Megally, Shafik, trans. *An Anthology of Modern Arabic Po-
           etry.* Zug: Inter Documentation Co., 1974.
OB   Bankier, Joanna, et al. *The Other Voice: Twentieth Century
           Women's Poetry in Translation.* New York: Norton, 1976.
SBL   *Selections from al-Babtain's Lexicon of Contemporary Arab
           Poets (Biographies and Poems of 101 Arab Poets.* Reviewed
           by Abdul-Wahid Lu'lu'ah. Kuwait: The Foundation of Ab-
           dulaziz Saud al-Babtain's Prize for Poetic Creativity, 2006.

SBOF   *The Space between Our Footsteps: Poems and Paintings from the Middle East.* Ed. Naomi Shihab Nye. New York: Simon & Schuster, 1998.

SICP   *Selection of Iraqi Contemporary Poetry.* Trans. George Masri. London: Iraqi Cultural Centre, 1977.

SSP   Badr Shakir al-Sayyab. *Selected Poems.* Trans. Nadia Bishai. London: Third World Centre and Beirut: Arab Institute for Research and Publishing, 1986.

TIGRIS   *Tigris.* A Journal of literature published in San Francisco and edited by Sargon Boulus in the early 1970s, perhaps 1971. Only issue no. 1 without date has been listed in several American libraries. For more information, see Shabaz under Studies and Interviews or http://almashriq.hiof.no/lebanon/700/780/legend/credit.html].

TISP   *Ten Iraqi Soldier-Poets: An Anthology.* Ed. Salman D. Al-Wasiti. Baghdad: Dar al-Ma'mun, 1988 [Includes poems by Ala' Madhlum Jawad, Abdul Jabbar al-Jubouri, Jalal Qadir Muhammad, Kamal Abdul Rahman, Ali Khamees Rahman, Abdul Karim Salman, Laith al-Sundooq, Fawzi al-Ta'i, Khalid Jabir Yousif, Ibrahim Zaidan].

UM   al-Udhari, Abdullah, trans. *Modern Poetry of the Arab World.* Harmondsworth, Middlesex, England: Penguin Books, 1986.

UNS   *Under the Naked Sky: Short Stories from the Arab World.* Trans. Denys Johnson-Davies. Cairo: AUCP, 2000 [Includes five short stories from Iraq, see Kachachi, Khudayyir, Mamduh, al-Nasiri, and Takarli].

VM   al-Udhari, Abdullah, trans. *Victims of a Map.* London: AL-SAQI Books, 1984.

WB   Boullata, Kamal, ed. *Women of the Fertile Crescent: Modern Poetry by Arab Women.* Washington, D.C.: Three Continents Press, 1978.

WP   Bankier, Joanna, and Deirdre Lashgari, eds. *Women Poets of the World.* New York: Macmillan, 1982.

I

SELECTED STUDIES AND OTHER WRITINGS

Abbas, Adnan. "Humanism and Exile as Subjects in the Poetry of Bilind [sic] al-Haydari." *Studia Arabistyczne I Islamistyczne.* 11 (2003): 5–29.

Abd al-Halim, M. A. S. "al-Sayyab: A Study of His Poetry." *Studies in Modern Arabic Literature.* Ed. R. C. Ostle. Warminster: Aris and Phillips, 1976, 69–85.

Abdrabou, Abdelrahman. "Poetry across Cultures: 'The City of Sindbad' and 'The Waste Land'." *Journal of English, Sana, Yemen* 15 (Sept. 1987): 47–57.

Abu Haidar, Farida. "A Voice from Iraq: The Fiction of Alia Mamdouh." *Women: A Cultural Review* 9:3 (1998): 305–11.

Abu Haidar, Jareer. "Buland al-Haidari: An Appreciation." *Ur,* Special Autumn Issue 1979: 38–39.

———. "Salah Niyazi: An Appreciation." *The Arab Cultural Scene.* Ed. C. Hourani. London: Namara Press, 1982, 66–68.

Abulaali, Wafa, and Danna A. Dhahir. "Translators' Prologue." *Contemporary Poetry from Iraq by Bushra al-Bustani: A Facing Page Translation.* Trans. Wafaa Abulaali and Sanna A. Dhahir. Lewiston, NY: Edwin Mellin Press, 2008, 1–23.

Ajami, Fouad. *The Dream Palace of the Arabs: A Generation's Odyssey.* New York: Pantheon Books, 1998, 3–9 [On Buland al-Haydari].

Ali, Nadje Sadiq al-. *Iraq Women: Untold Stories from 1948 to the Present.* London & New York: ZED Books, 2007.

———. "Afterword: The State of Exile." *Zubaida's Window.* By Iqbal Qazwini. Trans. Azza El Kholy and Amira Nowaira. New York: Feminist Press at the City University of New York, 2008, 123–37 [An informative essay on Qazwini and her novel *Zubaida's Window*].

Ali, SS [Ali, Salah Salim]. "Ideology, Censorship, and Literature: Iraq as a Case Study." *Primarjalna Knnjizevnost* 31 (2008): 213–20 [Among topics discussed is "the Baath Party's censorship . . . and the impact it had on Iraqi literature, along with a brief account of the literary categories that were placed out of circulation . . ."].

Allen, Roger. *Modern Arabic Literature.* New York: Ungar 1987 [Includes translations of Arabic reviews dealing with Yusuf al-Ani (42–45); Dhu al-Nun Ayyub (65–68); Abd al-Wahhab al-Bayati (78–84); Gha'ib Tu'mah Farman (96–100); Buland al-Haydari (136–40); Nazik al-Mala'ikah (204–08); Abd al-Rahman al-Rubay'i (262–64); Badr Shakir al-Sayyab (279–88), and Fu'ad al-Takarli (323–26)].

Altoma, Salih J. "Iraq and its Contemporary Arabic Literature." *AW* 7:10 (November 1961): 14–15.

——. "Postwar Iraqi literature: Agonies of Rebirth." *Books Abroad* 46 (1972): 211–13.

——. "Iraqi Literature." *Encyclopedia of World Literature in the 20th Century.* Vol. 2. New York: Frederick Ungar, 1981, 456–58.

——. "Nazik al-Mala'ika's Poetry and its Critical Reception in the West." Trans. Saadi Simawe. *Arab Studies Quarterly* 19:4 (1997): 7–20.

——. "America, the Gulf War and Arabic Poetry." *AlJadid* 3:21 (1997): 16–17.

——. "In Memoriam: Muhammad Mahdi al-Jawahiri (1900?–1997)." *Arab Studies Quarterly* 19:4 (1997): v–viii.

——. "Abd al-Wahhab al-Bayati: A Journey of Hopes, Disillusionment and Renewed Faith." *AlJadid* 5.26 (1999): 18–21.

——. "Iraqi Poets in Western Exile." *World Literature Today* 77.3 (October–December 2003): 37–42.

——. "Buland al-Haydari: 1926–1996." *Banipal* 18 (Autumn 2003): 30–31. Rpt. in http://www.masthead.net.au/issue9/iraqi.html.

——. "Iraq's Modern Arabic Literature in English Translation: 1950–2003." *JAL* 35.1 (2004): 88–138.

——. *Modern Arabic Literature in Translation: A Companion.* London: Saqi, 2005.

——. "Iraqi Memories: Selected Poems from Iraq." Poems by six Iraqi Poets [Abd al-Razzaq Abd al-Wahid, Zaki al-Jabir, Khalid al-Khazraji, Dunya Mikhail, Mujbil al-Maliki, and Ali-al-Shilah]. *WATA Journal of Languages and Translation* 4 (December 2007).

——. "Ghaib Tu'ma Farman: Baghdad 1927–Moscow 1990: Writing Iraq from Moscow." *Banipal* 29 (Summer 2007): 44–45.

————. "Lami'ah Abbas Amarah: Elegiac Reflections on the 1991 Gulf War." *International Journal of Contemporary Iraqi Studies* 1.3 (2007): 421–30.

————. Rev. of *Contemporary Iraqi Fiction: An Anthology*. Ed. and trans. Shakir Mustafa. *Sayyab Translation Journal* 1 (2008): 148–53.

————. "Translating Iraq's Contemporary Arabic Literature: Ten Years of *Banipal*'s Record 1998–2008." *International Journal of Contemporary Iraqi Studies* 3.3 (2009): 307–19.

Alwan, Muhammed B. "Philosophy, Psychology, Commitment, Elements in Craft of Iraqi Poet Buland Al-Haydari (1926–1996)." *AlJadid* 17 (April 1997): 6–9.

Amarah, Lami'ah Abbas. "An Interview with Iraq's Lamia Abbass Ammara [sic]." Interview by Samer M. Reno. *Arab Women: Between Defiance and Restraint*. Ed. Suha Sabbagh. New York: Olive Branch Press, 1996, 238–43.

Antoon, Sinan. "Muzaffar Al-Nawwab Remembers a Distant Childhood." *Al-Ahram Weekly Online*, 17–23 April 2003. http://weekly.ahram.org.eg/2003/634/bol.htm.

————. "They Came to Baghdad." *Al-Ahram Weekly Online*, 17–23 April 2003. http://weekly.ahram.org.eg/2003/634/bol.htm. Rpt. as "Dead Poets Society" in *The Nation* 26 May 2003. http://www.thenation.com/doc/20030526/antoon.

————. "Of Graves and Grievances." *Middle East Report* (Summer 2003): 34–37 [An Iraqi poet's early account of the American occupation of Baghdad].

————. "Nazik al-Mala'ika 23 August 1923–20 June 2007." *Banipal* 29 (2007): 3.

————. "Remembering Sargon Boulus: Bouquets on the Grave of Sargon Boulus." *Banipal* 30 (Autumn/Winter 2007): 4–11 [Tributes collected and translated by Sinan Antoon].

————. "The Divine Sponge." *The National* 2 Feb. 2009 www.thenational.ae/article/20090206/REVIEW/705714721/1008 [A Short Essay on Sargon Boulus: 1944–2007].

Assadi Al-, Jawad. See al-Asadi, Jawad.

Asadi, Jawad al-. "Jawad Al-Assadi: Director returns to Iraq to Find Nothing the 'Same'." Interview by Rebecca Joubin. *AlJadid* 11.52 (Summer 2005): 10–11, 17 [Regarding his experience in exile and his work as a playwright].

Asfour, John. "Refuge in the Lyrical Realm: Exiled Iraqi Explores Extremes of Human Experience." *The Gazette* 26 April 2008 [On Sa'di

Yusuf, recipient of the Blue Metropolis Montreal International Literary Festival Arab Prize].

Asfour, Mohammad. "The Translation of Poetry: An Example from Nazik al-Mala'ika." *International Journal of Arabic–English Studies* 1 (2000): 7–52. *From Silence to Sound: Studies in Literature and Language. Festschrift for Hussam el-Khateeb.* Ed. Mohammad Shaheen. Beirut: Dar al-Gharb al-Islamic, 2000, 508–458.

Attabi, Jamal al-. "The Poet Hussain al-Hussaini after a Long Fight . . ." Trans. Reem Kubba. *Gilgamesh* 4 (2006): 16–17.

Awf, Mu'mina al-. "The Den: A Novel by Abd al-Rahman al-Rubay'i." *Arab Society 1978–79: Reflections and Realities.* CEMAM Reports 6 (1978–79). Beirut: Saint Joseph University, 1981, 291–97.

Azma, Nazeer el-. "The Tammuzi Movement and the Influence of T. S. Eliot on Badr Shakir al-Sayyab." *JAOS* 88 (1968): 671–78.

Azouqa, Aida. "Al- Bayyati' [sic] and W. B. Yeats as Mythmakers: A Comparative Study." *JAL* 30.2 (1999): 258–99.

———. "Defamiliarization in the Poetry of 'Abd al-Wahhab al-Bayati and T. S. Eliot: A Comparative Study." *JAL* 32.2 (2001): 167–211.

———. "Metapoetry between East and West: Abd al-Wahhab al-Bayati and the Western Composers of Metapoetry." *JAL* 39.1 (2008): 38–71.

Azzawi, Fadhil al-. "'A Singer on the Side of the Road': Fadhil al-Azzawi Explores His Writing Process and Poetics." Trans. Khaled Mattawa. *AlJadid* 17 (April 1997): 12–13.

———. "Jalil al-Qaisi: Our Tree in Kirkuk." *Banipal* 21 (Autumn 2004): 92–93.

Badawi, M. M. *A Critical Introduction to Modern Arabic Poetry.* Cambridge: Cambridge UP, 1975 [Esp. on al-Zahawi, al-Rusafi, and al-Jawahiri, 47–67; al-Bayati, 210–16; Nazik al-Mala'ikah, 228–30; and al-Sayyab, 250–58].

———. "Two Novelists from Iraq: Jabra and Munif." *JAL* 23 (1992): 141–54 [Both lived for a long time in Iraq, but they are not included in this survey because of their non-Iraqi origins].

———. *A Short History of Modern Arabic Literature.* Oxford: Oxford UP, 1993 [Includes comments on al-Bayati, 59–67; al-Jawahiri, 32–33; al-Sayyab, 59–67; and Iraqi fiction, 220–25].

Baram, Amatzia. "Mesopotamian Identity in Ba'thi Iraq." *Middle Eastern Studies* 19 (1983): 426–55 [Includes references to al-Sayyab, al-Bayati, Buland al-Haydari, and other literary figures or works].

Bardenstein, Carol. "Stirring Words: Traditions and Subversions in the Poetry of Muzaffar Al-Nawwab." *Arab Studies Quarterly* 19.4 (1997): 37–63.

Bashkin, Orit. "'When Dwelling Becomes Impossible': Arab-Jews in America and in Israel in the Writings of Ahmad Susa and Shimon Ballas." *The Arab Diaspora: Voices of an Anguished Scream*. Ed. Zahia Small Salhi and Ian Richard Netton. London: Routledge, 2006, 83–107.

———. "'When Mu'awiya Entered the Curriculum'—Some Comments on the Iraqi Educational System in the Interwar Period." *Comparative Education Review* 50 (2006): 346–64 [Includes a section on Dhu Nun Ayyub's novel *Dr. Ibrahim* and other works].

———. "Representations of Women in the Writings of the Intelligentsia in Hashimite Iraq, 1921–1958." *Journal of Middle East Women's Studies* 4.1 (2008): 53–82.

———. "'Out of Place': Home and Empire in the Works of Mahmud Ahmad al-Sayyid and Dhu Nun Ayyub." *Comparative Studies of South Asia, Africa and the Middle East* 28.3 (2008): 428–42.

———. *The Other Iraq: Pluralism and Culture in Hashemite Iraq*. Stanford, CA: Stanford University Press, 2009.

Bayati, Abd al-Wahhab al-. "Spirit of Darkness, Spirit of Light." Interview by Riad Ismat. *The Middle East* 90 (April 1982): 34.

Bellem, Alex. "The Blind River: Self and Anxiety in Aziz Al-Samawi's Poetry." *Arab Studies Quarterly* 19.4 (1997): 111–29.

Ben Driss, Hager. "The Unholy Trinity: Politics, Sex and Mysticism in Aziz al-Sayyid Jasim's Narratives." *JAL* 35.1 (2004): 71–87.

———. "Women Narrating the Gulf: A Gulf of Their Own." *JAL* 36.2 (2005): 152–71 [Esp. 166–71 on the Iraqi novelist Hadiyyah Husayn].

Berg, Nancy. *Exile from Exile: Israeli Writers from Iraq*. Albany, NY: State University of New York Press, 1996 [Esp. 29–39 and 166–70].

Beydhoun, Abbas. "Poetics of the Real World." *Banipal* 7 (Spring 2000): 8 [On Sa'di Yusuf].

Biographical Encyclopedia of the Modern Middle East and North Africa [Electronic Resource]. Ed. Michael Fischback. Detroit: Gale Group, 2008 [Includes thus far entries on Sinan Antoon, Abd al-Wahhab al-Bayati, and Nazik al-Mala'ikah].

Birthed from Scorched Hearst: Women Respond to War. Ed. Marijo Moore. Golden, CO: Fulcrum Publishing, 2008 [Includes Bushra al-Bustani's "American Helmets"].

Bloom, Jessica. "[Samir Naqqash] Language, Dialects and Identity." *Banipal* 24 (Autumn/Winter 2005): 96.

Bouhabib, Amal. "Expatriate Iraqi Poet Returns Home to Find His Calling." *The Daily Star*, Beirut. 2 October 2004. http://www.dailystar.com.lb/features/10_02_04_b.asp [About Sinan Antoon].

Boullata, Issa J. "Badr Shakir al-Sayyab: A Life of Vision and Agony." *MEF* 46 2/3 (1970): 73–80.

———. Badr Shakir al-Sayyab and the Free Verse Movement." *IJMES* 1.3 (1970): 248–58.

———. "The Poetic Technique of Shakir al-Sayyab (1926–1964)." *JAL* 2 (1971): 104–15.

———. "The Masks of 'Abd al-Wahhab al-Bayati's Poetry." *JAL* 32.2 (2001): 107–18.

———. "Contemporary Arab Writers and the Literary Heritage." *IJMES* 15 (1983): 111–19 [Covers Badr Shakir al-Sayyab in addition to other Arab writers: Adonis, al-Ghitani, and al-Mas'adi].

———. "Bayati, Abd al-Wahhab al-." *Contemporary World Writers*. Ed. Tracy Chevalier. 2nd ed. Detroit: St. James, 1993, 48–50.

Boulus, Sargon. "It Just Grabbed Me, This Magic of Words, of Music." Interview by Margaret Obank. *Banipal* 1 (February 1998): 8–18. Print.

———. Interview. By Rayyan al-Shawaf. *Parnassus: Poetry in Review* 29: 1–2 (2005): 31–63. Print.

Brand, Hanita. "Three Arab Women Authors in their Quest for a Share in the Conceptualization of the Divine." *Feminist Theology* 16.1 (2007): 21–35 [Covers Buthaynah al-Nasiri, Nawal al-Sa'dawi, and Hanan al-Shaykh].

Caiani, Fabio. "Polyphony and Narrative Voice in Fu'ad al-Takarli's *al-Raj' al-ba'id*." *JAL* 35.1 (2004): 45–70.

———. *Contemporary Arab Fiction: Innovation from Rama to Yalu*. London: Routledge, 2007.

Caiani, Fabio, and Catherine Cobham. "The Other Shore: Dialogue and Difference in Mahdi Isa al-Saqr's al-Shati' al-thani." *Middle Eastern Literatures* 11.3 (2008): 265–81.

Campbell, Robert B. "Arab Literature and the Revolution: Some Contemporary Writers in Iraq, Syria, and Palestine 1974." *Vision and Revision in Arab Society 1974*. CEMAM Reports. Beirut: Saint Joseph University, Center for the Study of the Arab World: Dar El-Mashreq, 1975, 153–84 [Esp. 155–67 on some of Iraq's literary figures: Abd al-Razzaq Abd al-Wahid, Lami'ah Amarah, Abd al-Wahhab al-Bayati, Nazik al-Mala'ikah, Sa'di Yusuf, Bathinah [sic] (Buthaynah) al-Nasiri, Abd al-Sattar Nasir, Salimah Salih, Fu'ad al-Takarli, Abd al-Rahman al-Rabi'i [sic] Yusuf al-Ani, and Ghazi Majdi [The whole article, based on material published in selected Arabic dailies and weeklies, is historically significant].

Chalala, Elie. "Youssef al-Sayigh: Poet of Sorrows, Master of Contradictions." *AlJadid 11.53* (Fall 2005): 6–9.

Cobb, Jessica. Rev. of *Zubaida's Window: A Novel of Iraq Exile*, by Iqbal al-Qazwini. *Three Percent Review 5 May 2009*. http://www.rochester.edu/College/translation/threepercent/index.php?id=1907.

Cobham, Catherine. "The Long Way Back: Possibilities for Survival and Renewal in *al-Raj' al-ba'id* by Fu'ad al-Takarli." *Arabic and Middle Eastern Literatures* 5.2 (2002): 181–94.

——. "Reading and Writing in al-Masarrat wa'l-awja' by Fu'd al-Takarli." *JAL* 35.1 (2004): 25–44.

——. "Khazin al-la-mar'iyyat: Heroes for Our Time or 'He not Being Born is Busy Dying'." *Middle Eastern Literatures* 19.2 (2006): 217–23.

Cohen-Mor, Dalya. *A Matter of Fate: The Concept of Fate in the Arab World as Reflected in Modern Arabic Literature.* Oxford and New York: Oxford University Press, 2001 [Discusses Nazik al-Mala'ikah and Fu'ad al-Takarli].

"Combating the Culture of Death." *Irish Times* June 26, 2007 [Comments on Jawad al-Asadi and the European premier of his play *Bath of Baghdad.* See also the same paper's review June 28, 2007].

Contemporary World Writers. Ed. Tracy Chevalier. London; Washington, DC: St. James Press, 1993 [Includes two entries on Abd al-Wahhab al-Bayati (48–50) and Buland al-Haydari (239–40), in addition to twelve other Arab authors].

Cooke, Miriam. "Arab Women Arab Wars." *Cultural Critique* 29 (Winter 1994–1995): 5–29 [Covers works of three Iraqi novelists: Lutfiyyah al-Dulaymi, Suhaylah Salman, and Aliyah Talib]. Rpt. in *Reconstructing Gender in the Middle East: Tradition, Identity, and Power.* Ed. Fatma Müge Göçek and Shiva Balaghi. New York: Columbia University Press, 1994.

——. "Death and Desire in Iraqi War Literature." [Iran–Iraq War] In *Love and Sexuality in Modern Arabic Literature.* Ed. Roger Allen et al. London: Saqi Books, 1995, 184–99, 248–50.

——. *Women and the War Story.* Berkeley, CA: University of California Press, 1996 [Esp. 220–66 under the title "Flames of Fire in Qadisiya." Covers selected Iraqi works of fiction (by men and women) reflecting on Iran–Iraq War with a brief postscript on the first Gulf War].

——. "Baghdad Burning: Women Write War in Iraq." *World Literature Today* 81.6 (Nov.–Dec. 2007): 23–26.

Corrao, Francesca Maria. "The Autobiography of the Thief of Fire by 'Abd al-Wahhab al-Bayyati [sic]." In *Writing the Self: Autobiographical Writing in Modern Arabic Literature.* Ed. Robin Ostle, Ed de Moor and Stefan Wild. London: Saqi Books, 1998, 241–48, 324–25.

A Crack in the Wall: New Arab Poetry. Ed. Margaret Obank and Samuel Shimon. London: Saqi Books, 2001.

Dabbagh, Abdulla al-. "Poetics of Exile and Identity: The Case of Modern Iraqi Poetry." *International Journal of Arabic–English Studies* 6 (2005): 5–14 [Deals primarily with al-Sayyab, with additional comments on Abd al-Wahhab al-Bayati, Buland al-Haydari, and Sa'di Yusuf].

Darraj, Susan Muaddi. "A Searing Look at Iraqi Politics in the '60s: Fuad al-Takarli's 'Long Way Back'." *AlJadid* 8.38 (Winter 2002): 19.

Davis, Eric. *Memories of State: Politics, History, and Collective Identity in Modern Iraq.* Berkeley: University of California Press, 2005 [Offers an informative cultural background with references to numerous critics, poets, and literary and non-literary journals, especially under the Baathist regime. See 200–07].

DeYoung, Terri. "A New Reading of Badr Shakir al-Sayyab's 'Hymn of the Rain'." *JAL* 24.1 (1993): 39–61.

———. "Mu'arada and Modern Arabic Poetry: Some Examples from the Work of Badr Shakir al-Sayyab." *Edebiyât* 5:2 (1994): 217–45.

———. *Placing the Poet: Badr Shakir al-Sayyab and Postcolonial Iraq.* Albany, NY: SUNY Press, 1998.

Dhahir, Sanna. "Images of the Fall in Bushra al-Bustani's 'Andalusian Songs for the Wounds of Iraq'." In *Literatures of War*. Ed. Richard Pine and Eve Patten. Newcastle, UK: Cambridge Scholars, 2008, 418–28.

Dictionary of Oriental Literatures. Vol. III. Ed. Jaroslav Průšek and Jiři Bečka. New York: Basic Books, 1974 [Includes five entries "Abd al-Wahhab al-Bayati," "Muhammad Mahdi al-Jawahiri," "Nazik al-Mala'ika," and "Badr Shakir al-Sayyab," all by Karl Petráček and "Dhu'N-Nun Ayyub" by Jacob Landau].

Divine Inspiration: The Life of Jesus in World Poetry. Ed. Robert Atwan et al. New York: Oxford University Press, 1998, 177–80, 505–07 [On Badr Shakir al-Sayyab].

Dulaymi, Lutfiyah al-. "A Thousand and One Nights and the Fruits of the Earth." Trans. Max Weiss. *Banipal* 30 (Autumn/Winter 2007): 80–92 [A Personal Account of her readings and influences in her life].

Enany, Rasheed El-. "Poets and Rebels: Reflections of Lorca in Modern Arabic Poetry." *Third World Literature* 11.4 (1989): 254–64 [Covers four poems by Abd al-Wahhab al-Bayati, Badr Shakir al-Sayyab, Mahmud Darwish, and Salah Abd al-Sabur].

———. *Arab Representations of the Occident: East–West Encounters in Arabic Fiction.* London; New York: Routledge, 2006, 80–82 [A brief assessment of Dhu al-Nun Ayyub's novel *Dr. Ibrahim* and some of his short stories].

Encyclopedia of Arabic Literature. Ed. Julie Scott Meisami and Paul Starkey. 2 vols. London: Routledge, 1998 [See short entries on Daisy al-Amir, al-Aqlam, Dhu al-Nun Ayyub, Mir Basri, Abd al-Wahhab al-

Bayati, Gha'ib Tu'mah Farman, Buland al-Haydari, Muhammad Mahdi al-Jawahiri, Kazim Jawad, Muhammad Khudayyir, Nazik al-Mala'ikah, Husayn Mardan, Hilal Naji, Abd al-Malik Nuri, Ma'ruf al-Rusafi, Ali al-Sharqi, Badr Shakir al-Sayyab, Fu'ad al-Takarli, Jamil Sidqi al-Zahawi].

Enany, Rasheed El-. *Arab Representations of the Occident: East–West Encounters in Arabic Fiction.* London; New York: Routledge, 2006.

Encyclopedia of World Literature on the 20th Century. Ed. Steven Serafin. 3rd ed. 5 vols. Framingham, MI: St. James Press, 1999 [Includes entries on Abd al-Wahhab al-Bayati, Gha'ib Tu'mah Farman, Nazik al-Mala'ikah, and Badr Shakir al-Sayyab].

The Facts on File Companion to World Poetry: 1900 to the Present. Ed. R. Victoria Arana. New York: Facts on File, 2008 [Includes an entry on Sa'di Yusuf under "Youssef, Saadi" in addition to other Arab poets: Adonis, Andree Chedid, Mahmud Darwish, Gibran, Hafiz Ibrahim, Joyce Mansour, and Fadwa Tuqan].

Fartusi, Abd al-Hadi al-. "The Signified Structures and Their Historical Frame in Buland al-Haidari's Poem 'Confessions from the Year 1969[sic]=1961'." Trans. [Hana'a Khlaif?] *Gilgamesh* 4 (2006): 18–17.

Filali-Ansary, Abdou. "The Poet and the Prophet." *ISIM Newsletter*, Leiden. 14 (2004): 38–39. [Regarding Ma'ruf al-Rusafi's essay on prophecy in Islam].

Fondation, Larry. Rev. of *Zubaida's Window: A Novel of Iraqi Exile*, by Iqbal al-Qazwini. *Los Angeles Times* 19 October 2008. http://articles.latimes.com/2008/oct/19/entertainment/ca-iqbak-al-qazwini19.

Foster, Julie. "Isolated Iraqi Woman Longs for Better Times—*Absent.*" Review of Betool Khedairi's novel *Absent. San Francisco Chronicle* 29, July 2007.

Frangieh, Bassam K. "Modern Arabic Poetry: Vision and Reality." In *Tradition, Modernity and Postmodernity in Arabic Literature.* Ed. Kamal Abdel-Malek and Wael Hallaq. Leiden: Brill, 2000, 222–50 [See pp. 228–32, 238, 239 on -Bayati, Nawwab, and Sayyab].

Friedman, Susan Stanford. "The Futures of Feminist Criticism: A Diary." *PMLA* 121.5 (October 2007): 1704–10 [Includes sections on Iraqi war-related writings, *Baghdad Burning*, and an unpublished translation of Bushra al-Bustani's poem "Andalusiates for the Wounds of Iraq." The latter was published in 2008 with a slightly different title, "Andalusian Songs for the Wounds of Iraq." See Bushra al-Bustani under poetry section of this bibliography].

Furaih, Siham A. al-. *Creativity & Exuberance in Arab Woman's Poetry (From the Sixth to the Twentieth Centuries)*. Kuwait: Ministry of Information Government Printing Press, 2005 [Includes two chapters on Nazik al-Mala'ikah and Lami'ah Abbas Amarah].

Gabrieli, Franceso. "Contemporary Arabic Fiction." *Middle Eastern Studies* 2.1 (October 1965): 79–84 [Esp. 81–82 on Iraqi fiction as "an attractive novelty and a promise"].

Galvin, Rachel. "Of Poets, Prophets, and Politics." *Humanities* 23.1 (Jan.–Feb. 2002): 28–34.

Gawahri, Mohamed Mahdi el-. See al-Jawahiri.

Gee, Robert W. "Iraqis Find a Better Life in the Theater." *U.S. News & World Report* 2 July 2007, 31–32 [A brief reference to Iraqi plays produced in Damascus and noted actors].

Germanus, A. K. Julius. "Some New Arab Novelists." *Islamic Literature* 15 (1969): 217–29 [Esp. 228–29 regarding Ja'far al-Khalili, Idmun Sabri, and others].

Ghassani, Anwar al-. "The Kirkuk Group: Fifty Years of Presence in Iraqi Culture." December 2003. http://al-ghassani.net/an-kirkuk-and-kirkuk-group/kirkuk-group-essay-2003.html [An informative personal account of the history of the Kirkuk Group, which includes, among others, the author himself, Sargon Boulus, Fadhil al-Azzawi, Jalil al-Qaysi, Jan Dammou, and Salah Faiq during their years in Iraq and beyond in different countries].

Ghazoul, Ferial J. "The Poetics of the Political Poem." *Arab Studies Quarterly* 8 (1986): 104–19 [Focuses on Sa'di Yusuf].

———. "Cavafy and the Iraqi Poet Sa'di Yusuf." *Jusoor* 2/3 (Spring–Summer 1993): 98–104.

———. Rev. of "Hamid Sa'id, L'oiseau blanc." Trans. Odette Petit and Wanda Voisin (Paris: Edition Publisud, 1990). *IJMES* 25 (1993): 724–26.

———. "A Literary Passage to Besieged Iraq." *Al-Ahram Weekly Online,* 19–25 November 1998. weekly.ahram.org.eg/1998/404/cu1.htm.

———. "The Arabization of Othello." *Comparative Literature* 50.1 (1998): 1–31 [Esp.18–20 regarding Yusuf al-Sayigh's adaptation of Othello in his play *Desdemona*].

———. "A Forest of Symbols: Iraqi Fiction Today." *Banipal* 14 (Summer 2002): 3–4. Rpt. in "On Iraqi Fiction." *P.E.N. International* 52.2 (2002): 88–89.

———. "Tracking the Greco–Roman Trail in the Poetry of Nazik al-Mala'ika." *Muqaranat/Comparisons* 1 (2002): 19–28.

———. "Coming of Age in Iraq." Rev. of *A Sky So Close*, by Betool Khedairi, trans. Muhayman Jamil. *Al-Ahram Weekly Online*, 20–26 March 2003. weekly.ahram.org.eg/2003/630/bo2.htm.

———. *Postmarked Iraq: Inaam Kachachi, Paroles d'Irakiennes: Le drame irakien écrit par des femmes* (Iraqis Speak: The Iraqi Drama in Women's Writing). Paris: Le Serpent à Plumes, 2003, 213. *Al-Ahram Weekly Online*, 15–21 May 2003. weekly.ahram.org.eg/2003/638/bo2.htm.

———. "Duna Talib, Al-Nuqta Al-Ab'ad" (The Furthest Point). Damascus: Dar Al-Mada, 2000, 215; "Harb Nameh" (The Book of War). Damascus: Dar Al-Mada, 1998. pp. 204. *Al-Ahram Weekly Online*, 17–23 July 2003. weekly.ahram.org.eg/2003/647/bo3.htm.

———. "Iraqi Short Fiction: The Unhomely at Home and Abroad." *JAL* 35.1 (2004): 1–24.

———. "Afterword." *The Loved Ones.* By Aliya Mamdouh. New York: The Feminist Press at the City University of New York, 2007, 301–24.

———. "Iraq." In *Arab Women Writers: A Critical Reference Guide 1873–1999*. Ed. Radwa Ashour, Ferial Ghazoul, and Hasna Reda-Mekdashi. Trans. Mandy McClure. Cairo: The American University in Cairo Press, 2008, 178–203 [A concise and highly informative treatment of Iraqi women writers representing different generations and their contribution to poetry, fiction and drama].

Ghossein, Mirène. "The Dynamics of Motion in the Poetry of Sargon Boulus." *Arrival in Where-City: Sargon Boulus*. Washington, DC: Arab Cultural Foundation [1982?], 5–13.

Gohar, Saddik. "The Political Poetry of Le Roi Jones (Amiri Baraka) and Mudhaffar al-Nawwab: A Comparative Perspective." *DOMES* 15.2 (Fall 2006): 1–20.

———. "The Integration of Western Modernism in Postcolonial Arabic Literature: A Study of Abdul-Wahhab Al-Bayati's Third World Poetics." *Third World Quarterly* 29.2 (2008): 375–90.

———. "Toward a Hybrid Poetics: The Integration of Western/Christian Narratives in Modern Arabic Poetry." *Crossroads: An Interdisciplinary Journal for the Study of History, Philosophy, Religion and Classics* 3.1 (2008): 4–15 [Esp. 8–12 on Abd al-Wahhab al-Bayati, Muzaffar al-Nawwab, and Badr Shakir al-Sayyab].

Grace, Daphne. "Arab Women Write the Trauma of Imprisonment and Exile." In *Arab Women's Lives Retold: Exploring Identity through Writing*. Ed. Nawar Al-Hassan Golley. Syracuse: Syracuse University Press, 2007, 181–200 [Covers both Nawal al-Sa'dawi and Haifa Zangana].

Hafez, Sabry, "The Transformation of the Qasida Form in Modern Arabic Poetry." In *Qasida Poetry in Islamic Asia and Africa.* Ed. Stefan Sperl and Christopher Shackle. Vol. I. Leiden: Brill, 1996. 99–120 [Esp. 108–20 on Badr Shakir al-Sayyab's Rain Song].

Hage, George N el-. "Badr Shakir al-Sayyab and the Role of the Modern Arab Poet." *Dahish* 9.2 (Autumn 2003): 4–13.

———. "'Munajayat al-sab'in' ('Orisons of the Seventies'): 'Aziz al-Sayyid Jasim's Latest Prose Poems." *JAL* 37.2 (2006): 259–92 [See also under poetry Jasim, Aziz al-Sayyid].

Hamad, Wadood. "Muthaffar an-Nawwab: Portrait of a Poet, Activist, Painter, and, above All, Humanist." *Arab Review* 3.1 (1994): 22–26.

Hamarneh, Saleh K. "Ash-Shabibi: Poet and Scholar." *Folia Orientalia* 14 (1972–1973): 293–97.

Hamdar, Abir, "Marriage, Madness and Murder in Alia Mamdouh's Moth-balls and Salwa Bakr's *The Golden Chariot.*" *Raida* 18–19 (1993–1994): 47–49.

Hammoudi, Bassim A. "The Iraqi Short Story: The Artistic and Social Change." Trans. Ranin Khalid Saeed. *Gilgamesh* (2/1986): 73–81.

Hartman, Michelle. "Multiple Identities, Multiple Voices: Reading Andree Chedid's *La Maison sans Racines.*" *French Studies* 54.1 (2000): 54–66 [Underlines Chedid's use of epigraphs from Sayyab's and Gibran's works as a marker of her affiliation with Arabic literary tradition. ". . . Chedid's use of epigraphs not only pays homage to Gibran and Sayyab and links her texts to their works and ideas, but also posits her novel as a part of the tradition with which their works are identified."].

Hassan, Razzaq Ibrahim "The Iraqi Novel after the 17 July Revolution." *Ur* 4 (1980): 26–30.

Haydari, Buland al-. "Poetry through Painting." *Today Iraq* (Feb. 16–28, 1976): 22–23 [On Shafiq al-Kamali].

Haywood, John A. *Modern Arabic Literature: 1800–1970.* London: Lund Humphries, 1971 [See pp. 65–71, 105–14, 184–85, 213–15].

Higgs, Kerryn. "The Rhetoric and the Reality" Rev. of *What Kind of Liberation?: Women and the Occupation of Iraq*, by Nadje Al-Ali and Nicola Pratt and *City of Widows: An Iraqi Woman's Account of War and Resistance*, by Haifa Zangana. *Women's Review of Books* 26.4 (Jul.–Aug. 2009): 13–15.

Hijazi, Ahmad Abd al-Mu'ti. "Points of Reference." *Al-Ahram Weekly,* 12–18 August 1999 [On al-Bayati].

Howarth, James. "AL-BAYATI'S Perfect City." *Banipal* 18 (Summer 2003): 47.

Hurlbert, Claude Mark. "'From behind the Veil': Teaching the Literature of the Enemy." *Canadian Modern Language Review/La Revue canadienne des langues vivants*: 60.1 (September 2003): 55–68 [A revised version of the 1994 article with emphasis on the implications of teaching "literature for cross-cultural understanding" at a time when "the literature being taught is written by citizens of a country with which the students' country is at war"].

Hurlbert, Claude Mark, and Ann Marie Bodner. "Collective Pain: Literature, War, and Small Change." *Changing Classroom Practices: Resources for Literary and Cultural Studies*. Ed. David B. Downing. Albany, NY: SUNY at Albany, 1994, 202–31 [Based in part on the teaching of two Iraqi short stories: "From behind the Veil" by Dhu al-Nun Ayyub and "Clocks Like Horses" by Muhammad Khudayyir, in the fall of 1990, before the first Gulf War. The article deals with the implications of teaching "literature for cross-cultural understanding especially when the literature being taught is written by citizens of a country with which the students' country is at war."].

Huri, Yair. "'Perhaps I Disappointed You': On a Meta-Poetic Poem by Sa'di Yusuf." *Middle Eastern Literatures* 7.1 (2004): 77–83.

———. "'In Your Name this Death is Holy': Federico García Lorca in the Works of Modern Arab Poets." http://www.lehman.edu/faculty/guinazu/ciberletras/v13/huri.htm.

———. "'Seeking Glory in the Dunghills': Representations of the City in the Writings of Modern Arab Poets." *South Carolina Modern Language Review* 4.1 (2005): 49–73 [Covers al-Bayati, al-Sayyab, and Sa'di Yusuf in addition to Salah Abd al-Sabur and Adonis].

———. "'To Flee from All Languages': The Gap between Language and Experience in the Works of Modern Arab Poets." *Arab Studies Quarterly* 27.4 (Fall 2005): 1–16 [Includes Fawzi Karim].

———. *The Poetry of Sadi Yusuf: Between Homeland and Exile.* Brighton; Portland, Oregon: Sussex Academic Press, 2006.

Husni, Ronak. "Ambivalent Attitudes toward Nature in the Early Poetry of Nazik al-Mala'ika." *JAL* 38.1 (2007): 78–93.

Hussein, Ronak, and Yasir Suleiman. "Death in the Early Poetry of Nazik al-Mala'ika." *British Journal of Middle Eastern Studies* 20:2 (1993): 214–25.

Ingrams, Doreen. *The Awakened: Women in Iraq.* London: Third World Center, 1983 [Esp. 79–97 on "Pioneers" in support of women's rights, such as al-Zahawi and Rusafi, 129–54 "Women in Art and Literature" by Khalid Kishtainy].

Irwin, Robert. "Arab Countries." In *The Oxford Guide to Contemporary Writing.* Ed. John Sturrock. Oxford: Oxford University Press, 1996, 22–38 [Includes only a few general remarks about Iraq's literature without any specific reference to major writers except al-Bayyati [sic] and Ahmad Salih].

Izzidien, Yousif. See Izz al-Din, Yusuf.

Izz al-Din, Yusuf. "The Social Problem in Iraq and its Influence on Poetry." *Bulletin of the College of Arts and Sciences.* Baghdad 3 (1958): 73–80.

——. "The Emancipation of Iraqi Women and their Influence on Iraqi Life and Poetry." *Bulletin of the College of Arts.* Baghdad 1 (1959): 33–41.

——. *Modern Iraqi Poetry: Social and Political Influences.* Cairo: The Cultural Press, 1971.

——. *Poetry and Iraqi Society 1900–1945.* Baghdad: 1962.

Jabra, Jabra I. "The Rebels, the Committed and the Others: Transitions in Arabic Poetry Today." *Middle East Forum* 43.1 (1967): 19–32.

——. "Modern Arabic Literature and the West." *JAL* 2 (1971): 76–91.

Jamakani, Amira. "Narrating Baghdad: Representing the Truth of War in Popular Non-Fiction." *Critical Arts: A South–North Journal of Cultural and Media Studies* 21.1 (2007): 32–46 [Deals in part with Riverbend's *Baghdad Burning*].

Jawahiri, Muhammad Mahdi al-. "Address by LOTUS Award Winner." *L* 30 (Oct.–Dec. 1976): 132–34 [See also a brief biographical presentation, 128–31].

Jayyusi, Salma Khadra. *Trends and Movements in Modern Arabic Poetry.* Leiden: Brill, 1977.

——. "Modernist Poetry in Arabic." *Modern Arabic Literature.* Ed. M. M. Badawi. Cambridge; New York: Cambridge University Press, 1992, 132–75 [Covers Abd al-Wahhab al-Bayati, Buland al-Haydari, Nazik al-Mala'ikah, Badr Shakir al-Sayyab, and Sa'di Yusuf].

——. "al-Mala'ika, Nazik." *Encyclopedia of World Literature in the 20th Century.* Ed. S. R. Serafin. Vol. 3. Detroit: St. James, 1993, 166–67.

Jerome, Alexandra Izabela. Rev. of "Riverbend: Baghdad Burning II." *Arab Media & Society.* Cairo: The American University in Cairo. 2 (Summer 2007): 1–4.

Jihad, Kadhim. "Iraqi Literature: An Exemplary Multi-millennia Continuity." Trans. James Kirkup [From the French]. *Banipal* 17 (Summer 2003): 54–55.

——. "Mahmoud al-Braikan: The Poet of Long and Heroic Silence." *Banipal* 17 (Summer 2003): 40.

———. "The Iraqi Landscape in the Early Poems of Badr Shakir al-Sayyab." Trans. James Kirkup [From the French]. *Banipal* 19 (Spring 2004): 89–92.

Jubran, Sulaiman. "The Formula of Modernism in al-Bayati's *Abariq Muhashshamah.*" In *Writer, Culture, Text: Studies in Modern Arabic Literature.* Ed. A. Elad. Fredericton. Canada: York Press, 1993, 89–110.

———. "The Old and the New: Al-Jawahiri's Poetic Imagery." *Asian and African Studies* 26 (1992, 1994): 249–262.

Juburi, Amal al-. "Reflections/A Personal Vision of Poetry." Trans. Elie Chalala. *AlJadid* 31 (Spring 2000): 27.

Juma, Jamal. "Best of Times, Worst of Times." *Times Online* 6 May 2007. http://entertainment.timesonline.co.uk/tol/arts_and_entertainment/books/ [Juma's brief note regarding his poem "A Handshake in the Dark," which the British composer Michael Lyman used for his choral piece under the same title. See the *Sunday Times* 6 May 2007].

Kachachi, Inaam. "The American Granddaughter." Interview, by Antoine Jouki. *The National*, UAE. 16 March 2009. http://www.thenational.ae/article/20090316/ART/.../1093. [Regarding Kachachi's choice and view of the Iraqi–American heroine of her novel, *al-hafidah al-amrikiyyah* (The American Granddaughter). The novel appeared in French (Paris: L. Levi, 2009) under the title *Si je t'oublie Bagdad* (If I Forget You, Baghdad). See also under fiction Kachachi's entry].

Kadhim, Hussein. "False Heroes: A Study of Abd Al-Rahman Majid Al-Rubay'i's Novel *Al-Washm* (The Tattoo)." *Arab Studies Quarterly* 19.4 (1997): 95–110.

———. "Rewriting *The Waste Land*: Badr Shakir al-Sayyab's 'Fi al-Maghrib al-'Arabi." *JAL* 30.2 (1999): 128–70.

———. "Iraqi Literature." *Encyclopedia of World Literature on the 20th Century.* Ed. Steven Serafin. 3rd ed. Framingham, MI: St. James Press, 1999. Vol. II. 489–92.

———. "'Abd al-Wahhab al-Bayati's 'Ode to Jaffa'." *JAL* 32.2 (2001): 88–106.

———. "Iraq's Literary Contributions: An Overview." *Iraq: Its History, People, and Politics.* Ed. Shams Constantine Inati. Amherst, NY: Humanity Books, 2003, 103–10.

Khalil, Iman. "Arab–German Literature." *World Literature Today* 69.3 (1995): 521–27.

Khan, Zeba. "An Iraqi Poet, Al-Bayyati [sic] and a Reassessment of Commitment on the Themes of Liberation, Loneliness and Loss." *Culture: Unity and Diversity: Proceedings of the Annual Conference of the British Society for Middle Eastern Studies*, 12–14 July 1994. Manchester: University of Manchester, 1994, 357–65.

Khatib, Burhan al-. "The Experimental Trend in Iraqi Novels." *Iraq* 158 (April 15, 1982): 38–42.

Khazoum, Eliahu. "Ma'ruf al-Rusafi, Iraq's Conscience." *New Outlook*, Tel-Aviv 3.1 (October 1959): 50–52.

Khedairi, Betool. "Daughter of the Foreigner." Interview by Judith Gabriel. *AlJadid* 9.42/43 (Winter/Spring 2003): 31–32. Print.

Khoury, Dina Rizk. "Fragmented Loyalties in the Modern Age: Jamil Sidqi al-Zahawi on Wahhabism, Constitutionalism and Language." *International Congress on Learning and Education in the Ottoman World, Istanbul, 12–15 April 1999.* Ed. Ali Çaksu: Istanbul: Research Center for Islamic History, Art and Culture, 2001, 335–45.

———. "Looking for the Modern: A Biography of an Iraqi Modernist." [On Jamil Sidqi al-Zahawi]. *Auto/Biography and the Construction of Identity and Community in the Middle East.* Ed. Mary Ann Fay. New York: Palgrave, 2002, 109–24.

Khoury, Jeries N. "The figure of Job (Ayyub) in Modern Arabic Poetry." *JAL* 38.2 (2007): 167–95 [Focuses on Badr Shakir al-Sayyab].

Khulusi, Safa. "Ma'ruf al-Rusafi, 1875–1945." *Bulletin of the School of Oriental and African Studies* 13 (1949/50): 616–26.

———. "Contemporary Poetesses of Iraq." *The Islamic Review* (June 1950): 40–45 [Covers briefly Rabab al-Kazimi, Umm Nizar al-Mala'ika (Nazik's mother) and Nazik al-Mala'ika, Fatina al-Na'ib, and Lami'a Abbas Amarah].

———. "Atika (Al-Khazraji) a Modern Poetess." *Journal of the Royal Asiatic Society* 3–4 (1950): 149–57.

———. "Modern Arabic Literature in Iraq." *The Islamic Review* (February 1951): 35–39; (March 1951): 23–27.

———. "Modern Arabic Fiction with Special Reference to Iraq." *The Islamic Review* 30 (1956): 199–210.

———. "Poetry as a Vehicle of Social and Political Reform in Iraq." *New Iraq* 4 (April 1962): 14–15; 29–30. Rpt. in *Islamic Review* 50 (1962): 15–17.

———. "Ma'ruf ar-Rusafi in Jerusalem." In *Arabic and Islamic Garland: Historical, Educational, and Literary Papers presented to Abdul-Latif Tibawi by Colleagues, Friends, and Students.* Ed. Mahmud Akhal and Riadh el-Droubie. London: Islamic Cultural Centre, 1977, 147–52.

———. "Abdul Majid Lutfi's 'Rejuvenation of Words'." *JAL* 11 (1980): 66–67 [The author considers Lutfi as "the father of *vers libre* in Iraq and one of the founders of this genre in the Arab world"].

Kirkup, James. "The Voice Digs Deep Like Roots." *Banipal* 7 (Spring 2000): 6–7 [On Sa'di Yusuf].

Kishtainy, Khalid. *The Prostitute in Progressive Literature.* London; New York: Allusion and Busby, 1982 [Esp. 71–73 on Gha'ib Tu'mah Farman and Badr Shakir al-Sayyab].

———. "Women in Art and Literature." *The Awakened: Women in Iraq.* Ed. Doreen Ingrams. London: Third World Center, 1983, 129–54.

———. *Theatre with Commitment: Story of the Iraqi Theatre.* London: Iraqi Cultural Centre, 1980?

Klemm, V. "Ideals and Reality: The Adaptation of European Ideas of Literary Commitment in the Postcolonial Middle East—The Case of Abdalwahhab al-Bayati." *Conscious Voices: Concepts of Writing in the Middle East. Proceedings of the Berne Symposium July 1997.* Ed. S. Guth et al. Beirut: Orient-Institut der Deutschen Morgeniandischen Gesellschaft, 1999, 142–51.

Knight, Rolf. *Traces of MAGMA: An Annotated Bibliography of Left Literature.* Vancouver, BC, Canada: Draegerman Books, 2003, 232–33 [Includes questionable annotations of works (attributed at times inaccurately) by Yusuf al-Ani, Dhu al-Nun Ayyub, Abd al-Wahhab al-Bayati, Abd al-Malik Nuri, Fu'ad al-Takarli, and Munir Yasin. As the subtitle indicates, the focus of the annotations is leftist and communist trends in Iraqi literature.].

Langer, Jennifer. "Crossing Borders: The Extent to Which the Voices of Exiled and Refugee Women Have Adapted to Their New Western Diasporic Space." *Journal of International Women's Studies* 5.3 (May 2004): 66–74 [Includes references to Fawzi Karim, Samira al-Mana, and Haifa Zangana].

Lappin, Elena. "Exile's Return: The Story of One of Iraq's Most Important Poets." Thursday, 26 June 2003. http://slate.msn.com/id/2084880/ [Re: Fawzi Karim].

Leland, Mary. "Combating the Culture of Death." *Irish Times* 26 June 2007 [Comments on Jawad al-Asadi and the European premier of his play *Bath of Baghdad.* See also the same paper's review 28 June 2007].

Levy, Lital. "Self and the City: Literary Representations of Jewish Baghdad." *Prooftexts* 26 (2006): 163–211.

Lieberman, Laurence. "Dunya Mikhail: The Laggard Bird." *American Poetry Review* 37.3 (2008): 41–47.

Literature from the "Axis of Evil": Writings from Iran, Iraq, North Korea, and Other Enemy Nations. Ed. editors of *Words without Borders.* New

York; London: The New Press, 2006, 69–98 [Iraqi poems and fiction excerpts], 75–76.

Litvin, Margaret. "When the Villain Steals the Show: The Character of Claudius in Post-1975 Arab(ic) Hamlet Adaptations." *JAL* 38.2 (2007): 196–219 [Covers four Arabic adaptations including Jawad al-Asadi's *Forget Hamlet*].

Loloi, P. "Haydari, Buland al-." *Contemporary World Writers.* Ed. Tracy Chevalier. 2nd ed. Detroit: St. James, 1993, 239–41.

Loya, Arieh. "al-Sayyab and the Influence of T. S. Eliot." *The Muslim World* 61 (1971): 187–201.

Machut-Mendecka, Ewa. "The Warring Sheherezade: Tradition and Folklore in the Iraqi Drama." *Proceedings of the Arabic and Islamic Sections on the 35th International Congress of Asian and North African Studies.* Ed. K. Dévényi and T. Iványi. Budapest, Hungary: Chair for Arabic Studies, Eötvös Loránd University, 1998, 147–52.

———. "The Individual and the Community in Arabic Literary Autobiography." *Vers de nouvelles lectures de la literature arabe/Towards New Approaches of Arabic Literature* 46.3 (1999): 510–22; See also *Arabica* 46 (1999): 510–22 [Covers Alia Mamdouh among other Arab authors].

———. *Studies in Arabic Theatre and Literature.* Warsaw, Poland: Dialog Academic Publishing House, 2000, 99–104 [An overview of Iraqi theater's central themes as reflected in the works of Yusuf al-Ani, Qasim Muhammad, Adil Kazim, and Ghalib al-Muttalibi].

Mafraji, Ahmed F. al-. "Iraqi Theatre 1921–1958." Trans. Hassan Hafidh. *Gilgamesh* (2/1986): 65–69.

Mamdouh. Alia. "Creatures of Arab Fear." Trans. Shirley Eber and Fadia Faqir. *In the House of Silence: Autobiographical Essays by Arab Women Writers.* Ed. Fadia Faqir. Reading, UK: Garnet, 1998, 65–71.

———. "Baghdad: These Cities Are Dying." Trans. Marilyn Booth. *Autodafe* (*Journal of the International Parliament of Writers*) 2 (Autumn 2001).

———. "A Secret Language has formed inside of the Arabic Language." Trans. Michael Taylor. *Autodafe. Correspondence.* 2 (2001) [Conversation with Mona Chollet].

———. "Interview." By Iñaqui Gutiérrez de Terán. *Remebering for Tomorrow.* Amsterdam: European Cultural Foundation; Toledo, Spain: Escuela de Traductores de Toledo, 2000, 55–58.

———. "Smoke." Trans. Catherine Cobham. *New Literary History* 37.1 (2006): 57–64 [An account of the author's friendship with the French writer Hélène Cixous].

Mana, Samira al-. "Writing and the Notion of Searching for Female Identity." Trans. Shirley Eber and Fadia Faqir. *In the House of Silence: Autobiographical Essays by Arab Women Writers.* Ed. Fadia Faqir. Reading, UK: Garnet, 1998, 75–78.

Manguel, Alberto. *The City of Words.* Toronto: House of Anansi Press, 2007 [Cites remarks by Arab writers regarding the literary silence surrounding the Iraq War, 69–71].

Marashi, Ibrahim al-, and Abdul Hadi al-Khalili. "Iraqis' Bleak Views of the United States." *What They Think of Us: International Perceptions of the United States since 9/11.* Ed. David Farber. Princeton: Princeton University Press, 2007, 1–26.

Marmorstein, Emile. "Two Iraqi Jewish Short Story Writers: A Suggestion for Social Research." *The Jewish Journal of Sociology* 1 (1959): 187–200 [Includes summaries of short stories by Mir Basri and Anwar Sha'ul].

———. "An Iraqi Jewish Writer in the Holy Land." *The Jewish Journal of Sociology* 6 (1964): 92–100 [Includes a translation of a short story by Shalom Darwish written after he left Iraq].

Masliyah, Sadok. "Monorhyme, Stanzaic Poetry and Blank Verse in the Poetry of the Iraqi Poet Jamil S. Az-Zahawi (1863–1936)." *American Journal of Arabic Studies* 3 (1975): 14–36.

———. "Zahawi's Philosophy and His Views on Islam." *Middle Eastern Studies* 12 (1976): 177–87.

———. "Zahawi: A Muslim Pioneer of Women's Liberation." *Middle Eastern Studies* 32.3 (1996): 161–71.

Mason, Herbert. "Impressions of an Arabic Poetry Festival." *Religion and Literature* 20.1 (Spring 1988): 157–61 [Regarding the 8th annual Marbid Poetry Festival, Baghdad, November 1987].

Masumi, Saghir Hasan al-. "Rusafi, a Modern Poet of Iraq." *IC* 24 (1950): 50–59.

Mattawa, Khaled. "Wading through the Archipelago of Hope: On Translating the Poetry of Hatif Janabi." *AlJadid* 17 (April 1997): 10–11, 13. Fayetteville: University of Arkansas Press, 1996 [Adapted from the author's introduction to his translation of Janabi's poetry under the title *Questions and Their Retinue*].

———. "Sa'adi [sic]'s Continuum of Observation." *Banipal* 7 (Spring 2000): 4 [On Sa'di Yusuf].

———. "Remarkable Remembrances." *Banipal* 6 (Autumn 1999): 4–5 [On Fadhil al-Azzawi].

Maycock, Robert. "BBC SO/Storgards, Barbican, London." *Independent* 13 March 2007 [Regarding Micahel Nyman's adapatation of Jamal Juma's poems for his choral work *Handshake in the Dark*].

Mehta, Brinda. "Dissidence, Creativity, and Embargo Art in Nuha Al-Radi's *Baghdad Diaries.*" *Meridians: Feminism, Race, Transnationalism* 6.2 (2006): 220–35.

Melek, Maysoon. "The Poet Who Helped Shape My Childhood." *Intimate Selving in Arab Families: Gender, Self, and Identity.* Ed. Suad Joseph. Syracuse: Syracuse University Press, 1999: 77–91 [On Nazik al-Mala'ika].

Michael, Sami. "On Being an Iraqi–Jewish Writer in Israel." Trans. Imre Goldstein. *Prooftexts* 4.1 (1984): 23–33.

Milich, Stephan. "The Poetry of Sa'di Yusuf: From Exile to Post-Exile." *Al-Abhath* 55–56 (2008): 175–97.

———. "Will Iraq Perish? Concepts of Exile, Hybridity and Intertextuality in Saadi Youssef's Post-Colonial Poetry." *Bulletin of the Institute for Inter-faith Studies* 8.1–2 (2006).

Mohammed, Abd al-Wahid. "Punctuation in Modern Iraqi Short Story." *Bulletin of the College of Arts,* Baghdad. 20 (1977): 199–214.

Moosa, Matti. "Social Consciousness in the Iraqi Drama." *Muslim World* 71 (1981): 228–46.

Moreh, S. "Nazik al-Mala'ika and al-Shi'r al-Hurr in Modern Arabic Literature." *Asian and African Studies* 4 (1968): 57–84.

———. "The Influence of Western Poetry and Particularly T. S. Eliot on Modern Arabic Poetry (1947–1964)." *Asian and African Studies* 5 (1969): 1–50.

———. *Modern Arabic Poetry: 1800–1977.* Leiden: Brill, 1976.

———. "Samir Naqqash 1938–2004." *Banipal* 22 (Spring 2005): 135.

Mohsen, Fatma. See Muhsin, Fatimah.

Moor, Ed de. "The Humanized God in the Poetry of a Tammuzian: Badr Shakir al-Sayyab." *Representations of the Divine in Arabic Poetry.* Ed. Geert Borg and Ed de Moor. Amsterdam; Atlanta, GA: Rodopi, 2001, 193–210.

Mousa, Nedal M al-. "The Arabic Bildungsroman: A Generic Appraisal." *IJMES* 25 (1993): 223–40 [Esp. 226–28 dealing with Dhu al-Nun Ayyub's novel *Dr. Ibrahim*].

Muhalhal, Na'eem. "al-Sayyab's Memory and the Rain Song." Trans. Mohammed Darweesh. *Gilgamesh* 7 (2008): 3–7.

Muhanna, Nazim. "Where is the Iraqi War Literature?" *Asharq Al Wasat* 13 December 2006. www.aawsat.com/english/news.asp?section=3&id=7322.

Muhsin, Fatimah. "The Iraqi Migrant Novel." Trans. Falah Abd Al Jabar and Maysoon Batchachi. *Banipal* 2 (June 1998): 76–77.

Musawi, Muhsin Jassim. "Some Social Aspects of Iraqi Short Story." Trans. Mohammed Darweesh. *Gilgamesh* (1/1986): 64–72.

———. "The Modernist Trend in the Iraqi Short Story: The 1950s." *Gilgamesh* (2/1986): 59–64.

———. "The Sociopolitical Context of the Iraqi Short Story, 1908–1968." *Statecraft in the Middle East: Oil, Historical Memory and Popular Culture* Ed. Eric Davis and Nicolas Gavreilides. Miami: Florida International University Press, 1991, 202–27.

———. "Abd al-Wahhab al-Bayati's Poetics of Exile." *JAL* 32.2 (2001): 212–38.

———. "Writing in Exile: Which Sense of Be-Longing?" *English Studies in Canada* 27.4 (2001): 481–507.

———. *The Postcolonial Arabic Novel: Debating Ambivalence.* Leiden: Brill, 2003 [Covers briefly a few Iraqi writers: Dhu'l Nun Ayyub, Gha'ib Tu'mah Farman, Aziz al-Sayyid Jasim, Abd al-Majid al-Rubay'i, and Fu'ad al-Takarli].

———. *Arabic Poetry: Trajectories of Modernity and Tradition.* London; New York: Routledge, 2006 [Covers several Iraqi poets including Abd al Wahhab al-Bayati, Muhammad Mahdi al-Jawahiri, and Badr Shakir al-Sayyab].

———. *Reading Iraq: Culture and Power in Conflict.* London; New York: Tauris, 2006 [Discusses the contributions of numerous Iraqi literary figures].

Mushatat, Raad. [A pseudonym] "At Home and in Exile." Trans. Shirley Eber. *Index on Censorship* 2 (1986): 28–30 [An account about his personal experience and the political situation in Iraq].

Muthanna, Nazim. "Where is the Iraqi War Literature?" *Asharq Al Awsat* 13 December 2006.

Myers, Robert. "Blood on Both Hands: Jawad Al Assadi's *Baghdadi Bath.*" *Performing Arts Journal* 30.89 (2008): 108–11.

Naef, Silvia. "Literature and Social Criticism in the Iraqi Press of the First Half of the 20th Century: Ja'far al-Khalili and the Periodical Al-Hatif." *The Middle East Press as a Forum for Literature.* Ed. Horst Unbehaun. Frankfurt am Main: Peter Lang, 2004, 143–50.

Nasiri, Buthaynah al-. "Reflections on My Writings." *Barqiyya.* The American University in Cairo: The Middle East Studies Program. 7.3 (May 2003): 3–4, 6.

Nawwab, Muzaffar al-. "Muzaffar al-Nawwab Remembers a Distant Childhood." Interview by Sinan Antoon. *Al-Ahram Weekly* 17–23 April 2003.
Print.

Noorani, Yaseen. "Visual Modernism in the Poetry of 'Abd al-Wahhab al-
Bayati." *JAL* 32.3 (2001): 239–55.

Nowaira, Amira. "Outside Iraq." Rev. of *Zubaida's Window,* by Iqbal al-
Qazwini. *Al-Ahram Weekly Online*, 14–20 August 2008. http://weekly
.ahram.org.eg/2008/910/cu5.htm.

Nusayyer, Yassin. See Nusayyir, Yasin.

Nusayyir, Yasin. "The Iraqi Theatre in the 1970s." *Ur* 2–3 (1982): 50–51.

Nowaira, Amira. "Outside Iraq." Rev. of *Zubaida's Window,* by Iqbal al-
Qazwini. *Al-Ahram Weekly Online*, 14–20 August 2008. http://weekly
.ahram.org.eg/2008/910/cu5.htm.

Obank, Margaret. "Iraqi Poet Sargon Boulus: 'It Just Grabbed Me, This
Magic of Words, of Music'." *Banipal* 1 (February 1998): 8–18.

Ouyang, Wen-chin. "Intertextuality Gone Awry? The Mysterious (Dis) ap-
pearance of 'Tradition" in the Arabic Novel." *Intertextuality in Modern
Arabic Literature since 1967*. Ed. Luc-Willy Deheuvels et al. Durham,
UK: Durham University, Durham Modern Languages Series, 2006,
45–64 [Focuses on Abd al-Khaliq al-Rikabi's *Sabi' Ayyam al-Khalq*
(The Seventh Day of Creation) with a few introductory remarks on Salim
Matar's *The Woman of the Flask*].

———. "Text, Space and the Individual in the Poetry of Badr Shakir al-
Sayyab: Nationalism, Revolution and Subjectivity." *Sensibilities of
the Islamic Mediterranean: Self-Expression in a Muslim Culture from
Post-Classical Times to the Present Day*. Ed. Robin Ostle. London: I. B.
Tauris, 2008, 330–42.

Pannewick, Friederike. "The Martyred Poet on the Cross in Arabic Poetry:
Sacrifice, Victimization or the Other Side of Heroism." *Martyrdom in
Literature: Visions of Death and Meaningful Suffering in Europe and
the Middle East from Antiquity to Modernity*. Ed. Friederike Pannewick.
Wiesbaden: Reichter Verlag, 2004, 105–21.

Peled-Shapira, Hilla. "From Conventional to Personal or: What Happened
to Metaphor under the Influence of Ideology—The Case of Gha'ib
Tu'ma Farman." *Journal of Semitic Studies* 54.1 (2009): 227–49 [Dis-
cusses Farman's use of animal metaphors as a device to describe relations between intellectuals and the government].

Pinault, David. "Images of Christ in Arabic Literature." *Die Welt des Islams* 27. 1–3 (1987): 103–25 [Covers Badr Shakir al-Sayyab and Abd
al-Wahhab al-Bayati].

———. "Gods Wounded and Slain: Representations of Tammuz and Christ in Contemporary Iraqi and Syrian Literature." *Bulletin of Mary Henry Institute of Islamic Studies* 11.1–2 (1992): 40–54.

Pirie, Mark. "A Cry to the Gulf: The Poetry of Basim Furat Exiled Iraqi Poet." *Gilgamesh* 4 (2006): 24–32.

Radi, Nuha al-. *Baghdad Diaries.* London: Saqi, 1998. Rpt. as *Baghdad Diaries: 1991–2002.* London: Saqi, 2003.

———. ""Twenty Eight Days in Baghdad." *Granta* 83 (Fall 2003): 235–54.

Radi, Nuha al-, and Jasmina Tesanovic. "Globalization of Evil: Words from Baghdad and Belgrade." *Writing the World on Globalization.* Ed. David Rothenberg and Wandee J. Pryor. Cambridge, Mass.: MIT Press, 2005, 203–17.

Ramli, Muhsin al-. "Anti-Discrimination: Contribution on the Situation in Iraq." *Electronic Magazine of the Humanist Movement* (December 1997): 44–48.

Raphaeli, Nimrod. "The Revival of Cultural Life in Post-Saddam Iraq." *Middle East Media Research Institute,* no. 279, 6 June 2006 [Includes brief notes on current cultural/literary journals and professional periodicals published in Arabic and other languages].

———. "Culture in Post Saddam Iraq." *Middle East Quarterly* 14.3 (Summer 2007): 33–42 [A shorter account of the author's 2006 report].

Rakha, Youssef. "Youssef al-Ani: Stages of Development." *Al-Ahram Weekly,* 5–11 August 1999 [Based on an interview with al-Ani].

———. "Abdel-Wahab Al-Bayyati: Prometheus at the Sheraton." *Al-Ahram Weekly,* 11–17 February 1999.

———. "Badr Shakir al-Sayyab." *Al-Ahram Weekly,* 18–24 March 2004.

Rawi, Mouayed al-. "The Place of Origin." Trans. Basil Samara. *AlJadid* 11.52 (Summer 2005): 14–16 [On the poet's recollections of his city Kirkuk].

Rayhanova, Bajan. "The Concept of the Hero in Modern Arabic Prose." *Middle Eastern Literatures* 9.2 (August 2006): 169–78 [Includes reference to some of Shakir al-Anbari's works. Al-Anbari, an Iraqi exile in Syria, is presented among other Syrian writers].

Rejwan, Nissim. "Rejecting Europe's Cultural Influence: Protest of an Iraqi Poetess." *Jewish Observer and Middle East Review* 15.22 (June 3, 1966): 16–17 [On Nazik al-Mala'ikah].

———. Passage from Baghdad." *Keys to the Garden: New Israeli Writing.* Ed. Ammiel Alcalay. San Francisco: City Lights Books, 1996, 46–60.

———. *The Last Jews in Baghdad: Remembering a Lost Homeland.* Austin: University of Texas, 2004 [Esp. 139–50 regarding the author's association with a number of Iraqi poets and intellectuals during the forties before his departure to Israel: Buland al-Haydari, Najib al Mani', and Adnan Ra'uf].

Rich, Adrienne. "Iraqi Poetry Today." *Poetry International Web.* 4 July 2003. Rpt. in *A Human Eye: Essays on Art in Society: 1996–2008.* New York: W. W. Norton & Co., 2009, 6–18.

Riverbend. *Baghdad Burning: Girl Blog from Iraq.* New York: Feminist Press at the City University of New York, 2005 [Author's real name is not given; her blogs begin on 17th of August 2003 and stop on the 27th of October 2007].

———. *Baghdad Burning II: More Girl Blog.* Feminist Press at the City University of New York, 2006.

Rogers, Lynne. "Before Exile: Four Iraqi Narratives." *AlJadid* 50/51 (Winter/Spring 2005): 46–47. http://aljadid.com/reviews/BeforeExileFourIraqi NarrativesbyLynneRogers.html [Rev. of *The Woman of the Flask* by Salim Matar, *Saddam City* by Mahmoud Saeed, *The Last Jews of Baghdad: Remembering a Lost Homeland* by Nissim Rejwan, and *Two Grandmothers from Baghdad and Other Memoirs of Monkith Saaid* by Rebecca Joubin].

Rohde, Achim. "Opportunities for Masculinity and Love: Cultural Production in Ba'thist Iraq during the 1980s." *Islamic Masculinities.* Ed. Lahoucine Ouzgane. London; New York: Zed Books, 2006, 184–201 [See esp. 191–97 regarding writings by Yusuf al-Sayigh, Daisy al-Amir, and others].

Rosenthal, Peggy. "Christ in the Desert of Twentieth-Century Poetry." *Cross Currents* 47.1 (1997): 92–101 [Deals in part with al-Sayyab. See also her book below].

———. *The Poet's Jesus: Representations at the End of a Millennium.* New York: Oxford University Press, 2000 [See esp. 101–05 on al-Sayyab].

Ruston, Ursula. "Sadiq al-Saygh: A Two-Edged Sword." *Index on Censorship* 21.6 (1992): 24–26.

Sadka, Tova Murad. *Farewell to Dejla: Stories of Iraqi Jews at Home and in Exile.* Chicago, IL: Academy Chicago Publishers, 2008.

Saeed, Mahmoud. "Predicament of Iraqi Intellectuals: Victims of Domestic Repression and Sanctions." Ed. and trans. AlJadid editors. *AlJadid* 5.26 (Winter 1999): 13.

———. "A Legacy of Ruins: Iraqi Letters and Intellectuals under Saddam's Regime." *AlJadid* 42/43 (Winter–Spring 2003): 12–13.

Salama, Mohammad R. "The Mise-en-Scéne of 'Writing' in al-Bayati's Al-Kitabah 'Ala al-Tin." *JAL* 32.2 (2001): 142–66.

———. "The Interruption of Myth: A Nancian Reading of Blanchot and Al-Bayati." *JAL* 33.3 (2002): 248–86.

———. "A 'Salary' of Death: Aesthetics and Economy in Badr Shakir al-Sayyab's 'Haffar al-qubur' (the Gravedigger)." *JAL* 37.2 (2006): 190–205.

Samman, Hanadi Al-. "Out of the Closet: Representation of Homosexuals and Lesbians in Modern Arabic Literature." *JAL* 39.2 (2008): 270–310 [Includes brief discussion of Alia Mamdouh's 2007 novel *al-Tashahhi*].

Samarrai, Ghanim. "Hymn of the Rain: Assyaab's Decolonizing Task." *International Journal of Arabic–English Studies* 36.2 (2005): 35–46.

Saqr, Mahdi Isa al-. "On Mahmood Abdel Wahab." *Banipal* 21 (Autumn 2004): 76–77.

———, trans. "Testimony of Six Iraqi Authors: Life and Culture in Baghdad." *Banipal* 18 (Autumn 2003): 63–65 [Testimonies of Mahdi Isa al-Saqr, Saad Muhammed Raheem, Natiq Khaloosy, Wared Bader al-Salem, Mohammed Darwish Ali, and Taha Hamid Shabeeb].

Sbait, Dirgham H. "A Tribute to Nazik al-Mala'ikah, Poetess & Scholar Par Excellence." *Oregon Literary Review* 3.2 (2008).

Semaan, Khalil. "Islamic Mysticism in Modern Arabic Poetry and Drama." *IJMES* 10.4 (1979): 517–31 [See especially 519–23 on Abd al-Wahhab al-Bayati].

Shabaz, Stan. "Tribute to Sargon Boulus." http://www.zindamagazine.com/html/archives/2007/11.05.07/index_mon.php.

Shakarchi, Jawad al-. "Iraqi Actor Hopes for Theatre's Revival." Interview by Ahmed Janabi. http://english.aljazeera.net/NR/exeres/5AD360AF-9C7D-4183-99EA-96B2A2D15992. Web.

Shafiq, Hashim. Interview. By Soheil Najm. Trans. S. A. [Su'ad Ali]. *Gilgamesh* 1 (2005): 53–57.

Shawabikah, Muhammad 'Ali. *Arabs and the West: A Study in the Modern Arabic Novel, 1935–1985.* Karak: Mu'tah University, 1992 [Includes a brief discussion of three Iraqi novels by Dhu al-Nun Ayyub, Yusuf Izz al-Din, and Samira al-Mana along with a synopsis for each. See 53, 61–63, 89–93, 193, 208, and 220].

Sh'hadeh, Yousef. "Tormenting Thoughts on Exile: Hard Time and Alienation in Hatif al-Janabi's Poetry." *Rocznik Orientalistyczny* 56.2 (2003): 57–64.

Shimon, Samuel. "What's between the Poet and the Church?" Trans. Samuel Shimon and Margaret Obank. *Banipal* 2 (June 1998): 72–73 [A film script].

———. "A Travelling Tale: Steppenwolf Goes to San Francisco." Trans. Peter Clark. *Banipal* 23 (Summer 2005): 134–42.

Simawe, Saadi A., ed. *Modern Iraqi Literature in English Translation.*
A special issue of *Arab Studies Quarterly* 19.4 (Fall 1997) [Includes
articles by Salih J. Altoma, Carol Bardenstein, Alex Bellem, Hussein
Kadhim, Saadi Simawe, Wiebke Walther, and Salaam Yousif].

———. "The Politics and the Poetics of Sa'di Yusuf: The Use of the Ver-
nacular." *Arab Studies Quarterly* 19.4 (1997): 173–86.

———. "The Lives of the Sufi Masters in 'Abd al-Wahhab al-Bayati's Poetry." *JAL* 32.2 (2001): 119–41.

———. "Modernism and Metaphor in Contemporary Arabic Poetry." *World
Literature Today* 75.2 (2002): 275–284. Rpt. in *Twayne Companion to
Contemporary World Literature.* Ed. Pamela A. Genova. New York:
Twayne; Thomas Gale, 2003. 146–54 [Focuses on Badr Shakir al-
Sayyab and includes extracts of his poems "A Stranger at the Gulf" and
"The Book of Job"].

———. Rev. of *"Contemporary Iraqi Fiction: An Anthology,* ed. and trans.
Shakir Mustafa. *JAL* 40.1 (2009): 129–32.

Simon, Rachel. Rev. of *"Women on a Journey: between Baghdad and London.* Haifa Zangana; Trans. Judy Cumberbatch. Austin, TX: The Center
for Middle Eastern Studies, the University of Texas, 2007." *DOMES*
17.1, 210–11.

Smoor, Pieter. "Modern Poets of Iraq 1948–79: Cockroach or Martyr in the
Inn by the Persian Gulf." *Oriente Moderno* 9.1–6 (1990): 7–38.

———. "The Influence of T. S. Eliot on a Representative Modern Arab
Poet: Badr Shakir al-Sayyab." *Centennial Hauntings: Pope, Byron and
Eliot in the Year 88.* Ed. C. C. Barfoot and T. D'Haen. Amsterdam:
Rodopi, 1990, 341–62.

Snir, Reuven. "'We Were Like Those Who Dream': Iraqi–Jewish Writers
in Israel in the 1950s." *Prooftexts* 11 (1991): 153–73.

———. Rev. of Kazzaz, *The Jews in Iraq in the Twentieth Century. The
Jewish Quarterly Review, New Series* 84.4 (1994): 495–500.

———. "Forget Baghdad! The Clash of Literary Narratives among
Iraqi–Jews in Israel/Preview." *Orientalia Suecana: An International
Journal of Indological, Iranian, Semitic and Turkic Studies* 53 (2004):
143–63.

———. "'When Time Stopped': Ishaq Bar-Moshe as Arab–Jewish Writer in
Israel." *Jewish Social Studies* 11.2 (Winter 2005): 102–35.

———. "Arabic Literature by Iraqi Jews in the Twentieth Century: The
Case of Ishaq Bar-Moshe (1927–2003)." *Middle Eastern Studies* 41.1
(2005): 7–29.

———. "We Are Arabs before We Are Jews: The Emergence and Demise of Arab–Jewish Culture in Modern Times." *Electronic Journal of Oriental Studies* 8.9 (2005): 1–47.

———. "'Till Spring Comes': Arabic and Hebrew Literary Debates among Iraqi–Jews in Israel (1950–2000)." *Shofar: An Interdisciplinary Journal of Jewish Studies* 24.2 (2006): 92–123.

———. "'Arabs of the Mosaic Faith': Jewish Writers in Modern Iraq and the Clash of Narratives after Their Immigration to Israel." *Poetry's Voice-Society's Norms: Forms of Interaction between Middle Eastern Writers and Their Societies.* Ed. Angelika Neuwirth et al. Wiesbaden: Reichert, 2006.

———. "Arabic Journalism as a Vehicle for Enlightenment." *Journal of Modern Jewish Studies* 6.3 (2007): 219–37.

Somekh, Sasson. "Lost Voices: Jewish Authors in Modern Arabic Literature." *Jews among Arabs: Contacts and Boundaries.* Ed. Mark R. Cohen and A. L. Udovitch. Princeton: Darwin Press, 1989, 9–20.

———. "The Neo-Classical Arabic Poets." *Modern Arabic Literature.* Ed. M. M. Badawi. Cambridge; New York: Cambridge University Press, 1992, 36–81 [Covers Muhammad Mahdi al-Jawahiri, Ma'ruf al-Rusafi, and Jamil Sidqi al-Zahawi].

———. "Biblical Echoes in Modern Arabic Literature." *JAL* 26 (1995): 186–200.

———. *Baghdad, Yesterday: The Making of an Arab Jew.* Jerusalem: Ibis Editions, 2007.

———. From "Baghdad, Yesterday." *Gates of Reconciliation: Literature and the Ethical Imagination.* Ed. Barry Lopez. Honolulu: University of Hawaii Press, 2008, 128–36 [See *Mānoa* 20.1 (2008): 128–36].

Starkey, Paul. *Modern Arabic Literature.* Edinburgh: Edinburg University Press; Washington, D.C.: Georgetown University Press, 2006 [Offers a concise treatment of Iraqi traditional and modernistic poets, but limited information on Iraqi novelists].

Stevens, Simon. "Nazik al-Malaika (1923–2007): Iraqi Woman's Journey Changes Map of Arabic Poetry." *AlJadid* 58/59 (2007/2008).

Stewart, Desmond. "Abdul-Wahab Al-Bayati: A Poet of Exile." *New Middle East* (November 1972: 27–30).

"The Story of a Daring Publisher." Trans. Margaret Obank from German. *Banipal* 18 (Autumn 2003): 72–73 [Khalid al-Maaly's Camel Celebrates 20 Years of Publishing].

Sulaiman, Khalid A. *Palestine and Modern Arab Poetry.* London: ZED Books, 1984 [Includes numerous citations by neoclassical and modern Iraqi poets, such as al-Jawahiri, Rusafi, al-Bayati, and al-Sayyab].

Suleiman, Yasir. "Nationalist Concerns in the Poetry of Nazik al-Mala'ika." *British Journal of Middle Eastern Studies* 22: 1–2 (1995): 93–114.

———. "The Nation Speaks: On the Poetics of Nationalist Literature." *Literature and the Nation in the Middle East.* Ed. Yasir Suleiman and Ibrahim Muhawi. Edinburgh: Edinburg University Press, 2005, 208–231 [Focuses on Nazik al-Mala'ikah with a few references to the poetry of her mother and Atikah Wahbi al-Khazraji].

Sultani. Fadhil. "Badr Shakir al-Sayyab: One Heritage for Humankind." *Banipal* 5 Summer 1999): 11.

Taheri, Amir. "Book of the Book: An Iraqi Poet Finds a New Language: English." *Asharq Alawsat, English ed. May 3, 2006 [Regarding Jamal Juma's Book of the Book].*

Takarli, Fu'ad. Interview. By Nadhim al-Su'ood and Majid Tufan. Trans. Nibras Abdulhadi. *Gilgamesh* 3 (2005): 48–50.

———. "Iraq's Most Beloved Novelist, Fuad al-Takarli, Describes His Fine Balancing Act." An Interview by Rebecca Joubin. *AlJadid* 13 (58/59 2007).

Tami, Ahmed al-. "Arabic 'Free Verse': The Problem of Terminology." *JAL* 24.2 (1993): 185–98. [Discusses in detail "Free Verse" as defined or used by the Iraqi poet Nazik al-Mala'ikah and other Arab poets and critics].

Tatchell, Jo. *Nabeel's Song: A Family Story of Survival in Iraq.* London; Sceptre; New York: Doubleday, 2006 [A biography of Nabil Yasin]. See also *The Poet of Baghdad: A True Story of Love and Defiance.* New York: Broadway Books, 2008.

Tramontini, Leslie. "Fatherland, if Ever I Betrayed You . . . Reflections on Nationalist Iraqi Poetry of Thawrat al-'ishrin." *Al-Abhath* 50/51 (2002–2003): 161–86.

"Testimony of Six Iraqi Writers: Life and Culture in Baghdad." *Banipal* 18 (Autumn 2003): 63–65 [Mohammed Darwish Ali, Natiq Khaloosy, Saad Mohammed Raheem, Mahdi Issa al-Saqr, Wared Badr al-Salem, and Taha Hamid Shabeeb].

Thamir, Fadhil. "The Iraqi Story and Social Change." Trans. Salim Shamoun. *Gilgamesh* (1/1986): 72–75.

Thompson, Nissa. "Does the International Violence against Women Act Respond to Lessons from the Iraq War?" *Berkeley Journal of Gender, Law & Justice* 23 (2008): 1–17 [Discusses and incorporates standards derived from Haifa Zangana's *City of Widows: An Iraqi Woman's Account of War and Resistance* (2007)].

The Undergraduate's Companion to Arab Writers and Their Web Sites. Ed. Donna S. Straley. Westport, CT: Libraries Unlimited, 2004 [An informative guide that includes entries on the following Iraqi writers: Fadhil al-Azzawi, Abd al-Wahhab al-Bayati, Sargon Boulus, Muhammad Mahdi al-Jawahiri, Amal al-Juburi, Nazik al-Mala'ikah, Aliyah Mamduh, Dunya Mikhail, Samir Naqqash, Muzaffar al-Nawwab, Badr Shakir al-Sayyab, Fu'ad al-Takarli, and Sa'di Yusuf].

Valassopoulos, A. *Contemporary Arab Women Writers: Cultural Expression in Context.* London: Routledge, 2007 [Includes a brief discussion of Alia Mamdouh's *Mothballs*, see pp. 109–10].

Wallin, Birgitta. "Editor of Swedish Karavan, Birgitta Wallin: We Need More Translations." Interview by Samuel Shimon. *Banipal* 22 (Spring 2002): 132–133. Print [Includes remarks regarding Sa'di Yusuf].

Walther, Wiebke. "Distant Echoes of Love in the Narrative Work of Fu'ad al-Tikirli." *Love and Sexuality in Modern Arabic Literature.* Ed. Roger Allen et al. London: Saqi Books, 1995, 131–39, 244–43.

———. "From Women's Problems to Women as Images in Modern Iraqi Poetry." *Welt des Islam* 36.2 (1996): 219–41.

———. "Studies in Human Psyche and Human Behavior under Political and Social Pressure: The Recent Literary Works of Fu'ad Al-Takarli." *Arab Studies Quarterly* 19.4 (1997): 21–36.

———. "'My Hands Assisted the Hands of Events': The Memoirs of the Iraqi Poet Muhammad Mahdi al-Jawahiri. *"Writing the Self: Autobiographical Writing in Modern Arabic Literature.* Ed. Robin Ostle, Ed de Moor, and Stefan Wild. London: Saqi Books, 1998, 249–59, 325–27.

———. "The Beginnings of the Realistic School of Narrative Prose in Iraq." *Quaderni di Studi Arabi* 18 (2000): 175–98 [Focuses on Sulayman Faydi (1885–1951) and Mahmud Ahmad al-Sayyid (1901/3–1937)].

Wardani, Mahmoud. "When the Sea Changed Its Color." *Al-Ahram Online Weekly,* 451, 14–20 October 1999.

Wasiti, Salman D. al-. "Introduction." *Ten Iraqi Soldier-Poets: An Anthology.* Ed. Salman D. Al-Wasiti. Baghdad: Dar al-Ma'mun, 1988 [Includes extracts of war-related poems by Abd al-Razzaq, Abd al-Wahid, Yasin Taha Hafiz, Sami Mahdi, Hamid Sa'id, and Muhammad Jamil Shalash].

Weidner, Stefan. "Youssef's Place in Modern Arabic Poetry: The Art of the Stork." *Banipal* 7 (Spring 2000): 4 [On Sa'di Yusuf].

"What Will Be the New Future for the Literature and Culture of Iraq?" *Banipal* 17 (Summer 2003): 67–71 [Views of seven Iraqi authors and artists: Fadhil Assultani, Fadhil al-Azzawi, Fawzi Karim, Fatima Mohsen, Faisal Laibi Sahi, Hashem Shafiq, and Saadi Youssef].

Whitney, Eleanor. Rev. of *Zubaida's Window,* by Iqbal al-Qazwini. *Feminist Review* 5 May 2008. http://feministreview.blogspot.com/2008/05/

zubaidas-window-novel-of-iraqi-exile.html [With its unflinching treatment of the role power-hungry governments play in fueling war and oppression, *Zubaida's Window* is a must read for anyone looking for a fresh perspective on the war in Iraq and its effects on the lives of Iraqis].

Wild, Stefan. "National Socialism in the Arab Near East between 1933 and 1939." *Die Welts des Islams* 25 (1985): 126–1773 [Includes reference to Badr Shakir al-Sayyab's elegy "Martyrs of Freedom" in which he revealed, as a 16-year-old boy, pro-German sentiments and the anti-British orientation prevailing during the 1940s. Wild cites as an example al-Sayyab's verse: "The confederates of the English have shed their blood/ But in Berlin a lion is watching them." The article refers also to one of Anwar Sha'ul's poems that he wrote in 1941 against Axis propaganda].

Wiley, Joyce. "Alima Bint al-Huda, Women's Advocate." *The Most Learned of the Shia: The Institution of the Marja Taqlid.* Ed. Linda S. Walbridge. New York: Oxford University Press, 2001, 149–60 [A brief account of Bint al-Huda's writings including some of her short stories and novels].

Wynn, L. L. "Iraqi Resistance Literature." *Khaldoun.* http://khaldoun.wordpress.com/2008/09/12/iraqi-resistance-literature/.

The World Encyclopedia of Contemporary Theatre. Ed. Don Rubin et al. 5 vols. London; New York: Routledge, 2001 [Volume IV covers the Arab world including the section on Iraq (pp. 103–30), written originally in Arabic and translated by Maha and Tony Chehade. A few references are made to Yusuf al-Ani, Khalid al-Shawwaf, and Sa'dun al-Ubaydi].

Yazici, Huseyin. *The Short Story in Modern Arabic Literature.* Cairo: General Egyptian Book Organization, 2004, 81–94 [Includes references to numerous short-story collections by Iraqi authors and their subjects].

Yousif, Salaam. "The People's Theatre of Yusuf al-Ani." *Arab Studies Quarterly* 19.4 (1997): 65–93.

———. "The Struggle for Cultural Hegemony during the Iraqi Revolution." In *The Iraqi Revolution of 1958: The Old Social Classes Revisited.* Ed. Robert A. Fernea and Wm. Roger Louis. London: I. B. Tauris and Co. Ltd., 1991, 172–96.

———. «Le déclin de l'intelligentsia de gauche en Irak/On the Decline of the Leftist Intelligentsia in Iraq» *Revue des mondes musulmans et de la Méditerranée* 117–18 (2007): 51–79.

Yusuf, Sa'di. "On Reading the Earth." Trans. Ferial J. Ghazoul. *Alif* 13 (1993): 176–81 [Yusuf's speech delivered when he was awarded Sultan al-'Uways Poetry Prize for 1992]. Rpt. in *The View from Within: Writers and Critics on Contemporary Arabic Literature.* Ed. Ferial Ghazoul and

Barbara Harlow. Cairo: The American University in Cairo Press, 1994, 12–16.

———. Blessed Be the Quest." *Al-Ahram Weekly Online*, 376 7–13 May 1998 [On Nizar Qabbani].

———. "Iraqi Poet Saadi Youssef on 'Bullet Censorship'" An Interview by Jonathan Maunder. *Socialist Worker*, 26 August 2006. www.socialist worker.co.uk/art.php?id=9512.

———. "Interview" Lailah Nadir with James Byrne. *The Wolf* 15 (June 2007).

———. "An Interview with Poet Saadi Youssef." By Joy E. Stocke. *The Wild River Review*, September 2007.

Zangana, Haifa. "Iraqi Novelist Haifa Zangana: U.S. Troops Must Withdraw Now." Interview with Amy Goodman. *Democracy Now*, 9 March 2006 [Includes Zangana's translation of a poem by Nidal Abbas entitled "Sarre men ra'a [sic]"].

———. "Interview with Haifa Zangana." Wen-Chen Ouyang. *Comparative Critical Studies* 4.3 (2007): 447–53.

———. *City of Widows: An Iraqi Woman's Account of War and Resistance.* New York: Seven Stories Press, 2007 [Represents a leading woman activist's perspective and overview in regard to Iraqi women's role from the early 20th century until the present].

———. "Excerpt from *City of Widows: An Iraqi Woman's Account of War and Resistance.*" *Pen International* 52.2 (Winter 2007): 45–49.

Zeidan, Joseph T. *Arab Women Novelists: The Formative Years and Beyond.* New York: SUNY Press, 1995.

Zubaida, Sami. "The Fragments Imagine the Nation: The Case of Iraq." *International Journal of Middle East Studies 34.2* (2002): 205–15. [Deals in part with Muhammad Mahdi al-Jawahiri and his turbulent career].

———. "Entertainers in Baghdad, 1900–50." *Outside In: On the Margins of the Middle East.* Ed. Eugene L. Rogan. London; New York: L. B. Tauris, 2002, 212–30 [Includes selected relevant verses by al-Rusafi and other poets].

———. "Al-Jawahiri between Patronage and Revolution." *Revue des Mondes Musulmans et de la Méditerranée* 117–18 (2007): 81–97.

II

TRANSLATIONS

1

Autobiographical Essays

The following autobiographical essays are based on Arabic versions written by Iraqi authors who participated in a larger project undertaken in the 1980s at St. Joseph University's Center for the Study of the Modern Arab World, Beirut, Lebanon. They were originally published in a two-volume dictionary in 1996 covering more than 350 poets, novelists, playwrights, and critics from different Arab countries including Iraq. As listed in the 2004 updated two-volume English edition,[1] the essays present the original Arabic texts as provided by the authors themselves except in a few cases (marked by*) where the autobiographical section was extracted from other Arabic sources. The only exception is al-Khalili's essay, which was based on a doctorate dissertation presented to the University of Michigan, 1972 by J. Thomas Hamel under the title "Ja'far al- Khalili and the Modern Iraqi Short Story." Apart from the autobiographical component, each essay begins with a brief biographical section (full name, date of birth, education and career) and concludes with a list of the author's publications and other relevant items if available. In brief, these entries provide useful information on a wide range of trends that characterize Iraq's modern literature as viewed by more than thirty Iraqi authors who represent different genres, perspectives, and generations.

---

[1] *Crosshatching in Global Culture: A Dictionary of Modern Arab Writers: An Updated English Version of R. R. Campbell's "Contemporary Arab Writers."* John Donohue and Leslie Tramontini, eds. 2 vols. Beirut: Orient-Institut, 2004. For information on the history of the project, see the introduction XVII–XVIII.

VOLUME I

Amarah, Lami'ah, 505–508
Amir, Daisy al-, 107–110
Ani, Shuja'Muslim al-, 112–113
*Ani, Yusuf al-, 114–116 [Extracted from the playwright's introduction to his plays and an interview]
Ayyub, Dhu al-Nun, 174–178
Bayati, Abd al-Wahhab al-, 234–238
Boulus, Sargon, 263–266
Farman, Gha'ib Tu'mah, 332–334
al-Haydari, Buland, 446–448
Izz al-Din, Yusuf, 526–530
*Ja'far, Hasab al-Shaykh, 548–551 [Extracted from an interview]
*Jawahiri, Muhammad Mahdi al-, 554–558 [Extracted from two interviews]
Karim, Fawzi, 587–589
Kasid, Abd al-Karim, 594–596

VOLUME II

*al-Khalili, Ja'far, 619–623 [Based on Hamel's dissertation cited above]
Khayyat, Jalal Ayyub, 638–640
Khulusi, Abd al-Hamid, 653–656
*Khusbak, Shakir, 671–675 [Extracted from an interview]
Lu'lu'ah, Abd al-Wahid. 692–695.
*Mal'ikah, Nazik al-, 746–750 [Excerpted from two inteviews]
Mana (=Mani'), Samira al-, 756–757
Musawi, Muhsin Jasim al-, 813–817
Muttalibi, Abd al-Razzaq al-, 823–826
*Najafi, Ahmad al-Safi.al-, 826–830 [Excerpted from several sources]
*Nasir, Abd al-Sattar, 843–845 [Excerpted from an interview]
Nasir, Yasin Nazal al-. See Nusayyir, Yasin al-
Nusayyir, Yasin al-, 846–848
Niyazi, Salah, 869–871

2

Drama[1]

Ani, Yusuf al- (1927–).

———. "The Key." Trans. Salwa Jabsheh and Alan Brownjohn. *Modern Arabic Drama: An Anthology.* Ed. Salma Khadra Jayyusi and Roger Allen. Bloomington: Indiana University Press, 1995, 253–88.

———. "Three Plays of Yousif Al-`Ani: Translation and Introduction." by Waleed Shamil Hussain. Ph.D. dissertation. University of California, Los Angeles, 1989 [Includes translations of *Welcome Life*, *New Picture*, and *The Past Repeats Itself Anew*].

———. "Where the Power Lies." Trans. Lena Jayyusi and Thomas G. Ezzy. *Short Arabic Plays.* Ed. Salma Khadra Jayyusi. New York: Interlink Books, 2003, 1–19.

Asadi, Jawad.al-. *Forget Hamlet/Insu Hamlit.* Trans. Margaret Litvin. Brisbane: The University of Queensland, 2006.

———. "Baghdadi Bath." Trans. Robert Myers and Nada Saab. *Performing Arts Journal* 30.89 (2008): 112–23.

Assady, Jawad, al-. See Asadi, Jawad al-.

Hajaj, Kadhem al-. See Hajjaj, Kazim al-.

Hajjaj, Kazim al-. "The Actor." A One Act Play. Trans. Zainab Wadie, et al.*Gilgamesh* 1 (2005): 43–47.

Isma'il, Muhyi al-Din. "The Fall of the Black Wall." *Iraq Today* (Dec.16–31, 1977): 20–23.

---

[1] As noted earlier, in the introduction, of all genres, Iraqi drama is the least represented in English translations or studies. This marginal representation applies to Arabic drama in general. For related articles, see (under Part I) Ghazoul (1998); Litvin (2007); Machut-Mendecka (1999, 2000); Moosa (1981); Nusayyir (1982); Rakha (1999); and Yousif (1997, 2007).

Mana [al-Maniʿ], Samira al-. *Only a Half.* A play in two acts. Trans. Farida
    Abu-Haidar. London: Panorama Print, 1984.
Takarli, Fuʾad al-. "Coloured Telephones: A Dialogue." Trans. Catherine
    Cobham. *The Word* 1.3 (Mar. 2007). www.al-kalimah.com/English/
    2007/January/Edefault.html.

3

Fiction

A. ANTHOLOGIES AND NOVELS

Amir, Daisy al- (1935–). *The Waiting List: An Iraqi Woman's Journey toward Independence and Other Stories.* Trans. Barbara Parmenter. Austin: Center for Middle Eastern Studies, University of Texas, 1994.

Antoon, Sinan (1967–). *I'jam: An Iraqi Rhapsody.* Trans. author and Rebecca C. Johnson. San Francisco: City Lights, 2007.

Azzawi, Fadhil al- (1940–). *The Last of the Angels.* Trans. William M. Hutchins. Cairo: AUCP, 2007.

———. *Cell Block Five.* Trans. William M. Hutchins. Cairo: AUCP, 2008.

Badr, Ali. *Papa Sartre.* Trans. Aida A. Bamia. Cairo: AUCP, 2009.

Battlefront Stories from Iraq. Trans. A. W. Lu'lu'a. Baghdad: Dar al-Ma'mun for Translation and Publishing, 1982 [Includes a novella by Adil Abd al-Jabbar (pp. 7–90) and seven other short stories by Khudayyir Abd al-Amir, Latif Nasir Hasan, Ali Khayyun, Abd al-Sattar Nasir, Abd al-Khaliq al-Rikabi, Adnan al-Rubay'i, and Muhsin al-Thuwadi].

Contemporary Iraqi Fiction: An Anthology. Ed. and trans. Shakir Mustafa. Syracuse, NY: Syracuse University Press, 2008 [Includes selections from the works of sixteen authors: Ibtisam Abdullah, Ibrahim Ahmad, Lutfiyah al-Dulaimi, Maysalun Hadi, Muhammad Khudayyir, Samira al-Mana, Nasrat Mardan, Shmuel Moreh, Samir Naqqash, Abdul Sattar Nasir, Jalil al-Qaisi, Abdul Rahman, Majeed al-Rubaie, Mahmoud Saeed, Salima Salih, Mahdi Isa al-Saqr, Samuel Shimon].

Iraqi Short Stories: An Anthology. Ed. Yassen Taha Hafidh and Lutfiyah al-Dulaymi. Baghdad: Dar al-Ma'mun for Translation, 1988 [Includes thirty-eight short stories representing different generations of pre- and post-1950s writers].

Kachachi, Inaam. *The American Granddaughter.* Trans. Nariman Youssef. Doha: Bloomsbury Qatar Foundation; London: Bloomsbury, 2010.

Khedairi, Betool. (1965–). *A Sky So Close.* Trans. Muhayman Jamil. New York: Pantheon Books, 2001.

———. *Absent.* Trans. Muhayman Jamil. Cairo: AUCP, 2005; New York: Random House, 2007.

Khudayyir, Muhammad (1940–). *Basrayatha: Portrait of a City.* Trans. William M. Hutchins. Cairo: AUCP, 2007.

Mamdouh, Alia (1944–). *Mothballs.* Trans. Peter Theroux. Reading, UK: Garnet, 1996. Rpt. in *Naphtalene: A Novel of Baghdad.* New York: The Feminist Press at the City University of New York, 2005.

———. *The Loved Ones.* Trans. Marilyn Booth. Cairo: AUCP, 2006.

Mana, Samira al- (1935–). *The Umbilical Cord.* Trans. By the author; Ed. Charles Lewis. West Yorkshire, UK: Central Publishing Services, 2005.

———. *The Oppressors.* [An extract from the novella *The Oppressors.* Trans. Paul Starkey. London: Exiled Writers Ink, 2008.

Matar, Salim (1956–). *Woman of the Flask.* Trans. Peter Clark. Cairo: American University in Cairo Press, 2004.

Modern Iraqi Short Stories. Trans. Ali M. Cassimy [al-Kasimi] and W. McClung Frazier. Baghdad: Ministry of Information, 1971 [Includes eleven short stories by Daisy al-Amir, Dhu al-Nun Ayyub, Gha'ib Tu'mah Farman, Abd al-Majid Lutfi, Ja'far al-Khalili, Shakir Khusbak, Salah al-Din al-Nahi, Abd Allah Niyazi, Abd al-Malik Nuri, Mahmud al-Sayyid, and Fu'ad Takarli].

Mu'alla, Abd al-Amir (1942–1997). *The Long Days.* 3 vols. Volumes 1 and 2 trans. Mohieddin Ismail. London: Ithaca Press, 1979/1980. Volume 3 trans. Abd al Wahid Lu'lu'a. Baghdad: Dar al-Ma'mun for Translation, 1982.

Nasiri, Buthaynah al- (1947–). *Final Night: Short Stories.* Trans. Denys Johnson-Davies. Cairo: AUCP, 2002.

Qazwini, Iqbal (195?–). *Zubaida's Window.* Trans. Azza El Kholy and Amira Nowaira. New York: Feminist Press at the City University of New York, 2008.

Ramli, Muhsin al- (1967–). *Scattered Crumbs.* Trans. Yasmeeñ S. Hanoosh. Fayetteville: University of Arkansas Press, 2003.

Sadr, Aminah Haydar al- (1937/8–1980). *Friendly Letters.* Trans. M. N. Sultan. Tehran: Islamic Thought Foundation, 1985.

———. *In Search of Truth.* Trans. M. N. Sultan. Tehran: Islamic Thought Foundation, 1987.

———. *Two Women and a Man.* Trans. M. N. Sultan Tehran: Islamic Thought Foundation, 1987. [Reproduced by Ahlul Bayt Digital Islamic Library Project Team].

——. *Short Stories* [12 short stories]. Trans. M. N. Sultan. Tehran: Islamic Thought Foundation, 1987.

——. *Encounter at the Hospital.* Trans. M. N. Sultan. Tehran: Islamic Thought Foundation, 1987.

——. *Virtue Prevails.* Trans. M. N. Sultan. Tehran: Islamic Thought Foundation, 1991.

Saeed, Mahmoud (1939–). *Saddam City.* Trans. Ahmad Sadri. London: Saqi Books, 2004.

——. *Two Lost Souls.* Schaumburg, IL: Joshua Tree Publishers, 2006.

Shimon, Samuel (1956–). *An Iraqi in Paris: An Autobiographical Novel.* Trans. Samira Kawar et al. London: Banipal Books, 2005.

Takarli, Fu'ad (1927–2008). *The Long Way Back.* Trans. Catherine Cobham. Cairo: AUCP, 2001, 2007.

Zangana, Haifa (1950–). *Through the Vast Halls of Memory.* Trans. Paul Hammond and the author. Paris: Hourglass, 1991. Rpt. as *Dreaming of Baghdad.* New York: Feminist Press at the City University of New York, 2009.

——. *Women on a Journey between Baghdad and London.* Trans. Judy Cumberbatch. Austin, TX: The Center for Middle Eastern Studies, The University of Texas at Austin, 2007.

B. SHORT STORIES AND NOVEL EXTRACTS

Abbadi, Ghazi al- (1935/1940–1998).

——. "Five Rivers of Paradise." *ISS:* 109–125.

——. "The Game and Rules." Trans. Adil Abd al-Jabbar. *Iraq Today* (Jan. 1–15, 1978): 32.

Abbas, Lu'ay Hamza (1965–). "Two Short Stories" ["Closing His Eyes" and "A Much-Travelled Man"]. Trans. Yasmeen Hanoosh. *Banipal* 27 (Autumn/Winter 2006): 5–8.

Abdallah, Ibtisam (1943–).

——. "The Nursery." Trans. Shakir Mustafa. *Banipal* 18 (Autumn 2003): 53–54. Rpt. in *MC*: 182–85.

——. "The Other in the Mirror." *MC*: 185–90.

Abd al-Amir, Khudayyir (1934–).

——. "The Boy." Trans. Hrant Aghajan. *Gilgamesh* (2/1986): 47–52.

——. "The Castle." Trans. Yania S. Atallah. *Gilgamesh* (2/1986): 52–58.

——. "Clay Figures." Trans. Kadhim Saadedin. *Iraq Today* (Sept. 1–15, 1979): 31–32.

———. "Mud Structure." *ISS*: 85–91.
———. "A Soldier's Leave." *BS*: 133–49.
Abd al-Ilah. Lu`ay (1949–).
———. "The Ice Guard." Trans. Fiona Collins. *Banipal* 2 (July 1998): 18–19.
Abd al-Jabbar, Adil (1937–1991).
———. "After All That Time." *BS*: 7–90.
Abd al-Latif, Salah (1950–).
———. "The Supermarket." Trans. Salam Yousif. *Edebiyât* 8: 1 (1998): 125–27.
Abd al-Majid, Muhammad. "On Death and Joy." *ISS*: 225–34.
Abd al-Qadir, Abd al-Ilah (1940–).
———. "The Birthday Party." Trans. May Jayyusi and Christopher Tingley. *JMAF*: 144–49.
Abd al-Razzaq, Abd al-Ilah (1939–).
———. "Time for Bullets." *ISS*: 235–40.
———. "Voices from Near and Far." *Arabic Short Stories.* Trans. Denys Johnson-Davies. London: Quartet Books, 1983, 11–115.
Abdel Wahab, Mahmoud or Abdul Wahhab, Mahmood. See Abd al-Wahhab, Mahmud.
Abd al-Wahhab, Mahmud (1929–).
———. "Two Short Stories" ["A Different Kind of Women" and "An Exceptional Passer-by"]. Trans. Mahdi Isa al-Saqr. *Banipal* 21 (Autumn 2004): 74–77.
———. "Drucucu." Trans. Noor Abdul Jabbar. *Gilgamesh* 1 (2005): 34–35.
Abed, Kareem (1952–).
———. "Photographic Life." Trans. Fiona Collins. *Banipal* 3 (Oct. 1998): 26–27.
———. "Troubles, Laughter and Sparrows." Trans. Fiona Collins. *Banipal* 3 (Oct. 1998): 27.
Abdulilah, Luay. See Abd al-Ilah, Lu'ay.
Ahmad, Ibrahim (1946–).
———. "The Arctic Refugee." *MC*: 191–195.
———. "The Mailed Parcel." Trans. Lily al-Tai. *BR*: 14–18.
———. "The Man with the Umbrella." Trans. Peter Clark. *Banipal* 14 (2002): 22–24.
Ahmady, Kazim.al- "They Also Dream." Trans. Hashim G. Lazim. *Iraq Today* (June 16–30, 1978): 30–32.
Amin, Abd Allah Hamid al- "The Decision." Trans. Adil Abd al-Jabbar. *Iraq Today* (May 16–31, 1978): 30–32.

Amir, Daisy al- (1935–).

———. "An Andalusin Tale." *MISS*: 89–96.

———. "The Aunt of Rafiq." Trans. Tura Campanella. *Women and the Family in the Middle East: New Voices of Change.* Ed. Elizabeth Warnock Fernea. Austin: University of Texas Press, 1985, 209–14.

———. "The Cat, the Maid, and the Wife." *An Arabian Mosaic: Short Stories by Arab Women Writers.* Collected and trans. Dalya Cohen-Mor. Potomac, MD: Sheba Press, 1993, 115–20.

———. "The Doctor's Prescription." Trans. Barbara Parmenter. *AB*: 23–25.

———. "The Eyes in the Mirror." Trans. Miriam Cooke. *Opening the Gates: A Century of Arab Feminist Writing.* Ed. Margot Badran and Miriam Cooke. Bloomington: Indiana University Press, 1990, 115–18.

———. "The Future." *An Arabian Mosaic* (cited above): 41–48.

———. "The Future." Trans. Miriam Cooke. *BI*: 156–61. Rpt. in *Women on War: An International Anthology of Writings from Antiquity to the Present.* Ed. Daniela Gioseffi. New York: The Feminist Press at the City University of New York, 2003, 309–13.

———. "The Newcomer." *ISS*: 283–88.

———. "The Next Step." Trans. Sharif Elmusa and Thomas G. Ezzy. *JMAF*: 173–75.

———. "Tomorrow." Trans. Farida Abu Haidar. *Ur* (3/1981): 54; see also *MAS*: 26–29.

———. *The Waiting List: An Iraqi Woman's Journey toward Independence and Other Stories.* Trans. Barbara Parmenter. Austin: Center for Middle Eastern Studies, University of Texas, 1994.

Anbari, Shakir al- (1957–).

———. "Hidden Roads." Trans. Mohammed Darweesh. *Gilgamesh* 5 (2007): 54–56.

Antoon, Sinan (1967–).

———. "Diacritics" [An excerpt from the novel *Diacritics*]. Trans. by the author from his novel *I'jaam. Banipal* 19 (Spring 2004): 122–28.

———. *I'jam: An Iraqi Rhapsody.* Trans. author and Rebecca C. Johnson. San Francisco: City Lights, 2007.

Antun, Sinan. See Antoon, Sinan.

Asady, Fahd al- (1939–).

———. "Soil Revolution." Trans. Hashim. G. Lazim. *Iraq Today* (Sept. 15–30, 1977): 30–32.

Ayyub, Dhu'l-Nun (1908–1988).

———. "From behind the Veil." Trans. John Fletcher. *Ur* (Mar.–Apr. 1979): 35–38; see also *MAS*: 30–39. Rpt. in *The Graywolf Annual Six: Stories from the Rest of the World.* Ed. Scott Walker. S. Paul, MN: Graywolf Press, 1989, 97–105. [The translation is attributed incorrectly to "S. Al-Bazzazz"]; Rpt. in Reading *the World: Contemporary Literature from around the Globe.* Logan, Iowa: Perfection Learning, 2003, 119–20; *Modern World Literature.* Evanston, IL: Nextext, 2001.

———. "The Little Gods." *FK*: 223–25.

———. "The Little Gods." Trans. May Jayyusi and Christopher Tingley. *JMAF*: 77–80.

———. "A Pillar of the Tower of Babel." *Arab Stories: East and West.* Trans. R. Y. Ebied and M. J. L. Young. Leeds: Leeds University Oriental Society, 1977: 1–11.

———. "The Upright Tomb." *MISS*: 121–28.

———. "The Will of the Saint." Trans. and abridged by Pat Harvey. *Atlantic Monthly* 198 (Oct. 1956): 181–85 [Excerpted from the author's best-known novel *Dr. Ibrahim*, which was published in Arabic in 1936].

Azzawi, Fadhil al- (1940–).

———. "The Dead City." Trans. author. *Banipal* 21 (Autumn 2004): 16–27.

———. "Burhan Abdullah's Secret Chest" [An excerpt from *The Last of the Angels*]. Trans. William M. Hutchins. *Banipal* 26 (Summer 2006): 71–85.

———. "Hameed Nylon." Trans. William M. Hutchins. *Literature from the "Axis of Evil": Writings from Iran, Iraq, North Korea, and Other Enemy Nations.* Ed. editors of *Words without Borders.* New York; London: The New Press, 2006, 77–98.

———. *Cell Block Five.* Trans. William M. Hutchins. Cairo: AUCP, 2008.

———. *The Last of the Angels.* Trans. William M. Hutchins. Cairo: AUCP, 2007.

Bader, Ali. See Badr, Ali.

Badr, Ali (1964–).

———. "The Naked Feast" [An excerpt from the novel]. Trans. Mona Zaki. *Banipal* 20 (Summer 2004): 58–65.

Balasim, Hasan. See Blasim, Hassan.

Balbul, Ya'qub (1920–2003).

———. "Saida, the Midwife." *FK*: 220–22.

Bazzaz, Saad.al- "Arnoun." *MAS*: 54–69.

———. "Arnoun." *ISS*: 359–72.

Blasim, Hassan (1973–).

────. "Crossing Martyrs Bridge." Trans. Jonathan Wright. *Prospect* 153 (Dec. 2008): 66–69 [This is an edited version of the author's story that appeared in *Madinah: City Stories from the Middle East.* Ed. Joumana Haddad. London: Comma Press, 2008].

Bint al-Huda (1938–1980). See Sadr Aminah Haydar al-.

Contemporary Iraqi Fiction: An Anthology. Ed. and trans. Shakir Mustafa. Syracuse, NY: Syracuse University Press, 2008 [Inc. selections from the works of sixteen authors: Ibtisam Abdullah, Ibrahim Ahmad, Lutfiyah al-Dulaimi, Maysalun Hadi, Muhammad Khudayyir, Samira al-Mana, Nasrat Mardan, Shmuel Moreh, Samir Naqqash, Abdul Sattar Nasir, Jalil al-Qaisi, Abdul Rahman Majeed al-Rubaie, Mahmoud Saeed, Salima Salih, Mahdi Isa al-Saqr, Samuel Shimon].

Dabbagh, Ghanim al- "Fresh Water." Trans. Rosette Francis. *L* (Oct.–Dec. 1976): 60–65.

────. "That Night." *ISS*: 75–93.

Dhahir, Mahmud al-. "Orbit." *ISS*: 93–98.

Dulaimi, Lutfiyya al-. See Dulaymi, Lutfiyah al-.

Dulaymi, Lutfiyah al- (1942/1943?–).

────. "Clocks." Trans. Adnan Salman. *Gilgamesh* (1/1986): 37–43.

────. "The Date Harvest." Trans. Kadhim Saadedin. *Iraq Today* (Feb. 16–29, 1980): 28–32.

────. "A Day in a Woman's Life." Trans. Kadhim Saadedin. *Iraq* (Nov.1, 1981): 40–41.

────. "Diary on Tea-Green Leaves." *Iraq Today* (Mar. 1–15, 1981): 32–33.

────. "A Grandson." Trans. Yania S. Atallah. *Iraq Today* (Sept. 15, 1981): 32–35.

────. "Hayat's Garden" [Excerpt from the novel]. Trans. Shakir Mustafa. *Banipal* 26 (Summer 2006): 63–69. Rpt. in *MC*: 22–30.

────. "He Who Came." Trans. Saleh M. al-Hafidh. *Gilgamesh* (1/1986): 23–32.

────. "Lighter than Angels." Trans. May Jayyusi and Christopher Tingley. *JMAF*: 262–65.

────. "Lighter than Angels." *MC*: 39–43.

────. "Picking Season." *ISS*: 177–92 [Another translated version of "The Date Harvest"].

────. "What the Storytellers Did Not Tell." Trans. Shakir Mustafa. *Banipal* 19 (Spring 2004): 93–99. Rpt. under different title in "Shahrazad and Her Narrators."*MC*: 30–39.

Farman, Gha'ib Tu'mah (1927–1990).

———. "Five Voices" [Two chapters from the novel *Khamsat Aswat*]. Trans. Issa Boullata. *Banipal* 29 (Summer 2007): 46–62.

———. "Mr. Ma'ruf"s Woes" [An excerpt from the novella *Alaam* [sic] *al-Sayyid Ma'ruf*]. Trans. William M. Hutchins. *Banipal* 29 (Summer 2007): 63–77.

———. "Uncle Help Me Across." *MISS*: 45–56.

———. "Uncle, Please Help Me Get Across." Trans. Lena Jayyusi and Thomas G. Ezzy. *JMAF* 282–88.

Ghali, Duna (1963–).

———. "Sip." Trans. Shakir Mustafa. *Banipal* 23 (Summer 2005): 13–15.

———. "Helena Saba." A chapter from the novel *indama tastayqidh al-Ra'iha*. Trans. William M. Hutchins. *Banipal* 29 (Summer 2007): 94–99.

———. "The Psychiatrist." [A chapter from the novel *indama tastayqidh al-Ra'iha*]. Trans. William M. Hutchins. *Words without Borders: The Online Magazine for International Literature* Aug. 2008.

Haddad, Yusuf Ya'qub. "The Last Step on Ending the Sufferings." Trans. Kadhim Saadedin. *Iraq Today* (16 June–31 July 1979): 39–40.

Hadi, Maysalun (1954–).

———. "Calendars." *MC*: 73–76.

———. "The Fortune Teller and the Witness." *ISS*: 403–12.

———. "Her Realm of the Real." Trans. Shakir Mustafa. *Banipal* 14 (2002): 20–21. Rpt. in *MC*: 69–73.

———. "The Peep-hole." *Iraq* (Nov. 15, 1985): 34–37.

———. "Good Conduct." Trans. Hazim Malik. *Gilgamesh* 4 (2006): 74–76.

Hafiz, Safirah Jamil (1926–).

———. "The Ice-Cream Seller." *FK*: 236–38.

Hallaq, Kadhim al- (1959–).

———. "Three Short Stories: Boot, A Block of Ice, The Dead Man." Trans. author and Joshua Beckman. *Banipal* 19 (Spring 2004): 105–07.

———. "My One-Eyed Father and His Six Wives" [A chapter from the novel]. Trans by the author with thanks to Don Steinman. *Banipal* 26 (Summer 2006): 86–89.

Hariri, Ibrahim al-. "Books for Sale." Trans. Faisal Muhammad. *Jusoor* 7/8 (1996): 451–58.

Hasan, Latif Nasir (1956–).

———. "The Glitter." *BS*: 189–203.

Hayyawi, Muhammad. "The Lady of the Shack." *ISS*: 413–19.

Hillawi, Janan Jassim (1956–).

———. "Evening Descended Like a Bird." Trans. Paul Starkey. *Banipal* 17 (Summer 2003): 42–45.

Hussein, Hadiyya, or Hadiya. See Husayn, Hadiyyah.

Husayn, Hadiyyah (1956–).

———. "No One Knows That." Trans. Paul Starkey. *Banipal* 18 (Autumn 2003): 55–57.

———. "The Man Who Disappeared." Trans. S. A. [Su'ad Ali]. *Gilgamesh* 1 (2005): 29–30.

Hussein Jabbar Yasin. See Husayn, Jabbar Yasin.

Husayn, Jabbar Yasin. See Hussin, Jabbar Yassin the author's chosen name in French.

Hussin, Jabbar Yassin (1954–).

———. "Short Stories." Trans. Elizabeth Whitehouse. *Banipal* 14 (2002): 10–14 [Inc. "Fever," "Ashura Night," "The Mu'aydi Girl," "Nasser's House," "Return," "The Noise of the Mill," The Honey," "The Pearl," and "The Order of the Story"].

———. "The Day in Buenos Aires." Trans. Randa Jarrar. *Words without Borders: The World through the Eyes of Writers.* Ed. Samantha Schnee et al. New York: Anchor Books, 2007, 111–19.

'Iqabi, Hamid al- (1956–).

———. "The Banjo Player." Trans. Shakir Mustafa. *Banipal* 23 (Summer 2005): 66–68.

———. "The Thieves." Trans. Dunia Khalil. *Gilgamesh* 5 (2007): 65.

Isma'il, Muhyi al-Din. "Pestilence." Trans. Kadhim Saadedin. *Iraq Today* (16–31 Aug. 1979): 31–32.

Jaafar, Abid (1954–).

———. "A Maze of a House." Trans. Aida Bamia. *Banipal* 19 (Spring 2004): 108–14.

Jaza'iri, Zuhayr al- (1945–).

———. "In Hiding" *BR*: 48–51.

———. "The Scream." Trans. Samia Hosny and Robert Twigger. *Banipal* 15/16 (Autumn 2002/Spring 2003): 18–20 [A chapter from a novel].

Jebouri al- or Jibouri al-. Irada. See al-Juburi, Iradah.

Jezairy, Zuhair al-. See Jaza'iri, Zuhayr al-.

Jindari, Mahmud (1944–1995).

———. "Fire." *ISS*: 193–200.

al-Juburi, Iradah (1966–).

————. "Photos." Trans. Batool Ali. *Gilgamesh* 7 (2008): 33–35.

Kachachi, Inaam. "Streams of Hearts." Trans. Muhayman Jamil. *Banipal* 26 (Summer 2006): 90–95.

————. "Women in Fear." *UNS:* 36–45.

Kachachi, Inaam. "If I Forget You, Baghdad." Trans. William Hutchins. *IN Translation* Aug. 2009. http://intranslation.brooklynrail.org/arabic/if-i-forget-you-baghdad-by-inaam-kachachi

Kamil, Adil. "The Absentee." *ISS*: 317–322.

————. "The Child." Trans. Hashim G. Lazim. *Iraq Today* (Aug. 1–15, 1977): 26–28.

Kasimi, Ali al- (1942–).

————. "Fear." Trans. Ali Azeriah. *Kalimat* (Australia) 15 (Sept. 2003): 89–92.

————. "The Unknown Arriver." Trans. Ali Azeriah. *Kalimat* 21 (Mar. 2005): 67–72.

————. "Circles of Sorrow." Trans. Ali Azeriah. *Banipal* 24 (Autumn/Winter 2005): 62–64.

Khalaf, Ahmad. "Over There in the Rain." *ISS*: 213–24.

————. "Helmet for a Half-Dead Man." Trans. Hashim G. Lazim. *Iraq Today* (Mar. 1–15, 1978): 30–32.

Khalili, Ja'far al- (1914–1984).

————. "After Seventy." *MISS*: 57–63.

————. "Grace." *JMAF*: 93–96.

————. A Trivial Affair." Trans. Kadhim Saadedin. *Iraq Today* (16–31 Oct. 1979): 30–31.

Khasbak, Shakir. See Khusbak, Shakir.

Khatib, Burhan al- (1944–).

————. "Autumn Clouds." Trans. Dina Bosio and Christopher Tingley. *JMAF*: 446–467.

————. "The New Street." *ISS*: 273–82.

Khayyun, Ali. "Mourning Does Not Become the Martyrs." *BS*: 167–77.

Khedairi, Betool (1965–).

————. *A Sky So Close*. Trans. Muhayman Jamil. New York: Pantheon Books, 2001.

————. "From *A Sky So Close*." Trans. Muhayman Jamil. Rpt. in *AB*: 248–54.

————. *Absent*. Trans. Muhayman Jamil. Cairo: AUCP, 2005; New York: Random House, 2007.

Khidr, Muwaffaq. "The Pigeon and the Fountain and the Summer's Dream." *ISS*: 99–107.

Khisbak. See Khusbak.

Khodayyir, Muhammad. See Khudayyir, Muhammad.
Khudair, Diya'. See Khudayyir, Diya'.
Khudayr, Muhammad. See Khudayyir, Muhammad.
Khudayri, Batul. See Khedairi, Betool.
Khudayyir, Diya'. "When I Found Myself." Trans. Sharif Elmusa. *MERIP Middle East Report 148* (Sept.–Oct. 1987): 27–31.
Khudayyir, Muhammad (1940–).
———. "Autumn Vision." Trans. Yania S Atallah. *Gilgamesh* (1/1986): 46–47.
———. *Basrayatha: Portrait of a City.* Trans. William M. Hutchins. Cairo: AUCP, 2007.
———. "The Black Kingdom." Trans. Hashim G. Lazim. *Iraq Today* (Feb. 1–15, 1978): 30–31.
———. "Clocks Like Horses." Trans. Denys Johnson-Davies. *Azure* 7 (1980): 28–32; *Arabic Short Stories.* Ed. and trans. Denys Johnson-Davies. London: Quartet Books, 1983: 27–39. Rpt. in *JMAF*: 468–476; *The Graywolf Annual Six: Stories from the Rest of the World.* Ed. Scott Walker. St. Paul, MN: Graywolf Press, 1989, 134–47; *Vital Signs: International Stories on Aging.* Ed. Dorothy Sennett with Anne Czarniecki. St. Paul: Graywolf Press, 1991: 89–103; *Modern Literatures of the Non-Western World: Where the Waters Are Born.* Ed. Jayana Clerk and Ruth Siegel. New York: Harper Collins College Publishers, 1995: 466–76; and in *The Anchor Book of Modern Arabic Fiction.* Ed. Denys Johnson-Davies. New York: Anchor Books, 2006: 258–70.
———. "First Exploration" [Chapter One from the novel *Basrayatha*]. Trans. William M. Hutchins. *Banipal* 26 (Summer 2006): 53–61.
———. "Friday Bounties." Excerpts from Khudayyir's novel, [*Basriyatha*] Trans. Shakir Mustafa. *Edebiyât.* 13.1 (2002): 69–74. Rpt. in *MC*: 13–20.
———. "Hours Swift as Horses." Trans. Eva Elias. In *Flights of Fantasy: Arabic Short Stories.* Ed. Ceza Kassem and Malak Hashem. Cairo: Elias Modern Publishing House, 1985, 173–84 [Another translated version of "Clocks Like Horses"].
———. "The Marsh God." *Ur* (2/1980): 39–43; *MAS*: 78–87.
———. "Soldier's Message." Trans. Hadi al-Taie. *Gilgamesh* (1/1986): 33–34.
———. "The Swing." Trans. Kadhim Saadedin. *Iraq Today* (1–15 Aug. 1979): 29–32.
———. "The Turtle Grandmother." *MC*: 9–13.
———. "To the Night's Shelter." *UNS*: 153–65.
———. "The Window on the Yard." *ISS:* 201–11.

——. "Yusuf's Tales." Trans. Shakir Mustafa. *Banipal* 14 (2002): 5–9. Rpt. in *MC*: 2–8.

Khulusi, Natiq (1937–).

——. "Afternoon Tea." *ISS*: 301–08.

Khusbak, 'A'id (1946–).

——. "The Angels' Morning." Trans. Hadi al-Taie. *Gilgamesh* (1/1986): 44–45.

——. "The Tree." *ISS*: 249–260.

——. "Young Man, You Have a Promising Future." Trans. Yania S. Atallah. *Gilgamesh* (1/1986): 35–36.

Khusbak, Shakir (1930–).

——. "Buddies." *MISS*: 65–78.

——. "The Hyenas Invade Our Town." Trans. Nissim Rejwan. *New Outlook.* 10: 9 (Dec. 1967): 66–70. Rpt. in Rejwan's *Arabs in the Mirror: Images and Elf-Images from Pre-Islamic to Modern Times.* Austin: University of Texas Press, 2008, 183–88.

——. "In the Night." *FK*: 225–31.

——. "Summer." Trans. Olive Kenny and Thomas G. Ezzy. *JMAF*: 456–63.

Kraidi, Musa. See Kuraydi, Musa.

Kuraydi, Musa (1940–1996).

——. "The Eagle." Trans. Kadhim Saadedin. *Iraq Today* (16–30 Sept. 1978): 31–32.

——. "Midnight Corridor." *ISS*: 135–60.

——. "One Summer." Trans. May Jayyusi and Thomas G. Ezzy. *JMAF*: 480–88.

——. "Sindiyan." Trans. Kadhim Saadedin. *Iraq* (15 Nov. 1981): 42–43.

Lami, Jum'ah al-. "Who Killed Hikmat al-Shami?" Trans. Kadhim Saadedin. *Iraq Today* (1–15 Dec. 1977): 30–31.

Lutfi, Abd al-Majid (1905–1992).

——. "The Man Who Coughs." Trans. Kadhim Saadedin. *Iraq Today* (16–31 Dec. 1979): 27–28.

——. "The Lion Bohrmann." *MISS*: 137–47.

Majid, Jihad (1947–).

——. "The Bells." *ISS*: 379–90.

Mala'ikah, Nazik al- "Down Hill." *AW* (Oct.–Nov. 1966): 21.

Mamdouh, Alia (1944–).

——. "Crossing Over." Trans. Salwa Jabsheh and Christopher Tingley. *JMAF*: 512–13.

——. "The Dream." *Arab Women Writers: An Anthology of Short Stories.* Ed. and trans. Dalya Cohen-Mor. Albany, NY: State University of New York, 2005, 159–62.

————. *The Loved Ones.* Trans. Marilyn Booth. Cairo: AUCP, 2006.

————. *Mothballs.* Trans. Peter Theroux. Reading, UK: Garnet, 1996; Rpt. in *Naphtalene: A Novel of Baghdad.* New York: The Feminist Press at the City University of New York, 2005.

————. "Presence of the Absent One." *UNS*: 223–33. Rpt. in *AB*: 301–10.

Mamduh, Aliyah. See Mamdouh, Alia.

Mana, Samira al-. (1935–).

————. "The Billy Goat and the Menfolk." Trans. Farida Abu Haidar. *Ur* (Nov.–Dec. 1978): 25–26; see also *MAS*: 16–25. Rpt. without the translator's name in *AP* (Jan. 1982): 37–39.

————. "The Billy Goat and the Menfolk." Trans. Farida Abu Haidar and Christopher Tingley. *JMAF*: 514–518.

————. "Mrs. Collins." Trans. Farida Abu Haidar. *Azure* 11 (1982): 24–26. Rpt in *Gilgamesh* 7 (2008): 36–40.

————. "A Dormant Alphabet." Trans. Shakir Mustafa. *Edebiyât* 14.1/2 (2003): 130–31. Rpt. in *MC*: 94–95.

————. "A Kind of Dance." Trans. by the author; ed. Charles N. Lewis. *Crossing the Border: Voices of Refugee and Exiled Women.* Ed. Jennifer Langer. Nottingham: Five Leaves, 2002, 126–33 [An extract from the author's novel *Look at Me! Look at Me!*].

————. *The Oppressors.* [An extract from the novella *The Oppressors*] Trans. Paul Starkey. London: Exiled Writers Ink, 2008.

————. "Sexual Complacency." *MC*: 95–100.

————. "The Singing: A Short Story" [Trans. Farida Abu Haidar]. *Women's Rights are Human Rights Women's Rights are Universal.* The First Conference of the Middle East Centre for Women's Studies held on the 10th of December 2000. London: Al-Rafid, n.d., 71–74.

————. "The Soul." Trans. Shakir Mustafa. *Banipal* 17 (Summer 2003): 48–49. Rpt. in *MC*: 89–93.

————. "That Thing We Call Age." Trans. Shakir Mustafa. *Edebiyât* 14.1/2 (2003): 129–30. Rpt. in *MC*: 93–93.

————. "Tropical Jungle." Trans. Farida Abu Haidar. In *Exile Writers Ink: Voices in a Strange Land Online.*

————. "The Umbilical Cord." Trans. by the author and Charles Lewis. *Banipal* 1 (Feb. 1998): 53–54.

————. *The Umbilical Cord.* Trans. by the author; ed. Charles Lewis. West Yorkshire, UK: Central Publishing Services, 2005.

————. "The Umbilical Cord: The Novel of Exile." [An extract] *Gilgamesh* 5 (2007): 49–53.

Mani ', Samirah al-. See Mana, Samira al-.

Mardan, Nasrat (1948–).

———. "Bar of Sweet Dreams." *MC*: 171–75.

———. "Sufi Blessings." *MC*: 175–80.

Matar, Salim (1956–).

———. "Woman of the Flask." [Excerpt from the novel] Trans. Peter Clark. *Banipal* 9 (2000): 45–50.

———. *Woman of the Flask.* Trans. Peter Clark. Cairo: American University in Cairo Press, 2004.

Matti, Yusuf. "A Husband." Trans. Kadhim Saadedin. *Iraq Today* (1–15 Mar. 1980): 31–32.

Mirza, Fu'ad. "The Mare." Trans. Lily al-Tai. *BR*: 125–28.

Mizhir, Nadhum. See Muzhir, Nazim.

Mozany, Hussain al- (1954–).

———. "Trebeel." Trans. Lili al-Tai Milton. *Banipal* 4 (Spring 1999): 66–72.

Mu'alla, Abd al-Amir (1942–1997).

———. *The Long Days.* 3 vols. Volumes 1 and 2 trans. Mohieddin Ismail. London: Ithaca Press, 1979/1980. Vol. 3 trans. Abd al Wahid Lu'lu'a. Baghdad: Dar al-Ma'mun for Translation, 1982.

Mukhtar, Hameed al- "The Rabble." Trans. Faried Shkara. *Gilgamesh* 5 (2005): 33–36.

Muttalibi, Abd al-Razzaq al- (1943–).

———. "The Spectacles." *ISS*: 161–75.

Muzaffar, May (1940–).

———. "Matches to Dry Wood." Trans. May Jayyusi and Christopher Tingley. *JMAF*: 536–41.

———. "Personal Papers." Trans. Simone Fattal. In *Opening the Gates: A Century of Arab Feminist Writing.* Ed. Margot Badran and Miriam Cooke. Bloomington: Indiana University Press, 1990, 180–85.

———. "The Umbilical Cord." *ISS*: 309–315.

Muzhir, Nazim. "A Night Railway Station." Trans. by the author. *Gilgamesh* 5 (2007): 61–62.

Nahi, Salah al-Din al- (1914–).

———. "Madhi, the Magnanimous." *MISS*: 41–44.

Naqqash, Samir (1938–2004).

———. "Selections from Samir Naqqash, Tenants and Cobwebs (Nzulah u-Khait el-Shitan)." Trans. S Masliyah. *Edebiyât* 13.1 (2002): 49–67.

———. "Tantal." Trans. Shakir Mustafa. *Banipal* 24 (Autumn/Winter 2005): 85–95. Rpt. in *MC*: 115–129.

Nasir, Abd al-Sattar (1946–).

———. "Chubby Old Chum." *BS*: 179–88.

———. "Goodbye, Hippopotamus." Trans. Shakir Mustafa. *Banipal* 17 (Summer 2003): 52–53. Rpt. in *MC*: 102–05.

———. "Our Master, the Caliph: A Short Story." *Beirut: Université Saint Joseph. CEMAM Reports, 1975*, 247–54 [Part of an article entitled "Freedom of Expression: Theory and Practice" in which reference is made to the fact that Nasir was arrested in Iraq following the publication of the story's Arabic version in the Syrian periodical *al-Mawqif al-Adabi*].

———. "A Plain Talk." *ISS*: 242–48.

———. "al-Hussaini's Room." Trans. Dina Munther al-Mumaiez. *Gilgamesh* 7 (2008): 29–31.

Nasiri, Ali Khayyun al-. "Echoes." *Iraq Today* (16–31 Aug. 1980): 30–32.

Nasiri, Buthaynah al- (1947–).

———. "At the Beach." *Arab Women Writers: An Anthology of Short Stories*. Ed. and trans. Dalya Cohen-Mor. Albany, NY: State University of New York, 2005, 44–47.

———. *Final Night: Short Stories*. Trans. Denys Johnson-Davies. Cairo: AUCP, 2002.

———. "Homecoming." Trans. Denys Johnson-Davies. *Jusoor* 7/8 (1996): 443–50.

———. "I've Been Here Before." *AB*: 327–30.

———. "Man and Woman." Trans. Nirvana Tanoukhi. *Paintbrush: A Journal of Poetry and Translation* 28 (2001/2002): 284–290.

———. "The Return of the Prisoner." *UNS*: 211–18.

———. "The Short History of Samah." Trans. Nirvana Tanoukhi. *Banipal* 10/11 (Spring/Summer 2001): 111–12.

Nasser, Abdul Sattar. See Nasir, Abd al-Sattar.

Niyazi, Abd Allah. (1907–)

———. "The Book." Trans. Kadhim Saadedin. *Iraq Today* (Oct.1–15, 1979): 30–31.

———. "One Dirham." *MISS*: 129–37.

———. "When the Clouds Were on the Point of Tears." *Ur* (Special Autumn Issue, 1979): 80–83; *MAS*: 98–109.

Nouri, Abdel Malik. See Nuri, Abd al-Malik.

Nuri, Abd al-Malik (1921–1992?).

———. "Abbas Lost." Trans. Prudence Seymour. *MEF* 37 (1961): 38–40.

———. "Fatouma." Trans. Ali M. Cassidy [sic]/Cassimy [=Kasimi] and W. M. Frazier. *Ur* (Jan./Feb.1979): 50–56; *MISS*: 25–39; *MAS*: 110–25.

———. "Sickness." *ISS:* 19–27.

———. "Song of the Earth." Trans. Angele Boutros. *L* (Apr. 1970): 98–99.

———. "The South Wind." Trans. Denys Johnson-Davies. In *Modern Arabic Short Stories.* London: Oxford University Press, 1967, 120–29. See also the 1993 edition published by The American University in Cairo Press, 1993, 118–27.

———. "The Waitress, the Newspaper Boy, and the Spring." Trans. Salwa Jabsheh and Christopher Tingley. *JMAF:* 549–57.

———. "The Wind from the South." *FK:* 231–36.

Qaisi, Jaleel al-. See Qaysi, Jalil al-.

Qaysi, Jalil al- (1937–2006).

———. "Zulaikha." Trans. Shakir Mustafa. *Banipal* 21 (Autumn 2004): 88–94. Rpt. in *MC:* 107–14.

———. "The Kingdom of Light Reflections." Trans. May Salih. *Gilgamesh* 4 (2006): 64–72.

Qazwini, Iqbal al-. *Zubaida's Window.* Trans. Azza El Kholy and Amira Nowaira. New York: Feminist Press at the City University of New York, 2008.

Ramli, Muhsin al- (1967–).

———. "Boredom." Trans. Adam Gaise. *Banipal* 8 (Summer 2000): 66–67.

———. *"Scattered Crumbs."* [Excerpt from chapter 1 of the novel] Trans. Yasmeen S. Hanoosh. *Banipal* 17 (Summer 2003): 56–59.

———. *Scattered Crumbs.* Trans. Yasmeen S. Hanoosh. Fayetteville: University of Arkansas Press, 2003.

———. "from *Scattered Crumbs.*" Trans. Yasmeen S. Hanoosh. *Literature from the "Axis of Evil": Writings from Iran, Iraq, North Korea, and Other Enemy Nations.* Ed. by editors of *Words without Borders.* New York; London: The New Press, 2006, 69–74.

Rawdhan, Abd Awan al- (1939–).

———. "A Curse." Trans. Yania S. Atallah. *Iraq* (1 Oct. 1985): 32–35.

Rikabi, Abd al-Khaliq al-. "Balzac's Apple." Trans. Yania S. Atallah. *Gilgamesh* (2/1986): 42–46.

———. "The Book of Alif." [Excerpt from the novel *The Seventh Day of Creation*] Trans. Wen-chin Ouyang. *Banipal* 32 (Summer 2008): 106–25.

———. "The Cavalier." *BS:* 91–116. Rpt. in *Gilgamesh* (2/1986): 32–41.

———. "al-Faddy." *ISS:* 289–99.

———. "Mad Dog Disease." Trans. Wen-chen Ouyang. *Banipal* 18 (Autumn 2003): 35–37.

———. "The Siren." Trans. Kadhim Saadedin. *Iraq* (1 Oct. 1981): 42–45.

Rubaie, Abdul Rahman Majeed al-. See Rubay'i, Abd al-Rahman Majid al-.

Rubay'i, Abd al-Rahman Majid al- (1939–).

———. "The Hero and the City." *ISS*: 127–34.

———. "The Kingdom of Bulls." Trans. May Jayyusi and Naomi Shihab Nye. *JMAF*: 612–15.

———. "A Man and a Woman." Trans. Shakir Mustafa. *Banipal* 17 (Summer 2003): 64–66. Rpt. in *MC*: 83–87.

———. "The Odour of the Land." Trans. Kadhim Saadedin. *Azure* 2 (1978): 42–44.

———. "The Tattoo." [Excerpt from the novel *Al-Washm*, chapter ten] Trans. Shakir Mustafa. *Banipal* 17 (Summer 2003): 63–64. Rpt. in *MC*: 80–83.

Rubay'i, Adnan al-. "Another Cup of Coffee." *BS*: 151–65, see also *ISS*: 335–48.

———. "The Tree and the Black Bird." Trans. Kadhim Saadedin. *Iraq* (1 Nov. 1981): 43–45.

Ruznamaji, Muhammad. "An Improvised Story." Trans. Kadhim Saadedin. *Iraq Today* (Sept. 16–30, 1979): 31–32.

Sabri, Idmun (1921–1975).

———. "Government Bread." *ISS*: 41–48.

Sadr, Aminah Haydar al- (1938–1980).

———. *Friendly Letters*. Trans. M. N. Sultan. Tehran: Islamic Thought Foundation, 1985.

———. *In Search of Truth*. Trans. M. N. Sultan. Tehran: Islamic Thought Foundation, 1987.

———. *Two Women and a Man*. Trans. M. N. Sultan Tehran: Islamic Thought Foundation, 1987 [Reproduced by Ahlul Bayt Digital Islamic Library Project Team].

———. *Short Stories* [12 short stories]. Trans. M. N. Sultan. Tehran: Islamic Thought Foundation, 1987.

———. *Encounter at the Hospital*. Trans. M. N. Sultan. Tehran: Islamic Thought Foundation, 1987.

———. *Virtue Prevails*. Trans. M. N. Sultan. Tehran: Islamic Thought Foundation, 1991.

Saeed, Mahmoud (1939–).

———. "Bitter Morning." Trans. Shakir Mustafa. *Banipal* 19 (Spring 2004): 115–17. Rpt. in *MC*: 157–60.

———. "A Figure in Repose." *MC*: 160–69.

———. *Saddam City*. Trans. Ahmad Sadri. London: Saqi books, 2004.

———. *Two Lost Souls.* Schaumburg, IL: Joshua Tree Publishers, 2006.
Sa'id, Mahmud. See Saeed, Mahmoud.
Salih, Salimah. (1942–).
———. "The Barrier." Trans. May Jayyusi and Christopher Tingley. *JMAF*: 640–42.
———. "The Enemy." Trans. Mona Zaki. *Banipal* 10/11 (Spring/Summer 2001): 97–98.
———. "Those Boys." Trans. Shakir Mustafa. *Banipal* 19 (Spring 2004): 118–121. Rpt. in *MC*: 131–35.
———. "Two Short Stories" ["Forgiveness Tree" and "The Revenant"]. Trans. William M. Hutchins. *Banipal* 27 (Autumn/Winter 2007): 73–78.
———. "The Wheat Watchmen." Trans. Mona Zaki. *Banipal* 10/11 (Spring/Summer 2001): 96–97.
Salman, Suhaylah Dawud (1937–).
———. "Aunt Um[m] Malik Bitten by a Horse." *ISS*: 261–72.
Salim, Nizar (1925–1983).
———. "Song of the Turnip Vendor." *ISS*: 29–40.
Salim, Warid Badr al- (1956–).
———. "The Dream of the Red Anemones." *ISS*: 391–402.
Saqr, Mahdi Isa al- (1927–2006).
———. "Breaking Away." Trans. Shakir Mustafa. *Banipal* 14 (2002): 16–18. Rpt. in *MC*: 49–56.
———. "A Compound Figure." *ISS*: 59–73.
———. "A Dreamer in Dark Times." *MC*: 59–67.
———. "Fresh Blood." Trans. May Jayyusi and Jeremy Reed. *JMAF*: 656–59.
———. "The Horse." *Iraq Today* (Mar. 16–31, 1978): 30–32.
———. "Morning Exercises." Trans. Shakir Mustafa. *Edebiyât* 12.2 (2001): 260–63. Rpt. in *MC*: 56–58.
———. "Please, No More Flags." A chapter from the novel *A House on the Tigris*. Trans. by the author. *Banipal* 18 (Autumn 2003): 40–44.
———. "The Returnee." Trans. Shakir Mustafa. *Banipal* 14 (2002): 19; *Index on Censorship* 32.1 (2003). Rpt. in *MC*: 47–49.
———. "Some New Blood." *FK*: 241–43.
———. "Waiting." Trans. Shakir Mustafa. *Edebiyât* 12.2 (2001): 260–63. Rpt. in *MC*: 45–47.
Sayyid, Mahmud al- (1901–1937).
———. "Baddaai Alfaaiz." *MISS*: 79–88.
Shimon, Samuel (1956–).

———.The Assyrian Bear" [An excerpt from an autobiographical novel]. Trans. Samira Kawar. *Banipal* 21 (Autumn 2004): 122–25.

———. "Carpenter" [An excerpt from an autobiographical novel *Samuel the Third*]. *Banipal* 1 (Feb. 1998): 57–61.

———. "The Hedgehog" [An Excerpt from an autobiographical novel]. Trans. Paul Starkey. *Banipal* 20 (Summer 2004): 68–74.

———. *An Iraqi in Paris: An Autobiographical Novel.* Trans. Samira Kawar et al. London: Banipal Books, 2005.

———. "Royal Silver." [Excerpt from an autobiographical novel] Trans. Fiona Collins. *Banipal* 7 (Spring 2000): 34–36.

———. "The Street Vendor and the Movies." *MC*: 137–55.

———. "Toulouse." Trans. Fiona Collins. *Banipal* 3 (Oct. 1998): 38–39.

———. "Two Royalists on Quatorze Juillet." Trans. Paul Starkey. *Banipal* 18 (Autumn 2003): 66–71.

Simawe, Saadi (1946–).

———. "Thrill." Trans. from the Arabic by the author. *The Toronto South Asian Review* 9 (2/Winter 1991): 40–47.

Takarli, Fu'ad al- (1927–2008).

———. "The Boil." Trans. Dalya Cohen-Mor. In *A Matter of Fate: The Concept of Fate in the Arab World as Reflected in Modern Arabic Literature.* Oxford and New York: Oxford University Press, 2001, 210–18.

———. "The Cloud." *UNS*: 65–70.

———. "The Dying Lamp." Trans. Denys Johnson-Davies. In *Modern Arabic Short Stories.* London: Oxford University Press, 1967, 51–55. See also the 1993 edition published by the American University in Cairo Press, 1993, 50–54.

———. "The Extinguished Lantern." *FK*: 271–73.

———. "Green Eyes." Trans. Farida Abu Haidar. *Ur* (3/1985): 46–49.

———. "A Hidden Treasure." Trans. Ronak Husni and Daniel L. Newman. In *Modern Arabic Short Stories: A Bilingual Reader.* London: Saqi, 2008, 222–43 [Bilingual: Arabic and English].

———. *The Long Way Back.* Trans. Catherine Cobham. Cairo: AUCP, 2001; 2007.

———. "from *The Long Way Back*" [An excerpt]. Trans. Catherine Cobham. *AB*: 430–33.

———. "The Others." *ISS*: 49–57.

———. "The Oven." Trans. Catherine Cobham. *Azure* 8 (1981): 29–31.

———. "Ring of Sand" [Excerpt]. Trans. Issa J. Boullata. *Banipal* 14 (2002): 25–29.

———. "The Road into Town." *MISS*: 97–120.

———. "Silence and Thieves." Trans. Nihad Salem. *L* (Apr. 1972): 82–88. Rpt. in *Afro-Asian Short Stories: An Anthology.* Cairo: Permanent Bureau of Afro-Asian Writers, 1973. Vol. II. 355–70.

———. "The Truth." Trans. May Jayyusi and Elizabeth Fernea. *JMAF*: 721–25.

Talib, Aliya (1957–).

———. "Greening." Trans. Miriam Cooke and Rkia Cornell. *BI*: 192–95.

———. "A New Wait." Trans. Miriam Cooke and Rkia Cornell. *BI*: 80–85.

Tawfiq, Amjad (1950–).

———. "Death of the Young Birds Seller." *ISS*: 349–57.

Tekerli, Fouad. See Takarli, Fu'ad al-.

Tikerli, Fu'ad al-. See Takarli, Fu'ad al-.

Thuwadi, Muhsin. "Mission Delayed to Zero Hour." *BS*: 117–32.

Wali, Najm (1956–).

———. "Edward and the First Geography Lesson." Trans. Jennifer Kaplan. http://www.wordswithoutborders.org/article.php?lab=Edward.

———. "To Teresa, with Regards." Trans. Lily Al-Tai Milton. *Banipal* 3 (Oct. 1998): 18–23

———. "Waltzing Matilda." Trans. Marilyn Booth. *Words without Borders* (Oct. 2003). Rpt. in *Writing the World: On Globalization.* Ed. David Rothenberg and Wandee J. Pryor. Cambridge, MA: MIT Press, 2005, 203–17.

———. "Wars in Distant Lands." Trans. Raymond Stock. *Harper's Magazine* 316.1899 (Feb. 2008): 75–80.

Yahya, Hasaballah. See Yahya, Hasab Allah.

Yahya, Hasab Allah (1944–).

———. "A City Heading to the Unknown." Trans. Mohammed Darweesh. *Gilgamesh* 3 (2005): 30–32.

Yasin, Faraj. "The Rope." *ISS*: 373–78.

Yasin, Najman. "The Minaret." *ISS*: 323–34.

———. "The Thieves." Trans. Farida Abu Haidar. *Ur* (3/1981): 52–53.

Youssef, Saadi. See Sa'di.

Yusuf, Sa'di (1934–).

———. "Fadhil al-Marzoog" [An excerpt from the novel *Triangle of the Circle*]. Trans. by the author. *Banipal* 26 (Summer 2006): 40–52.

Zangana, Haifa. (1950–).

———. "Parallel Lives." Trans. Mundher al-Adhami. *Banipal* 17 (2003): 50–52.

———. *Through the Vast Halls of Memory.* Trans. Paul Hammond and the author. Paris: Hourglass, 1991. Rpt. in *Dreaming of Baghdad.* New York: Feminist Press at the City University of New York, 2009.

———. "What Choice?" *Surrealist Women: An International Anthology.* Ed. Penelope Rosemont. Austin: University of Texas Press, 1998, 416–19. [An excerpt from *Through the Vast Halls of Memory* cited above].

———. "Through the Vast Hall of Memory 1." *BR:* 71–74.

———. "Through the Vast Hall of Memory 2." *BR:* 110–13.

———. *Women on a Journey between Baghdad and London.* Trans. Judy Cumberbatch. Austin, TX: The Center for Middle Eastern Studies, The University of Texas at Austin, 2007.

———. "The Journey of Exiled Iraqi Writers." Trans. Judy Cumberbatch. *Exiled Ink* 9 (Spring/Summer 2008): 18–19.

4

Poetry

A. ANTHOLOGIES

Abd al-Wahid, Abd al-Razzaq (1930?–).

———. *Poems.* Comp. Ali Ja`far Allaq. Trans. Mohammed Darweesh. Baghdad: Dar al-Ma'mun, 1989.

Allaq, Ali Ja'far al- (1945–).

———. *Poems.* Trans. Mohammed Darweesh. Baghdad: Dar al-Ma'mun, 1988.

Arabic Poetry in Iraq/Min al-shi'r al-'Arabi fi al-'Iraq. Bilingual Selections. Trans. Abd al-Wahid Lu'lu'ah. Kuwait: Muassasat Jaizat Abd al-Aziz Sa'ud al-Babtin lil-Ibda' al-sh'ri, 2004 [Includes selected poems of thirty Iraqi poets born between 1863 and 1954].

Azzawi, Fadhil al- (1940–).

———. *In Every Well a Joseph Is Weeping.* Trans. Khaled Mattawa. *Quarterly Review of Literature. Poetry Book Series* 36 (1997).

———. *Miracle Maker: Selected Poems.* Trans. Khaled Mattawa. Rochester, NY: BOA Editions, 2003.

Bayati, Abd al-Wahhab al- (1926–1999).

———. *Lilies and Death.* Trans. Mohammed B. Alwan. Baghdad: al-Adib Printing Press, 1972.

———. *Love, Death, and Exile.* Trans. Bassam K. Frangieh. Washington, DC: Georgetown University Press, 1990.

———. *Poet of Iraq: Abdul Wahab al-Bayati.* An introductory essay with translations by Desmond Stewart. London: Gazelle, 1976.

———. *The Singer and the Moon.* Trans. Abdullah al-Udhari. London: TR Press, 1976.

Boulus, Sargon (1944–2007).

———. *Arrival in Where-City.* Washington, DC: Arab Cultural Foundation [1982?] [Published as a limited special program on the occasion of the poet's readings at Kevorkian Middle East Center, New York University and the Center for Contemporary Arab Studies, Georgetown University, Mar. 9–10, 1982. It includes, in addition to Mirène Ghoussein's introduction, ten poems translated by the author and Issa Boullata, Michael Beard, Adnan Haydar, Admer Gouryh, and Mirène Ghossein.].

———. *Knife Sharpener: Selected Poems.* London: Banipal Books, 2009 [According to the publisher this book is "a collection of poems, written between 1991 and 2007 that he translated himself, together with an essay, "Poetry and Memory," written a few months before he died in October 2007"].

Braikan al-, or al-Breikan. See al-Buraykan, Mahmud.

Buraykan, Mahmud al- (1934–2002).

———. *Mahmud al-Braikan: Selected Poems 1953–1995.* Bilingual Edition. Trans. Shihab Ahmed al-Nassir. Baghdad: Dar al-Ma'mun for Translation and Publishing, 2005 [A bilingual selection of thirty poems by one of the most important Iraqi poets and the least represented in translation. The poems are arranged according to their dates in descending order from 1993 to 1954: Homage to Ephemeral Things; Ghost to Ghost; The Voice; The Possessed; A World in Lighting; Rooms for Nothingness; The Bottomless Cave; Unpeopled City; The River under the Earth; Fade-out of the Screen; The Stage Backroom; The Desertification; Destinies; The Face; Lighting, I, II; Labyrinth of the Butterfly; The Bedouin None Has Seen His Face; The Night; Visitant; Windows; The Lion in the Circus; The Journey of the Monkey Guard of the Lighthouse; A Requiem on the Spirit of the Poet on the Brink of the World; The Ghosts Session; Quiet Horror: A Song; The Art of Torture; Myth of the Sleeper-walker; Presentiments of Issa Bin Azraq on the Way to Hard Labour; Mown Down in the Street.]

Faiq, Salah. *Another Fire Befitting a City.* Trans. Haifa Zangana and A. M. al-Abbas aided by John Digby and Paul Hammond. London: Melmoth, 1979 [See also *The Lode, the Word: Poems and Collages.* Trans. "The poet's friends with Paul Hammond." London: Melmoth, 1985].

Flowers of Flame: Unheard Voices of Iraq. Ed. Sadek Mohammed et al. East Lansing: Michigan State University Press, 2008 [Includes poems by more than thirty Iraqi poets born between the early 1950s and 1970s].

Furat, Basim (1967–).

———. *Here and There: A Selection.* Trans. Muhieddein Assaf et al. Ed. Mark Pirie. Wellington, New Zealand: Headworx Publishers, 2004.

———. *The Moon That Excels in Nothing but Waiting.* Trans. Muhieddein Assaf. Ed. Mark Pirie. Paekakariki, New Zealand: Earl of Seacliff Art Workshop, 2006.

Hafiz, Yasin Taha (1936–).

———. *Poems.* Trans. Mohammed Darweesh. Baghdad: Dar al-Ma'mun, 1989.

Haydari, Buland al- (1926–1996).

———. *Dialogue in Three Dimensions.* Trans. Husain Haddawy. London: Pan Middle East Graphics and Publishing, 1982.

———. *Songs of the Tired Guard.* Trans. Abdullah al-Udhari. London: TR Press, 1977.

Hilli, Ali al- (1930–).

———. *The Candle Tears.* n.p., n.d. [198?].

Iraqi Poetry Today. Ed. Saadi Simawe. A special issue of *Modern Poetry in Translation* 19 (2003) [Includes works by 40 poets. Among them are six who write in Kurdish and two in Hebrew].

Janabi, Hatif. *Questions and Their Retinue: Selected Poems.* Trans. Khaled Mattawa. Fayetteville: University of Arkansas Press, 1996.

Mahdi, Sami (1939/1940–).

———. *Poems.* Selected and intro. by Hatim al-Saqr. Trans. Mohammed Darweesh. Baghdad: Dar al-Ma'mun, 1988.

Mikhail, Dunya (1965–).

———. *Diary of a Wave Outside the Sea.* Trans. by the author and ed. by Louise I. Hartug. Cairo: Ishtar Publishing House, 1999.

———. *The War Works Hard.* New York: New Directions, 2005; Carcanet, London, 2006.

Modern Iraqi Poetry. Ed. Yaseen Taha Hafiz. Trans. Abdul Wahid Lu'lu'a. Baghdad: Dar al-Ma'mun, 1989.

"The Poetry of Iraq." Ed. Sadek R. Mohammed, Soheil Najim, Haidar Al-Kabi. *Atlanta Review* 13.2 (Spring/Summer 2007): 20–89 [Includes poems by more than thirty poets]. See also *Flowers of Flame.*

Sa'id, Hamid (1941–).

———. *Poems.* Selected and intro. by Majid al-Samarraie. Trans. Salman D. al-Wasiti. Baghdad: Dar al-Ma'mun, 1988.

Sayyab, Badr Shakir al- (1926–1964).

———. *Selected Poems.* Trans. Nadia Bishai. London: Third World Center, 1986 [Reissued in 2001 without reference to the 1986 edition. Cairo: General Egyptian Book Organization, 2001].

Selection of Contemporary Iraqi Poetry. Trans. George Masri. London: Iraqi Cultural Centre, 1977 [Poems by al-Haydari, Shafiq al-Kamali, and Hamid Sa'id. See below under their respective names.].

Ten Iraqi Soldier-Poets: An Anthology. Ed. Salman D. Al-Wasiti. Baghdad: Dar al-Mamun, 1988 [Includes poems by Ala' Madhlum Jawad, Abdul Jabbar al-Jubouri, Jalal Qadir Muhammad, Kamal Abdul Rahman, Ali Khamees Rahman, Abdul Karim Salman, Laith al-Sundooq, Fawzi al-Ta'i, Khalid Jabir Yousif, Ibrahim Zaidan].

Twenty One Iraqi Poets. Ed. Margaret Obank. www.masthead.net.au/issue9/iraqi.html [Mar. 2005].

Yusuf, Sa'di (1934–).

———. *Without an Alphabet, Without a Face: Selected Poems of Saadi Youssef.* Trans. Khaled Mattawa. St. Paul: Graywolf Press, 2002.

B. OTHER TRANSLATED POEMS

Abd, Karim. See Abed Kareem.

Abd Allah, Adil (1955–).

———. "A Country out of Work." Trans. Soheil Najm. *IP*: 58. Rpt. in *FF*: 43.

———. "The Prey." Trans. Soheil Najm. *IP*: 40. Rpt. in *FF*: 3.

Abd Allah, Najat (1969–).

———. "If the Spring Came Late." Trans. Gailan. *World Words: An Anthology of International Writers in New Zealand.* Ed. T. M. Schaeffer. Wellington, NZ: Writers International in Association with Headwork, 2006, 115.

Abd al-Amir, Ali (1955–).

———. "The Hanging Gardens of Death." Trans. Siham Abdul Kareem. *Gilgamesh* 3 (2005): 25–26

———. "The Hanging Gardens of Death." Trans. Soheil Najm. *IP*: 83–85. Rpt. in *FF*: 86–88.

Abd al-Aziz, Talib (1952–).

———. "My Brother's War." Trans. Haider Al-Kabi. *IP*: 82. Rpt. in *FF*: 84–85.

Abd al-Husayn, Ahmad. "The Last Air." Trans. Khalida Hamed. *Gilgamesh* 1 (2005): 26–28.

Abd al-Hurr, Mundhir (1961–).

———. "We Are Not Dead." Trans. Sadek Mohammed. *IP*: 55. Rpt. in *FF*: 36.

Abd al-Latif, Husayn. "Three Poems: Matador, A Freight Train's Song, Windswept." Trans. Najah Abbas Raheem. *Gilgamesh* 5 (2007): 41–42.

Abd al-Latif, Nu'man Thabit. "Night at its Stillest." Trans. Sami Khamou. *GAP:* 490.

Abd al-Qadir, Ra'd (1953–).

———. "The Transient Things." Trans. Soheil Najm. *IP*: 78–80.

Abd al-Razzaq, Wafa'. "The Judge." In *Exile Writers Ink: Voices in a Strange Land Online.*

———. "A Search," "The Judge." Trans. Jennifer Langer and Ziba Karbassi. *Exiled Ink* 8 (Winter 2007/2008) 25.

Abd al-Wahid, Abd al-Razzaq. "Dreaded Road." Trans. Diana Der Hovanessian and Lena Jayyusi. *JM*: 128.

———. "The Door-Knocker." *SBL:* 27–28.

———. "A Drop of Fear." *Ur* (3/1981): 59.

———. "Drop of Sadness." *FH:* 204.

———. "Estrangement." *Ur* (3/1981): 59.

———. "Fingers of Fear." *Ur* (3/1981): 59.

———. "The Fire Fountain." *MIP*: 53.

———. "The Fire Fountain." Trans. A. W. Lu'lu'a. *Gilgamesh* (2/1986): 23.

———. "A Fugitive from the Museum." *MIP:* 54–57.

———. "A Fugitive from the Museum." Trans. A. W. Lu'lu'a. *Gilgamesh* (2/1986): 24–26.

———. "A Homeland." Trans. Salih J. Altoma. *WATA Journal of Languages and Translation* 4 (Dec. 2007).

———. "Job's Patience." *The Arab Review* 5 (1/1996): 29.

———. "A Letter to President Bush." Trans. Salih J. Altoma. *WATA Journal of Languages and Translation* 4 (Dec. 2007).

———. "Martyrdom at the Threshold of the Age of Forty." *SBL*: 26–27.

———. "A New Year's Wish." *Ur* (3/1981): 59.

———. *Poems.* Selected by Ali Ja'far Allaq and Trans. Mohammed Darweesh. Baghdad: Dar al-Ma'mun, 1989.

———. "Reaching Forty." Trans. Diana Der Hovanessian and Lena Jayyusi. *JM*: 129–30.

———. "Two Languages." Trans. Salman al-Wasiti. *Gilgamesh* (2/1986): 23–24.

———. "Warning." *Ur* (3/1981): 59.

———. "You Rise among Truths." Trans. Diana Der Hovanessian and Lena Jayyusi. *JM*: 130–32.

Abdoullatif, Hussien. See Abd al-Latif, Husayn.

Abdul-ameer, Ali. See Abd al-Amir, Ali.

Abdul-Hur, Munthir. See Abd-Hurr, Mundhir.

Abdulqadir, Ra'ad. See Abd al-Qadir, Ra'd.
Abdulhussein, Ahmed. See Abd al-Husayn.
Abdul Rahman, Kamal. "from 'the Traitor'." Trans. Sahba' Abdul Ghani. *TISP*: 53–54.
———. "An Iraqi Woman." Trans. Sahba' Abdul Ghani. *TISP*: 55–57.
Abdul Razak, Wafaa. See Abd al-Razzaq, Wafaa.
Abed, Kareem (1952–).
———. "Three Poems: Fear, Invitation, Your Face." Trans. Dunya Mikhail. *Banipal* 6 (Autumn 1999): 72.
Abed al-Razzaq, Wafaa. See Abd al-Razzaq, Wafa'.
Addam, Majid (1972–).
———. "From the poem 'On the Street, I Repeat "Good Night."'" Trans. Camilo Gomez-Rivas. *Banipal* 24 (Autumn/Winter 2005): 52–55.
Alfaker, Muniam [al-Faqir, Mun'im]. "Five Poems." Trans. Khaled Mattawa. *Banipal* 8 (Summer 2000): 55.
Ali, Ahmed Asheikh. See Ali, Ahmad al-Shaykh.
Ali, Ahmad al-Shaykh. "From Her Book, One More Time." Trans. Soheil Najm. *IP*: 49. Rpt. in *FF*: 22.
Ali, Mahdi Muhammed. "An Upside Down Picture." Trans. Salaam Yousif. *IPT*: 12. Rpt. in *The Poker* 2 (Spring 2003): 58 and *Poetry International* 10 (2006): 104.
———. "Five Poems: Condition, Expatriation, Flight, Heritage, and Homeland." Trans. Salaam Yousif. *IPT*: 13–14.
Allaq, Ali Ja'far al-. "Ashes of Chants." *SBL*: 81–83.
———. "Departure." *MIP*: 126–27.
———. "The Face of the Pleiades a Book." Trans. Kadhim Saadedin. *Iraq Today* (Jan.1–15, 1979): 30–31.
———. "Finished Relation." *MIP*: 127–28.
———. "Homeland for Water Birds." Trans. Kadhim Saadedin. *Iraq Today* (1–15 Jan. 1979): 30.
———. "How Did Night Surprise Us?" *API* 115–16.
———. "Lady of Chaos." Trans. Sharif Elmusa and Thomas G. Ezzy. *JM*: 153.
———. *Poems.* Selected and intro. by Hatim al-Saqr. Trans. Mohammed Darweesh. Baghdad: Dar al-Ma'mun, 1988 [Includes: The Dreamer's Flower . . . the Body's Flower; Exeter; Face of Ember and Water; Family Trees; Fruit of the Past; Home for the Water Birds; The Low Cloud; The New Babylon; New Elegy to Cordova; Rain for the Hopeless Villages; Something Green; Three States; Two Lovers; and Two Women].

———. "Poet." Trans. Sharif Elmusa and Thomas G. Ezzy. *JM*: 152–53.

Amara, Lamea Abbas. See Amarah, Lami ʿah Abbas.

Amarah, Lamiʿah Abbas (1929–).

———. "Amarah." Trans. Salih J. Altoma. *International Journal of Contemporary Iraqi Studies* 1.3 (2007): 422.

———. "Amara [Amarah]." Trans. Marcia Hermansen and Lamea Abbas Amara. In *Food for Our Grandmothers: Writings by Arab–American and Arab–Canadian Feminists.* Ed. Joanna Kadi. Boston: South End Press, 1994, 113.

———. "Baghdad." Trans. Salih J. Altoma. *International Journal of Contemporary Iraqi Studies* 1.3 (2007): 421.

———. "Basrah." Trans. Salih J. Altoma. *International Journal of Contemporary Iraqi Studies* 1.3 (2007): 422.

———. "But I." Trans. Basima Bezirgan and Elizabeth Fernea. *FW*: 332.

———. "The Commandments." Trans. Mike Maggio. *The Poetry of Arab Women.* Ed. Nathalie Handal. New York: Interlink Books, 2001, 80–81.

———. "The Curse of Discrimination." Trans. Marcia K. Hermansen. In *Mandaee.* La Mesa, California. (8/June 1992): 39.

———. "Diogenes." Trans. Basima Bezirgan and Elizabeth Fernea. *IPT*: 92–93. Rpt. in *Poetry International* 10 (2006): 114–15.

———. "Enemy." Trans. Salih J. Altoma. *International Journal of Contemporary Iraqi Studies* 1.3 (2007): 424–25.

———. "The Fortune-teller." Trans. Basima Bezirgan and Elizabeth Fernea. *FW*: 331–32.

———. "Frouzanda Mahrad." Trans. Mike Maggio. *Pig Iron* 15 (1988): 28 [Relevant to the Iran–Iraq War: 1980–1988].

———. "Had the Fortune-teller Told Me." *MIP*: 62–63.

———. "If the Fortune Teller Had Told Me." Trans. Sara Marsden. *Ur* (2–3/1982): 136.

———. "Image." *FH: 20.* Rpt. as "His Image." In the *Bulletin of the Arab American Club of Southern California* 1 (Nov. 1994): 13.

———. "Lee Anderson." Trans. Salih J. Altoma. *International Journal of Contemporary Iraqi Studies* 1.3 (2007): 422–23.

———. "The Lost One." Trans. S.A. Khulusi. *The Islamic Review* (June 1950): 44–45.

———. "The Path of Silence." Trans. Basima Bezirgan and Elizabeth Fernea. *FW:* 333.

———. "San Diego on a Rainy Day." Trans. Mike Maggio with Nathalie Handal. *The Poetry of Arab Women.* Ed. Nathalie Handal. New York: Interlink Books, 2001: 79–80.

———. "The Seasons of the Coloured Trees." Trans. Sara Marsden. *Ur* (2–3/1982): 136.

———. "Suspension Bridge." Trans. Salih J. Altoma. *International Journal of Contemporary Iraqi Studies* 1.3 (2007): 423.

———. "Tears on a Sad Iraqi Face." Trans. Salih J. Altoma. *AlJadid* 21 (Fall 1997): 17. Rpt. in *International Journal of Contemporary Iraqi Studies* 1.3 (2007): 423–424.

———. "Travel Game." *MIP*: 63–64.

———. "Untitled Poem." Trans. Rose Ghurayyib. *AGH*: 90. Rpt. in *Al-Raida* (Feb. 1990): 13.

———. "Untitled Poem." Trans. Rose Ghurayyib. *AGH*: 91.

———. "Untitled Poem" [Concerning Palestine]. Trans. Safa Khulusi. *The Islamic Review* (Mar. 1951): 25.

———. "Where Is Thy Sting, O Death?" *al-Raida* 4 (May 1, 1985): 7.

Amil, Adil al-. "Once" and "A Window." *Gilgamesh* 7 (2008): 21.

Amil, Rushdi al- (1934/1935–1990).

———. "Daily Scene." *MIP*: 88–90.

———. "From the Notebook." Trans. Mohammed Darweesh. *BO*. (23 July 1985): 6.

———. "Three Poems." Trans. Mohammed Darweesh. *BO*. (12 Mar. 1985): 6.

———. "Two Poems." *MIP*: 87–88.

Antoon, Sinan. "[Four Poems] The Milky Way, Phantasmagoria, A Prisoner's Song, and Wars I." Trans. author S. Antoon. *IPT*: 16–17.

———. "Necropolis." Trans. S. Antoon. *Banipal* 29 (Summer 2007): 107–09.

———. "A Prism: Wet with War." Trans. S. Antoon. *IPT*: 15–16. Rpt. in *The Poker* 2 (Spring 2003): 56–57.

———. "Strings." Trans. S. Antoon. *Banipal* 18 (Autumn 2003): 60–61.

———. "Wrinkles on the Wind's Forehead." *Banipal* 18 (Autumn 2003): 61–62.

Asadi, Khalil al- (1950–).

———. "Illusory Village." Trans. Sadek Mohammed. *IP*: 50–51. Rpt. in *FF*: 23–25.

Asadi, Salam al-. "Fragments of a Memory. 1. The Clay's Memory. 2. Gunpowder." Trans. Salih J. Altoma. *Free Verse: A Journal of Contemporary Poetry and Poetics* [A bi-annual electronic journal] (Winter 2002).

———. "The Clay's Memory." Trans. Salih J. Altoma. *Poets Against the War*. Ed. Sam Hamill. New York: Thunder's Mouth Press/Nation Books, 2003, 15–16. Rpt. in *Orion* (May–June 2004): 20.

Asheikh, Ahmed. See Ali, Ahmad al-Shaykh.

Assaieg, Sadiq. See al-Sayigh, Sadiq.

Assultani, Fadhil, al-Sultani, Fadhil.

Ataymish, Abd al-Latif (1948–).

———. "[Two Poems] A Homeland without Friends, The Dead Know No Fear." Trans. Salih J. Altoma. *World Literature Today* 77.3 (Oct.–Dec. 2003): 39.

Azzawi, Fadhil al- (1940–).

———. "Bedouins under an Alien Sky." Trans. Khaled Mattawa and the author. *Banipal* 6 (Autumn 1999) 3–7. [thirteen poems: Ash; Guide; Listen; Noah!; I Want to Change Myself; The Wise Man in Our House; Feast in Candlelight; Bedouins; Newton's Apple; Events; Lenin Platz in Berlin; Everything Turned Out Well in the End; Go, Fadhil, to Heaven, and thou, al-Azzawi, Straight to Hell] See also: *A Crack in the Wall: New Arab Poetry.* Ed. Margaret Obank and Samuel Shimon. London: Saqi Books, 2001: 30–37 [Includes seven of the poems listed above].

———. "Crossing the Valley." Trans. Saadi Simawe and Ralph Savarese. *IPT*: 24.

———. "Every Morning the War Gets Up from Sleep." Trans. Salaam Yousif. *IPT*: 32–39.

———. "Every Morning the War Gets Up from Sleep" [Section 7 of the Poem cited above with no reference to the translator]. *Twilight of Empire: Responses to Occupation.* Ed. Viggo Mortensen et al. Santa Monica, CA: Perceval Press, 2005, 121.

———. "Farewell." Trans. Khaled Mattawa. *AlJadid* 17 (Apr. 1997): 12.

———. "Feast in Candlelight." *Blooming through the Ashes: An International Anthology on Violence and the Human Spirit.* Ed. Clifford Chanim and Aili McConnon. New Brunswick, NJ: Rutgers University Press, 2006, 278.

———. "A Film in a Railway Station." Trans. Saadi Simawe and Ralph Savarese. *IPT*: 24–25.

———. "For Everyone His Own Tree." Trans. Saadi Simawe and Ralph Savarese. *IPT*: 26.

———. "How to Write a Magical Poem." *Banipal* 1 (Feb. 1998): 66. Rpt. in *Poetry International Web* 2007.

———. "In a Magic Land." Tans. Saadi Simawe. *IPT*: 40.

———. *In Every Well a Joseph Is Weeping.* Trans. Khaled Mattawa. *Quarterly Review of Literature. Poetry Book Series.* 36 (1997) [Includes: Always; The Apple; Arriving Late; Betrayal; Brotherliness; The Computer's Exhortation; The Dream Walker; Escaping, I Reach a River; Explosions; Farewell; The Frog; The General's Last Night; Good Morning; God; How to Write a Magical Poem; In Captivity; In the Court of Honor; In Every Well a Joseph Is Weeping; Intersections; Journey of the Banished; The King and His Donkey; Life with Rats; The Lost Son's Return Home; Magician's Hat; A Man in Memory; The Monster; Napoleon's Horse; No Matter How Far; An Old Continent; On a Distant Island; On the Evenings of Victory; On a Night in Winter; Out of Habit; Party, The Party; Questions; Questions Again; Robinson Crusoe; Silent Parade; Solitude; Song of Myself; Those Beautiful Days; Vision on a Bus; and When We Reached Kafka's House Late].

———. "In My Spare Time." Trans. Khaled Mattawa. *Poetry International Web* 2007.

———. "The Last Iraq." Trans. Salaam Yousif. *IPT*: 40.

———. "Leave the Earth behind You." Trans. Saadi Simawe and Ralph Savarese. *IPT*: 25–26. Rpt. in *Poetry International* 10 (2006): 108.

———. "The Lion and the Apostle." Trans. Saadi Simawe and Ralph Savarese. *IPT*: 29. Rpt. in *Poetry International* 10 (2006): 107.

———. *Miracle Maker: Selected Poems.* Trans. Khaled Mattawa. Rochester, NY: BOA Editions, 2003.

———. "The Night with the Vampire." Trans. Saadi Simawe and Ralph Savarese. *IPT*: 30–31.

———. "On a Dying Planet." Trans. Saadi Simawe and Ralph Savarese. *IPT*: 26–27.

———. "Poems from a UFO Window." Trans. F. al-Azzawi. *Banipal* 12 (Autumn): 52–55 [The Book of My Life, I Confess that I Have Lived My Life, Inside a Black Hole, A Journey to Distant Planets, The Lion and the Apostle, Memory of Sand, A Statue in a Square, and When the Sky Still Had No Name].

———. "The Poet." Trans. Saadi Simawe and Ralph Savarese. *IPT*: 29–30.

———. "Political Prisoner." Trans. Salaam Yousif and Melissa Brown. *IPT*: 32.

———. "The Self-Defeating Poem." Trans. by the poet. *IPT*: 31.

———. "Shipping Out." Trans. Saadi Simawe and Ralph Savarese. *IPT*: 27–28.

———. "Songs for Jerusalem, War and Revolution." Trans. Shafik Magar. *L* (Apr. 1970): 82–85.

———. "The Song of the Slave Girl." Trans. Saadi Simawe and Ralph Savarese. *IPT*: 28–29.

———. "The Unknown Man." Trans. Saadi Simawe. *IPT*: 39–40.

Baghdadi, Tajia al-. "Has Your Throat Gone Dry Shehrezad." Trans. M. T. Ali. *Exiled Ink* 9 (Spring/Summer 2008): 8.

———. "The Treacheries of Devastation." Trans. Muhammad Tawfiq Ali. *Exiled Ink* 8 (Winter 2007/2008): 22.

Bahr al-'Ulum, Muhammad Salih. (1908–1992).

———. "Lenin and the October Revolution." Trans. Nihad A. Salem. *L* (Apr. 1970): 160.

Barikan, Mahmud al-. See al-Buraykan, Mahmud.

Basir, Muhammad Mahdi al- (1895–1974).

———. "Here I Am O Fatherland." Trans. Leslie Tramontini. *Al-Abhath* 50/51 (2002–2003): 161–86.

———. "Long Live Science and Its Renewer!" Trans. Leslie Tramontini. *Al-Abhath* 50/51 (2002–2003): 181–82.

———. "Science and Us." *FK*: 83.

Bayati, Abd al-Wahhab al-. "'Ain-al-shams': or The Metamorphoses of Ibn-'Arabi in His Translation of Desires." Trans. with notes by Desmond Stewart. *Encounter* 39 (Oct. 1972): 26–27.

———. *Abdul Wahab al-Bayati* [a short introduction and four poems]. London: Iraqi Cultural Centre, 1979 [Poems include: Eye of the Sun (Trans. Desmond Stewart); I am Born and Burnt in Love; Lament for the June Sun; Love under the Rain (Trans. George Masri)].

———. "Aisha's Garden." *SBL:* 29–30.

———. "Aisha's Profile." Trans. Bassam K. Frangieh. *LFAN*: 554–55.

———. "Apology for a Short Speech." *BM*: 17. Rpt.in *AP* (July 1980): 53.

———. "An Apology for a Short Speech." *UM*: 38.

———. "The Arab Refugee." *UM*: 36–37.

———. "The Arab Refugees." Trans. Hashim Lazim. *Iraq Today* (16–31 Aug. 1980): 19.

———. "Art for Life." Trans. M. M. Badawi. *JAL* 6 (1975): 134.

———. "Bab ash-Sheikh, Poem, Poet's Childhood, The Unknown Man." Trans. Adnan Salman. *BO* (July 7, 1985): 6.

———. "The Bad Sorcerer." Trans. Mohammad Salama. *JAL* 32.2 (2001): 160.

———. "Basrah." *API* 69–70.

———. "The Birth and Death of Aisha." Trans. Bassam Frangieh. *Banipal* 17 (Summer 2003): 36–38.

———. "The Birth of Aisha and Her Death." Trans. Sargon Boulus and Christopher Middleton. *JM:* 171–76.

———. "The Book of Poverty and Revolution." *AK:* 111–15.

———. "Broken Pitchers." Trans. M. M. Badawi. *JAL* 6 (1975): 133.

———. "Broken Urns." *AWW*: 84–85.

———. "Childhood." Trans. Aida Azouqa. *JAL* 32.2 (2002): 206.

———. "Death and the Lamp." Trans. James Howarth. *Banipal* 18 (Autumn 2003): 46–47.

———. "The Descent of Orpheus to the Underworld." Trans. Nihad A. Salem. *Afro-Asian Poetry*. Cairo: Atlas Press, 1971: 150–51.

———. "The Descent of Orpheus to the Underground." *L* (Jan. 1972): 142–43.

———. "Diaries of Poor Lovers." Trans. Salah Nasrawi. *Iraq Today* (Feb. 1–15, 1978): 32.

———. "The Dragon." Trans. Noel Abdulahad. *AlJadid* 9.42/43 (Winter/ Spring 2003): 33.

———. "The Dragon." Trans. Farouk Abdel Wahab. *IPT*: 48–49.

———. "The Dragon." *API*: 64–66.

———. "Elegies." Trans. Salih J. Altoma [From al-Bayati's elegies dedicated to his daughter Nadiya who died in California in 1990]. *AlJadid* 5.28 (Summer 1999): 20.

———. "Elegies of Lorca." Trans. Rasheed el-Enany. *Third World Quarterly* 10.4 (1989): 254–56.

———. "Elegy for Aisha." Trans. Sargon Boulus and Christopher Middleton. *JM*: 176–79.

———. "Elegy to Aisha." Trans. Farouk Abdel Wahab. *IPT*: 52–53.

———. *Eye of the Sun*. Copenhagen: 1978 [Includes: About Those Who Refuse to 'Play the Part of the Actor'; An Apology for a Short Speech; The Civilization of the West; Eye of the Sun; Greetings to Athens; I Was Born in the Age of Betrayals; Loneliness; A Poem to My Son Ali; Profile of the Lover of the Great Bear; To Ernest Hemingway; To Anna Seghers; The Wall; and Words That Will Not Die].

———. "The Face and the Mirror." *FH*: 36.

———. "The Fire of Poetry." *API*: 67–68.

———. "From 'The Death and the Candelabrum'." *Iraq* (Dec. 1, 1981): 45.

———. "From Al-Hallaj." Trans. Khalil I. Semaan. *JAL* 10 (1979): 65–69. Rpt. in *IJMES* 10 (1979): 520–523.

———. "The Fugitive." *UM:* 36.

———. "Glory to Children and the Olive Tree." *APR* 4 (12/Dec. 1972).

———. "The Greek Poem." Trans. Mohammed Darweesh. *BO* (27 Nov. 1985): 5.

———. "Greetings to Athens." Trans. Abdullah al-Udhari. *A Mirror for Autumn*. London, 1974.

———. "The Gypsy Symphony." Trans. A. W. Lu'lu'a. *Gilgamesh* (2/1986): 20–22.

———. "The Gypsy Symphony." *MIP*: 48–50.

———. "Al Hallag's [sic] Agony." Trans. Shafiq Megally. *L* (Apr. 1970): 100–01. Rpt. in *Afro-Asian Poetry*. Cairo, 1971: 147–149 and in *MMAP*: 1–4.

———. "Hamlet." *UM*: 37–38.

———. "I & II 'Two Poems to My Son Ali'." Trans. M. A. Khouri and H. Algar. *JAL* 1 (1970): 80–82. Rpt. in *AK*: 109–11.

———. "I Am Born and I Burn in My Love." Trans. Farouk Abdel Wahab. *IPT*: 41–43.

———. "I am Born and Burnt in Love." Trans. G. Masri. *UR* (Autumn 1979): 40–45.

———. "The Impossible." Trans. Salma Khadra Jayyusi and Christopher Middleton. *JM*: 170–71.

———. "Lament for the June Sun." Trans. [with notes] by Desmond Stewart. *Encounter* 37 (Oct. 1971): 22–23.

———. "Lamentation." Trans. Aida Azouqa. *JAL* 32.2 (2002): 207.

———. *Lilies and Death*. Trans. Mohammed B. Alwan. Baghdad: al-Adib Printing Press, 1972. [Includes: Absence; An Apology for a Short Speech; A Baghdad Mawal; The Child and the Dove; The City; The Civilization of the West; Consolation; Death at Noon; Death and Time; Enamored Butterfly; Fugitive; Lilies and Freedom; Loneliness; My Father in the Path of the Sun; A Poem to My Son Ali; A Postcard to Damascus; A Prayer to the Unreturning; Rain; Rendezvous at Ma'rra, The Road of Return; The Singer and the Moon; The Sorrow of Violets; The Spring and the Children; A Starless Sky; The Village Market; The Wall; and Words That Will Not Die].

———. "Lorca Elegies" Trans. S. Boulus. *MA* 10 (1/1977): 64–66. Rpt. in *AP* 1 (July 1980): 54.

———. *Love, Death, and Exile*. Trans. Bassam K. Frangieh. Washington, DC: Georgetown University Press, 1990 [Includes: About Waddah of Yemen; Aisha's Mad Lover; Aisha's Orchard; Aisha's Profile; Another Paper; al-Basra; The Birth in Unborn Cities; The Birth; The Blind Singer; A Conversation of a Stone; Death and the Lamp; The Deceiver; The Earthquake; Elegy to Khalil Hawi; Elegy to the Unborn City; Eye of the Sun; The Face; False Cities; The Fire of Poetry; First Symphony of the Fifth Dimension; For Rafael Alberti; From the Papers of Aisha; The Great Wall of China; The Greek Poem; The Gypsy Symphony; I Shall Reveal My Love for You to the Winds and the Trees; I Am Born and Burn in My

Love; The City, Lament for the June Sun; Labor Pains; The Lady of the
Seven Moons; Light Comes from Granada; Love and Death; Love Poems
at the Seven Gates of the World; Love under the Rain; The Lover; The
Magus; A Man and a Woman; Metamorphoses of Netrocres in the Book
of the Dead; The Nightmare of Night and Day; The Peacock; The Poem;
Poems on Separation and Death; Portrait of the Lover of the Great Bear;
The Princes and the Gypsy; A Profile of a City; Reading from the Book of
al-Tawasin by al-Hallaj; Secret of Fire; Shiraz's Moon; A Smoke Dancer;
Something about Happiness; Three Watercolors; The Unknown Man;
Variations on the Suffering of Farid al-Din al-Attar; and A Woman].

———. "Love in the Rain." Trans. Mohammed Darweesh. *BO* (30 Apr.
1985): 6.

———. "Love Poems to Astarte." *MMAP*: 4–7.

———. *Love under the Rain*. Madrid: Editorial Oriental, 1985 [Includes:
Eye of the Sun (Trans. Desmond Stewart); Love under the Rain; I am
Born and Burnt in Love (Trans. George Masri); Lament for the June
Sun].

———. "Love under the Rain." Trans. Farouk Abdel Wahab. *IPT*: 43–45.

———. "Luzumiyya." Trans. Khadra Salma Jayyusi and Christopher
Middleton. *JM*: 171.

———. "A Man and a Woman." *Paintbrush: A Journal of Poetry and
Translation* 28 (2001/2002): 132.

———. "The Master and His Disciple." Trans. Salih J. Altoma. *Edinburgh
Review* 127 (2009): 64–65.

———. "The Nightmare." Trans. Shafik Magar. *Baghdad* (5 July 1972):
13–15.

———. "Nightmare." Trans. M. M. Badawi. *JAL* 6 (1975): 134–36.

———. "The Nightmare." Trans. Farouk Abdel Wahab. *IPT*: 45–46.

———. "The Nightmare." Trans. Salih J. Altoma. *Free Verse: A Journal
of Contemporary Poetry and Poetics* [A bi-annual electronic journal]
(Winter 2002).

———. "Nine Ruba'iyat." Trans. Najat Rahman and Carolina Hotchandi.
IPT: 55–56.

———. "Orpheus Descent into the Underworld." Trans. Mohammad Salama. *JAL* 32.2 (2001): 161.

———. "Passages from Prokofiev's Fifth Symphony." *MMAP*: 8–9.

———. "Poems of Separation and Death." *MIP*: 46–48.

———. "Poems of Separation and Death." Trans. A. W. Lu'lu'a. *Gilgamesh*
(2/1986): 19–20.

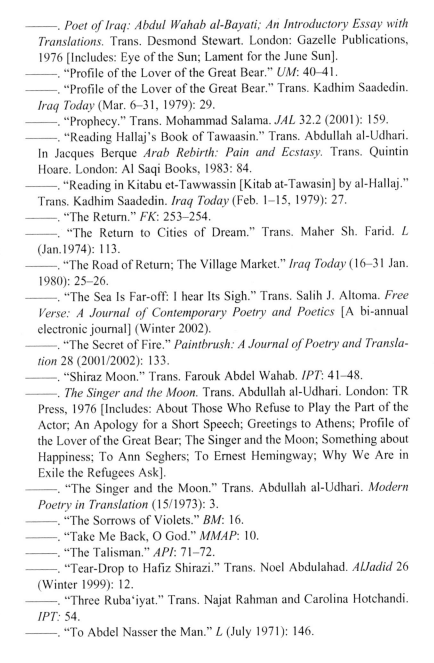

——. *Poet of Iraq: Abdul Wahab al-Bayati; An Introductory Essay with Translations.* Trans. Desmond Stewart. London: Gazelle Publications, 1976 [Includes: Eye of the Sun; Lament for the June Sun].

——. "Profile of the Lover of the Great Bear." *UM*: 40–41.

——. "Profile of the Lover of the Great Bear." Trans. Kadhim Saadedin. *Iraq Today* (Mar. 6–31, 1979): 29.

——. "Prophecy." Trans. Mohammad Salama. *JAL* 32.2 (2001): 159.

——. "Reading Hallaj's Book of Tawaasin." Trans. Abdullah al-Udhari. In Jacques Berque *Arab Rebirth: Pain and Ecstasy.* Trans. Quintin Hoare. London: Al Saqi Books, 1983: 84.

——. "Reading in Kitabu et-Tawwassin [Kitab at-Tawasin] by al-Hallaj." Trans. Kadhim Saadedin. *Iraq Today* (Feb. 1–15, 1979): 27.

——. "The Return." *FK*: 253–254.

——. "The Return to Cities of Dream." Trans. Maher Sh. Farid. *L* (Jan.1974): 113.

——. "The Road of Return; The Village Market." *Iraq Today* (16–31 Jan. 1980): 25–26.

——. "The Sea Is Far-off: I hear Its Sigh." Trans. Salih J. Altoma. *Free Verse: A Journal of Contemporary Poetry and Poetics* [A bi-annual electronic journal] (Winter 2002).

——. "The Secret of Fire." *Paintbrush: A Journal of Poetry and Translation* 28 (2001/2002): 133.

——. "Shiraz Moon." Trans. Farouk Abdel Wahab. *IPT*: 41–48.

——. *The Singer and the Moon.* Trans. Abdullah al-Udhari. London: TR Press, 1976 [Includes: About Those Who Refuse to Play the Part of the Actor; An Apology for a Short Speech; Greetings to Athens; Profile of the Lover of the Great Bear; The Singer and the Moon; Something about Happiness; To Ann Seghers; To Ernest Hemingway; Why We Are in Exile the Refugees Ask].

——. "The Singer and the Moon." Trans. Abdullah al-Udhari. *Modern Poetry in Translation* (15/1973): 3.

——. "The Sorrows of Violets." *BM*: 16.

——. "Take Me Back, O God." *MMAP*: 10.

——. "The Talisman." *API*: 71–72.

——. "Tear-Drop to Hafiz Shirazi." Trans. Noel Abdulahad. *AlJadid* 26 (Winter 1999): 12.

——. "Three Ruba'iyat." Trans. Najat Rahman and Carolina Hotchandi. *IPT*: 54.

——. "To Abdel Nasser the Man." *L* (July 1971): 146.

———. "To Anna Seghers, Author of 'The Dead Stay Young'." Trans. Abdullah al-Udhari. *TR* (Winter 1974): 54–56.

———. "To Ernest Hemingway." *UM*: 38–40.

———. "To Naguib Mahfouz." Trans. Farouk Abdel Wahab. *IPT*: 41.

———. "To Rafael Alberti." Trans. Kadhim Saadedin. *Iraq Today* (Aug. 1–15, 1977): 26–27.

———. "To T. S. Eliot." Trans. Najat Rahman and Carolina Hotchandi. *IPT*: 55.

———. "To Whom Does the Homeland Belong?" Trans. Salih J. Altoma. *AlJadid* 28 (Summer 1999): 19.

———. "Transformations of Aisha's Birth and Death in the Magical Rituals Inscribed in Cuneiform on the Nineveh's Tablets." Trans. Farouk Abdel Wahab. *IPT*: 49–52.

———. "A Traveller without Luggage." *AWW*: 85–86.

———. "Two Poems for My Son." Trans. Najat Rahman and Carolina Hotchandi. *IPT*: 57–58.

———. "The Village Market." *BM*: 15. Rpt. in *AP* 1 (July 1980): 55.

———. "The Wall." Trans. M. Bakir Alwan. *BA* 46 (1972): 249.

———. "Who Owns the Homeland?" Trans. Farouk Abdel Wahab. *IPT*: 41.

———. "Why Are We in Exile the Refugees Ask." Trans. Abdullah al-Udhari. *A Mirror for Autumn*. London: 1974. Rpt. in *AP* 1 (July 1980): 53. Rpt. in *BSOF*: 70.

———. "A Woman in Love." Trans. Mohammed Darweesh. *BO* (8 Feb. 1986): 6.

———. "Writing on Aisha's Tomb." Trans. Farouk Abdel Wahab. *IPT*: 54.

———. "Writing on Al-Sayyab's Tomb." Trans. Saadi A. Simawe. *AlJadid* 4.24 (Summer 1998): 9.

Bazaz, Ali al-. See al-Bazzaz, Ali.

Bazzaz, Ali al- (1958–).

———. "Oh Humanity." Trans. Soheil Najm. *IP*: 86. Rpt. in *FF*: 92.

Boulus, Sargon (1944–2007).

———. "A Butterfly's Dream." Trans. Kees Nijland. *Poetry International Web* 2007.

———. "Configuration, 4," "Configuration on Skin, 6," and "Configuration on Skin, 12." *Tigris* 1. n.p.

———. "Earth Is neither a Mother nor a Flower." Trans. Issa Boullata. *Arrival in Where-City: Sargon Boulus*. Ed. Mirène Ghossein. Washington, DC: Arab American Cultural Foundation, 1982: 26.

———. "Eight Poems." Trans. S. Boulus. *Banipal* 12 (Autumn 2001): 3–7 [The Dream of Childhood, A Key to the House, The Legend of Al-Sayyab and the Silt, News about No One, The Story Will Be Told, Tea with Mouayed al-Rawi in a Turkish Café after the Wall Came Down, and The Ziggurat Builders].

———. "Eight Poems." Trans. S. Boulus. *Banipal* 29 (Summer 2007): 12–17 [The Borders, A Conversation with a Painter in New York after the Tower Fell, Incident in a Mountain Village, Knife Sharpener, The Letter Arrived, The Siege, Widow Maker, Mother of Woes, Witness on the Shore].

———. "An Elegy for Sindbad Cinema." Trans. Kees Nijland. *Poetry International Web* 2007.

———. "Entries for a Possible Poem." *A Crack in the Wall: New Arab Poetry.* Ed. Margaret Obank and Samuel Shimon. London: Saqi Books, 2001, 71–73.

———. "Executioner." Trans. Mirène Ghossein. *Arrival in Where-City*: 20.

———. "Feast of Ice." Trans. Basima Bezirgan and Elizabeth Fernea. *CE*: 283–284.

———. "How Middle-Eastern Singing Was Born." Trans. Kees Nijland. *Poetry International Web* 2007.

———. "How Middle-Eastern Singing Was Born." Trans. the author. *LFAN*: 467–469.

———. "I Came from There." Trans. Kees Nijland. *Poetry International Web* 2007.

———. "Kneel in the Sand." Trans. by the poet. *Arrival in Where-City: Sargon Boulus*: 19.

———. "Korfu." Trans. by the poet. *Arrival in Where-City*: 18.

———. "Lighter." Trans. by the poet and Alistair Elliot. *JM*: 183–184.

———. "Magic." Trans. by the poet. *Arrival in Where-City: Sargon Boulus*: 23.

———. "A Man Fell on His Knees." Trans. Kees Nijland. *Poetry International Web* 2007.

———. "Master." *A Crack in the Wall: New Arab Poetry.* Ed. Margaret Obank and Samuel Shimon. London: Saqi Books, 2001, 70.

———. "Mr. America." http://lanaturnerjournal.com/article=sargon_boulus_mr_america

———. "My Father's Dream." Trans. the poet and Alistair Elliot. *JM*: 185–186. Rpt. in *BR*: 123–24.

———. "No Matter Where I Am." Trans. Michael Beard and Adnan Haydar. *Arrival in Where-City*: 21.

———. "Poem." Trans. S. Boulus and Alistair Elliot. *JM*: 184–185.

———. "Poem." Trans. Admer Gouryh. *Arrival in Where-City: Sargon Boulus*: 22.

———. "Poem." Trans. Mirène Ghossein. *Arrival in Where-City*: 27.

———. "A Refugee Talking." Trans. Kees Nijland. *Poetry International Web* 2007.

———. "Remarks to Sinbad from the Old Man of the Sea." *A Crack in the Wall: New Arab Poetry.* Ed. Margaret Obank and Samuel Shimon. London: Saqi Books, 2001, 74–75.

———. "The Secret of Fire." *SBL*: 30–31.

———. "Siege." Trans. by the poet and Alistair Elliot. *JM*: 186–187.

———. "Six Poems." Trans. S. Boulus. *Banipal* 8 (Summer 2000): 48–49 [The Corpse, The Face, Hulague, The Hun's Exaltation, Remarks to Sinbad from the Old Man of the Sea, A Song for the One Who Will Walk to the End of the Century, and This Road Alone].

———. "Six Poems." S. Boulus. *Banipal* 18 (Autumn 2003): 38–39 [A Boy against the Wall, Butterfly Dream, The Execution of the Hawk, The Executioner's Feast, The Pouch of Dust, and The Skylight].

———. "Story." Trans. S. Boulus. *Arrival in Where-City: Sargon Boulus*: 25.

———. "Tu Fu in Exile." Trans. Kees Nijland. *Poetry International Web* 2007.

———. "Water at My Threshold." Trans. Issa Boullata. *Arrival in Where-City*: 24.

———. "Whenever I Take a Step." Trans. S. Boulus. *Arrival in Where-City*: 17.

———. "Who Knows the Story." Trans. by the author. *Banipal* 4 (Spring 1999): 92. Rpt. in *A Crack in the Wall: New Arab Poetry.* Ed. Margaret Obank and Samuel Shimon. London: Saqi Books, 2001, 75–77.

Braikan, Mahmoud/Mahmood al-. See al-Buraykan, Mahmud.

Buraykan, Mahmud al- (1934–2002).

"Affiliation." Trans. Haider Al-Kabi. *IP*: 67. Rpt. in *FF*: 55.

———. "Another City." Trans. Sargon Boulus. *Banipal* 17 (Summer 2003): 40–41.

———. "The Bottomless Cave." Shihab Ahmed [al-Nassir]. *Gilgamesh: Journal of Iraqi Culture* 1 (2005): 23.

———. "Deserted City." Trans. Sargon Boulus. *Banipal* 17 (Summer 2003): 39.

———. "An Empty City." Trans. Saadi Simawe and Ralph Savarese. *IPT*: 65.

———. "The Ever-Present Dead." Trans. Sargon Boulus. *Banipal* 17 (Summer 2003): 41.

———. "The Face." Trans. Saadi Simawe and Ralph Savarese. *IPT*: 66.

———. "The Face." Trans. Shihab Ahmed [al-Nassir]. *Gilgamesh: Journal of Iraqi Culture* 1 (2005): 22.

———. "Kings." Trans. Sargon Boulus. *Banipal* 17 (Summer 2003): 41.

———. "The Knocker." Trans. Sargon Boulus. *Banipal* 17 (Summer 2003): 40.

———. "Man of the Stone City." Trans. Lena Jayyusi and Naomi Shihab Nye. *JM*: 191–193.

———. "The Manner of Sand." Trans. Abdul Settar Al-Assady. *GAP: 337*.

———. "Meditations on a World of Stone." Trans. Saadi Simawe and Ralph Savarese. *IPT*: 64–65.

———. "The Monkey's Journey." Trans. Saadi Simawe and Ralph Savarese. *IPT*: 66–67.

———. "Of Freedom." Trans. Haider Al-Kabi. *IP*: 66. Rpt. in *FF*: 54.

———. "On Freedom." Trans. Noel Abdulahad. *AlJadid* 8.41 (Fall 2002): 8.

———. "The Possessed." Trans. Saadi Simawe and Ralph Savarese. *IPT*: 67–68.

———. "Room for Nothingness." Shihab Ahmed [al-Nassir]. *Gilgamesh: Journal of Iraqi Culture* 1 (2005): 23.

———. "Shaping." Trans. Haider Al-Kabi. *IP*: 64. Rpt. in *FF*: 51.

———. "A Song of a Quiet Fear." Trans. Omar Sabry. *L* (Jan. 1973): 136–137.

———. "Tale of the Assyrian Statue." Trans. Lena Jayyusi and Naomi Shihab Nye. *JM*: 188–191.

———. "The Underground River." Trans. Sargon Boulus. *Banipal* 17 (Summer 2003): 39.

———. "Unpeopled City." Shihab Ahmed [al-Nassir]. *Gilgamesh: Journal of Iraqi Culture* 1 (2005): 23.

———. "Vacant City." Trans. Salih J. Altoma. *Free Verse: A Journal of Contemporary Poetry and Poetics* [A bi-annual electronic journal] (Winter 2002).

———. "The Voice." Trans. Sargon Boulus. *Banipal* 17 (Summer 2003): 39–40.

———. "A World of Lightning." Trans. Saadi Simawe and Ellen Watson. *IPT*: 68.

Bustani, Bushra al- (1950–).

———. "American Helmets." Trans. Wafa A Zeanal' Abidin. *Birthed from Scorched Hearst: Women Respond to War*. Ed. Marijo Moore. Golden, CO: Fulcrum Publishing, 2008.

———. *Contemporary Poetry from Iraq by Bushra al-Bustani: A Facing Page Translation*. Trans. Wafaa Abulaali and Sanna A. Dhahir. Lewiston, NY: Edwin Mellin Press, 2008.

Chellab, Abdulla Hussain. See Jallab, Abd al-Allah Husayn.

Dawai, Salam. See Dawway, Salam.

Dawway, Salam (1970–).

———. "When He Exploded." Trans. Soheil Najm. *IP*: 46. Rpt. in *FF*: 40.

Dixon, Zuhur (1933–).

———. "Dialogue of the Night of the Roses." Trans. Patricia Alanah Byrne and Salma K. Jayyusi. *JM*: 210–11.

———. "Overture." Trans. Patricia Alanah Byrne and Salma K. Jayyusi. *JM*: 210.

———. "Season of Beginning and End." Trans. Patricia Alanah Byrne and Salma K. Jayyusi. *JM*: 211–12.

———. "Two Hands on the Water." Trans. Patricia Alanah Byrne and Salma K. Jayyusi. *JM*: 212–13. Rpt. in *SBOF*: 60.

Faiq, Salah (1945–).

———. *Another Fire Befitting a City.* Trans. Haifa Zangana and A. M. al-Abbas aided by John Digby and Paul Hammond. London: Melmoth, 1979 [Includes Another Fire Befitting; a City; Days; Night Compositions; and seventeen Poems].

———. "17 Poems." *Azure* 5 (1980): 46–47.

———. "Poems." Trans. Patricia Alanah Byrne and Salma K. Jayyusi. *JM*: 218–219 [Includes five untitled short poems].

———. "Untitled" [Poem no. 2 selected from *JM* cited above]. *BSOF*: 32.

Faqir, Mun'im al-. See Alfaker, Muniam.

Furat, Basim (1967–).

———. "Coming to Be." Trans. Abdul Monem Nasser. *World Words: An Anthology of International Writers in New Zealand.* Ed. T. M. Schaeffer. Wellington, NZ: Writers International in Association with Headwork, 2006, 124.

———. "Jeanette." Trans. Abbas El Sheikh. *World Words: An Anthology of International Writers in New Zealand.* Ed. T. M. Schaeffer. Wellington, NZ: Writers International in Association with Headwork, 2006, 125.

———. "Me." Trans. Abbas el-Sheikh. *GAP*: 494.

———. "My Father." Trans. Abbas el-Sheikh. *GAP*: 495.

———. "No Looking Back." Trans. Abdul Monem Nasser. *World Words: An Anthology of International Writers in New Zealand.* Ed. T. M. Schaeffer. Wellington, NZ: Writers International in Association with Headwork, 2006, 126.

———. "Oh. Blackness, Guide Me." Trans. Abdul-Settar Al-Assady. *GAP*: 538.

———. "The Samurai." Trans. Soheil Najem. *GAP*: 493.
Ghassani, Anwar al- (1937–2009).
———. "Beautification after My Birth in Ur" and "Nomadic Kurds." Trans. A. Ghassani and Ellen Dore Watson. *Poetry International* 10 (2006): 109.
———. "Family Talk." *Horizon 5—International Peace Poetry* 2002. http://www.iflac.com/horizon/horizon5/horizion5_poetry.html.
———. "Nomadic Kurds." Trans. the author and Ellen Dore Watson *Poetry International* 10 (2006): 110–111.
———. "Two Poems: The Bay of El Coco; Dresden." Trans. the poet. *Banipal* 3 (Oct. 1998): 61.
Habash, Ali (1965–).
———. "Rockets Destroying a Happy Family." *Voices in Wartime: Anthology; A Collection of Narratives and Poems.* Ed. Andrew Himes and Jan Bulthmann. Seattle, Washington: White Press, 2005, 122.
Hadithi, Kamal al- (1939–).
———. "A Fighter's Dream." Trans. Mohammed Darweesh. *BO* (16 Sept. 1985): 5.
Hafiz, Yasin Taha (1936–).
———. "About the Gun." Trans. Karam Helmy. *Gilgamesh* (1/1986): 17.
———. "Baqouba." *MIP*: 103–106.
———. "Before and After the Bridge." *Iraq* (Dec. 15, 1984): 42; *Ur* 2 (1985): 51–53.
———. "Breaking the Precepts." Trans. Salma Khadra Jayyusi and John Heath-Stubbs. *JM*: 241.
———. "The Day Star." Trans. Kadhim Saadedin. *Iraq* (1 Aug. 1981): 42–43.
———. "A Face in Arbil's Market." Trans. Shihab Ahmed. *Gilgamesh* (1/1986): 22.
———. "The Gazelle." Trans. Sharif Elmusa and Christopher Middleton. *JM*: 237–238.
———. "I Like the Mountains." Trans. Kadhim Saadedin. *Iraq* (15 June 1981): 42–43.
———. "Leaves." Trans. Karam Helmy. *Gilgamesh* (1/1986): 20.
———. *Poems.* Trans. Mohammed Darweesh. Baghdad: Dar al-Ma'mun, 1989 [Includes: Abdullah and the Dervish; Baqouba; Beauty; Carriages; Dreams; Life on a Bench; A New Method to Catch Light; Night of Glass (Extract); A Quiet Gulf for Fishing; Return of Gilgamesh; Sarhan; Special Meeting with Myself; and Wartime Poems].
———. "Sarhan." *MIP*: 106–107.

———. "Two Poems." *MIP*: 102–103.
———. "Visit to Apologize." Trans. Mohammed Darweesh. *BO* (29 Dec. 1985): 5.
———. "Wind Flower." *Ur* 2 (1984): 40–41.
———. "A Woman." Trans. Salma Khadra Jayyusi and John Heath-Stubbs. *JM*: 240.
———. "Words and Truth." Trans. Sharif Elmusa and Christopher Middleton. *JM*: 238–240.
Haidar, Jalil. See Haydar, Jalil.
Haidari, Buland al-. See al-Haydari, Buland.
Haider, Faisal Abdul Waheb. See Haydar, Faysal Abd al-Wahhab.
Haider, Majid el-. See Haydar, Majid al-.
Hamdani, Fa'iz al-. "The Heart of a Singer" [and other poems] *Gilgamesh* 7 (2008): 24–26.
Hamdani, Salah al-. *Baghdad, Mon Amour.* Trans. from the French by Sonia Alland. Williamantic, CT: Curbstone, 2008.
Hantoosh, Gzar. See Hantush, Kazar.
Hantush, Kazar (?–2006).
———. "Celebration." Trans. Saadi Simawe and Ellen Dore Watson. *IPT*: 75.
———. "Destinies." Trans. Saadi Simawe. *Poetry International* 10 (2006): 112.
———. "A Glass of Ancient Wine." Trans. Saadi Simawe and Ellen Dore Watson. *IPT*: 74–75. Rpt. in *The Poker* 2 (Spring 2003): 55.
———. "The Happiest Man in the World." Trans. Saadi Simawe and Ellen Dore Watson. *IPT*: 73.
———. "From 'The Leaves of Autumn.'" Trans. Saadi Simawe and Brenda Hillman. Rpt. in *Poetry International* 10 (2006): 113.
———. "Love in the Time of Cholera." Trans. Saadi Simawe and Ellen Dore Watson. *IPT*: 75–76.
———. "Poems for Rasmia." Trans. Saadi Simawe and Ellen Dore Watson. *IPT*: 76–77.
———. "Take Me, Loneliness." Trans. Saadi Simawe and Ellen Dore Watson. *IPT*: 73–74.
Harbi, Tariq (1957–).
———. "The Bullet." Trans. Abdul-Settar Al-Assady. *GAP*: 533.
Hasan, Falihah (1967–).
———. "At the Margin of the War." Trans. Soheil Najm with poetic editing by Susan Bright. http://earthfamilyalpha.blogspot.com/2007/12/iraqi-poet-faliha-hassan.html.

Hasan, Salah (1960–).

———. "An Old Song about the Plains." Trans. Sinan Antoon. *Banipal* 22 (Spring 2005): 42–43.

———. "Three Poems. 1. Running Away from the Family. 2. The Statue of the Poet. 3. Reception Party." Trans. Soheil Najm. *Gilgamesh: Journal of Iraqi Culture* 3 (2005): 28.

Hassan, Faliha. See Hasan, Faliha.

Hatem, Adam. See Hatim, Adam.

Hatim, Adam [Pen name for Sa'dun Hatim] (1957–1993).

———. "This Is My Life." Trans. Haider Al-Kabi. *IP*: 44–46. Rpt. in *FF*: 37.

Hattab, Jawad al- (1950–).

———. "An Attempt to Explain Bewilderment." *API* 123–24.

Haydar, Faysal Abd al-Wahhab. "Interpretation of the Day." *GAP*: 380.

———. "The Lustrous Grief." *GAP*: 379.

———. "The Precursors of Death" *GAP*: 422.

Haydar, Jalil (1945–).

———. "Two Poems: 1. Long-Haired Sorrow. 2. Texts." Trans. Rachel Lawal. *Banipal* 5 (Summer 1999): 82.

Haydar, Majid al-. "Poets." Trans. Abdul Settar Al Assady. *GAP*: 532.

Haydari, Buland al-. "Accused Thou Innocent." Trans. Nihad A. Salem. *L* (Apr. 1972): 102–03.

———. "Abandoned Gate." Trans. Mohammed Bakir Alwan *JAL* 9 (1978): 151.

———. "Age of Rubber Seals." Trans. Patricia Alanah Byrne and Salma Khadra Jayyusi. *JM*: 243–44.

———. "The Age of Rubber Stamps." Trans. Nihad A. Salem. *L* (July 1972): 108.

———. "The Age of Rubber Stamps." Trans. Mohammed B. Alwan. *Al-Jadid* 17 (Apr. 1997): 8.

———. "Arrogance." Trans. Desmond Stewart in collaboration with Ali Haidar al-Rikabi. *New World Writing* 5 (1954): 285–86.

———. "Assassination." *API*: 62–63.

———. "Baghdad: Who Knows?" Trans. Salih J. Altoma. *Banipal* 18 (Autumn 2003): 29–30.

———. "Barrenness." *AK*: 127–29.

———. "Barrenness." Trans. Issa J. Boullata. *MA* 9 (1/1976): 73. Rpt. in *BM*: 25–26 and in *AP* 1 (4 July 1980): 49.

———. "Between Two Distances." Trans. Abdullah al-Udhari. *A Mirror for Autumn*. London: Menard Press, 1974. Rpt. in *Pagitica* 2.1 (Winter 2002): 132.

———. "Between Two Marks." Trans. Salih J. Altoma. *Banipal* 18 (Autumn 2003): 30–31.

———. "A Bitter Land." *MMAP*: 35–36.

———. "A Branch, a Desert and Mothaffar." *MMAP*: 37–38.

———. "A Call to Sleep." Trans. Abdullah al-Udhari. *TR* 2 (1975): 66–69.

———. "A Call to Sleep." Trans. Abdullah al-Udhari. *Modern Poetry in Translation* 17 (2002): 153–154.

———. "Confessions from 1961." Trans. Abd al-Hakim Amin. *Gilgamesh: Journal of Iraqi Culture* 3 (2005): 17–19.

———. "Conversation at the Bend in the Road." Trans. Abdullah al-Udhari. *Modern Poetry in Translation* (15/1973): 3. Rpt. in *UM*: 42–43 and *BR*: 68.

———. "The City Ravaged by Silence." Trans. Hussein Kadhim and Christopher Merrill. *IPT:* 78–80.

———. "The Dead Witness." Trans. Abdullah al-Udhari. *A Mirror for Autumn*. London: 1974. Rpt. in *HN*: 68–69 and *UM*: 45–46. Rpt. in *Pagitica* 2.1 (Winter 2002): 45–46.

———. "The Dead Witness." Trans. Patricia Alanah Byrne and Salma Khadra Jayyusi. *JM*: 242–243.

———. "Death in Four Voices." Trans. Hussein Kadhim and Christopher Merrill. *IPT*: 85–87.

———. "Depths." Trans. Sargon Boulus. *MA* 10 (1/1977): 56–57. Rpt. in *AP* 1 (4 July 1980): 51.

———. "Dialogue of the Colours." Trans. Hussein Kadhim and Christopher Merrill. *IPT*: 80–82.

———. *Dialogue in Three Dimensions*. Trans. Husain Haddawy. London: Pan Middle East Graphics, 1982. Rpt. partially in Jacques Berque. *Arab Rebirth: Pain and Ecstasy*. London: 1983: 85–86.

———. "Dialogue." Trans. Patricia Alanah Byrne and Salma Khadra Jayyusi. *JM*: 245–246.

———. "The Disappointment of Ancient Man." *AWW*: 82.

———. "A Dream." *MMAP*: 38.

———. "Dream." Trans. Sargon Boulus. *MA* 10 (1/1977): 58. Rpt. in *AP* 1 (4 July 1980): 51.

———. "A Dream in Four Shots." Trans. Abdullah al-Udhari. *Modern Poetry in Translation* 17 (2002): 152–53.

———. "The Dream of Returning." Trans. Mohammed B. Alwan. *AlJadid* 17 (Apr. 1997): 7.

———. "Dreaming of Snow." Trans. Mohammed Bakir Alwan *JAL* 9 (1978): 150–51.

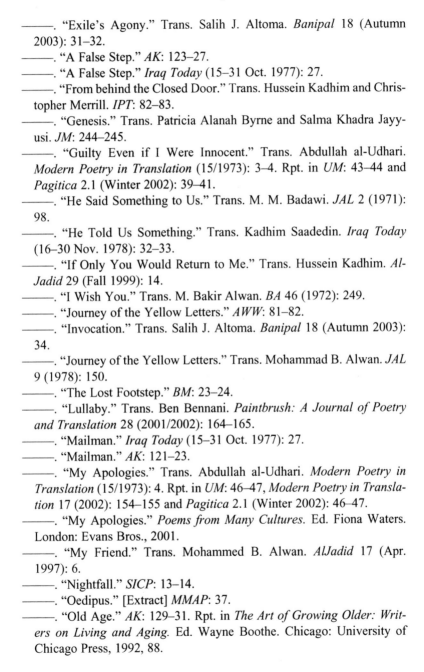

——. "Exile's Agony." Trans. Salih J. Altoma. *Banipal* 18 (Autumn 2003): 31–32.

——. "A False Step." *AK*: 123–27.

——. "A False Step." *Iraq Today* (15–31 Oct. 1977): 27.

——. "From behind the Closed Door." Trans. Hussein Kadhim and Christopher Merrill. *IPT*: 82–83.

——. "Genesis." Trans. Patricia Alanah Byrne and Salma Khadra Jayyusi. *JM*: 244–245.

——. "Guilty Even if I Were Innocent." Trans. Abdullah al-Udhari. *Modern Poetry in Translation* (15/1973): 3–4. Rpt. in *UM*: 43–44 and *Pagitica* 2.1 (Winter 2002): 39–41.

——. "He Said Something to Us." Trans. M. M. Badawi. *JAL* 2 (1971): 98.

——. "He Told Us Something." Trans. Kadhim Saadedin. *Iraq Today* (16–30 Nov. 1978): 32–33.

——. "If Only You Would Return to Me." Trans. Hussein Kadhim. *Al-Jadid* 29 (Fall 1999): 14.

——. "I Wish You." Trans. M. Bakir Alwan. *BA* 46 (1972): 249.

——. "Journey of the Yellow Letters." *AWW*: 81–82.

——. "Invocation." Trans. Salih J. Altoma. *Banipal* 18 (Autumn 2003): 34.

——. "Journey of the Yellow Letters." Trans. Mohammad B. Alwan. *JAL* 9 (1978): 150.

——. "The Lost Footstep." *BM*: 23–24.

——. "Lullaby." Trans. Ben Bennani. *Paintbrush: A Journal of Poetry and Translation* 28 (2001/2002): 164–165.

——. "Mailman." *Iraq Today* (15–31 Oct. 1977): 27.

——. "Mailman." *AK*: 121–23.

——. "My Apologies." Trans. Abdullah al-Udhari. *Modern Poetry in Translation* (15/1973): 4. Rpt. in *UM*: 46–47, *Modern Poetry in Translation* 17 (2002): 154–155 and *Pagitica* 2.1 (Winter 2002): 46–47.

——. "My Apologies." *Poems from Many Cultures*. Ed. Fiona Waters. London: Evans Bros., 2001.

——. "My Friend." Trans. Mohammed B. Alwan. *AlJadid* 17 (Apr. 1997): 6.

——. "Nightfall." *SICP*: 13–14.

——. "Oedipus." [Extract] *MMAP*: 37.

——. "Old Age." *AK*: 129–31. Rpt. in *The Art of Growing Older: Writers on Living and Aging*. Ed. Wayne Boothe. Chicago: University of Chicago Press, 1992, 88.

———. "Old Age." "Sterility." Trans. D. Stewart. *Ur* (Sept.–Oct. 1978): 40–45.

———. "Old Age." *SICP*: 7–9.

———. "Old Age." *GAP*: 347.

———. "An Old Picture." Trans. M. Bakir Alwan. *The Literary Review* 13 (1970): 529–30.

———. "On the Way of Migration from Baghdad." Trans. Salih J. Altoma. *Banipal* 18 (Autumn 2003): 33.

———. "The Parcel." Trans. Abdullah al-Udhari. *A Mirror for Autumn*. London: 1974. Rpt. in *HN*: 69–70.

———. "The Postman." *BM*: 19.

———. "The Postman." *UM*: 42.

———. "Postman." *MIP*: 51–52.

———. "Premature Elegy." Trans. Hussein Kadhim and Christopher Merrill. *IPT*: 87–88.

———. "A Premature Elegy." *FH*: 58.

———. "The Return of the Victim." Trans. Salih J. Altoma. *Banipal* 18 (Autumn 2003): 34.

———. "Scream in a Long Night." Trans. Salih J. Altoma. *Banipal* 18 (Autumn 2003): 32.

———. "Shame." *FK*: 284.

———. "Sleeping Pills." Trans. Abdullah al-Udhari. *TR* 3 (1976): 36–38. Rpt. in *Pagitica* 2.1 (Winter 2002): 41–43.

———. "Sleeping Pills." Extracts. Trans. Mohammed B. Alwan. *AlJadid* 17 (Apr. 1997): 7.

———. "So That We Do Not Forget." Trans. Hussein Kadhim and Christopher Merrill. *IPT:* 83–85.

———. *Songs of the Tired Guard*. Trans. Abdullah al-Udhari. London: TR Press, 1977 [Includes: Between Two Distances; A Call to Sleep; Conversation at the Bend in the Road; The Dead Witness; A Dream in Four Shots; Dying; Guilty Even if I Were Innocent; If You But Slept with Me Once; My Apologies; Nirvana; The Parcel; Sleeping Pills; Talking; Tell Me . . . Can I; They . . . and I].

———. "Spring Is Gone." *MMAP*: 36.

———. "Steps in Strange Lands." *BM*: 27–28. Rpt. in *AP* (July 1980): 49.

———. "Sterility." Trans. M. Bakir Alwan. *The Literary Review* 13 (1970): 531.

———. "Sterility." Trans. Desmond Stewart in collaboration with Ali Haidar al-Rikabi. *New World Writing* 5 (1954): 284–85.

———. "Stolen Frontiers." *API*: 59–61.

———. "The Sun Will Rise Again." Trans. Salih J. Altoma. *Banipal* 18 (Autumn 2003): 32.
———. "From 'The Ten IDs'." *SBL*: 99–101.
———. "Talking in a Long Street." Trans. Abdullah al-Udhari. *Pagitica* 2.1 (Winter 2002): 143–145.
———. "They Departed." Trans. Hussein Kadhim. *AlJadid* 29 (Fall 1999): 14.
———. "Today I Come Back." *MMAP*: 35.
———. "Tomorrow Here." *BM*: 20.
———. "Tomorrow. If They Erupt." Trans. Salih J. Altoma. *Banipal* 18 (Autumn 2003): 33.
———. "To a Negro from Alabama." *SICP*: 10–11.
———. "Twenty Thousand Killed . . . Old News." *BM*: 21–22. Rpt. in *AP* 1 (4 July 1980): 50.
———. "Waiting Sails." *AWW*: 83.
———. "Why Didn't They Apologize . . ?" Trans. Hussein Kadhim and Christopher Merrill. *IPT*: 88–89.
———. "The Will." Trans. Hussein Kadhim and Christopher Merrill. *IPT*: 78.
———. "A Woman's Shadow and I." *API*: 58.
Hilli, Ali al- (1930).
———. "Cafe Chardagh." *MIP*: 73–74.
———. "Cafe Latafa." *MIP*: 72–73.
———. *The Candle Tears*. n.p. n.d. (198?) [Includes: A Vision after Death, A Hymn for the Coming Era, The Smashed Idol, A Story, Baghdad, Disobedience, A Sunny Dream, The Music of Silence, A Queer Master, Returned as a Child, Zanzibar and the Other Sorrow, A Message to Tashkent, The Prisoner, A Trance, Rites in a Greek Temple, Beirut . . . My Lady!, The Eternal Shine, Death and Staying, Who Are You? Abstraction, A Burning, Conversation, Tender Love, The Surprise, Wounded Perfume, Lake of Dreams, Remnants of Prayer].
———. "Gallows Food." *API*: 89.
———. "A Hymn for the Coming Era." Trans. M. Ismail. *Iraq Today* (Aug. 1–15, 1978): 29.
———. "O Guardian of Fire." *API*: 88.
———. *Selected Poems*. Baghdad: Baghdad Observer, 1971 [Microform/Library of Congress].
———. "The Surprise." Trans. Salah Nasrawi. *Iraq Today* (1–15 Aug. 1978): 29.

Hilli, Khalid al- (1945–).

———. "Five Poems." Trans. Raghid Nahhas. *Kalimat* 22 (Sept. 2005): 57.

Husayni, Husayn al-. "The Cell." Trans, Kadhim Sa'deddin. *Gilgamesh: Journal of Iraqi Culture* 4 (2006): 57–58.

Imara, Lamiah Abbas. See Amarah, Lami'ah Abbas.

Imarah, Ali al- (1970–).

———. "Calendar." Trans. Sadek Mohammed. *IP*: 72. Rpt. In *FF*: 68.

———. "Creation." Trans. Sadek Mohammed. *IP*: 72. Rpt. in *FF*: 67.

Iskandar, Gharib. See Isknader, Gareeb.

Isknader, Gareeb. "[Three Poems] Uruk-Mandaly-Basra." *Exiled Ink* 8 (Winter 2007/2008): 24.

Izz al-Din, Yusuf (1922–).

———. "Murmurs of Memories." Trans. Thoraya Mahdi Allam. *Echoes of Arabic Poetry in English Verse.* Cairo: General Egyptian Book Organization, 1986, 102–103.

Jabbar, Emad (1968–).

———. "Do Not Live a Day in a Homeland's Memory." *Creativity in Exile.* Ed. Michael Hanne. Amsterdam; New York: Rodopi, 2004, 206–207.

———. "O Fire Be Peaceful." *Creativity in Exile.* Ed. Michael Hanne. Amsterdam; New York: Rodopi, 2004, 207–10.

Jabbar, Siham (1963–).

———. "Like Hypatia in Ancient Times." Trans. Soheil Najm. *Gilgamesh: Journal of Iraqi Culture* 5 (2007): 43–44.

———. "Like Hypatia in Ancient Times." Trans. Soheil Najm with poetic editing by Susan Bright. http://earthfamilyalpha.blogspot.com/2008/01/iraqi-poet-siham-jabbar.html.

Jabir, Zaki al- (1932–).

———. "For Twenty Years." Trans. Salih J. Altoma. *WATA Journal of Languages and Translation* 4 (Dec. 2007).

———. "Husayn, O My Lord." Trans. Salih J. Altoma. *WATA Journal of Languages and Translation* 4 (Dec. 2007).

———. "The Other." Trans. Salih J. Altoma. *WATA Journal of Languages and Translation* 4 (Dec. 2007).

———. "Our Homeland." Trans. Noel Abdulahad and Raghid Nahhas. *Kalimat* 9 (Mar. 2002): 110.

———. "Sindbad." Trans. Salih J. Altoma. *WATA Journal of Languages and Translation* 4 (Dec. 2007).

Jabiri, Muslim al-. "Poem [Umm Sa'd]." Trans. Kadhim Saadedin. *Iraq Today* (1–15 May 1979): 31–32.

Al-Jabouri, Amal. See al-Jubouri, Amal.

Jabr, Fadel K. (1960–).

———. "Waiting for the Marines." Trans. by the Poet. *100 Poets against the War*. Ed. Todd Swift. Cambridge, UK: SALT Publishing, 2003, 69–71.

Ja'far, Hasab al-Shaykh. See Shaykh Ja'far, Hasab al-.

Jallab, Abd al-Allah Husayn. "Tablets." Trans. Abdul Settar Al-Assady. *GAP*: 526.

Jamal al-Din, Mustafa (1927–1996).

———. "Awake." *API*: 78–79.

———. "A Gulf Damsel." *API*: 77.

———. "A Night on the Euphrates." *API*: 75–76.

Jamaluddeen, Mustafa. See Jamal al-Din, Mustafa.

Jamil, Hafiz (1908–1984).

———. "Lebanon." *API*: 32.

———. "Poetic Salutation." *API*: 31.

Jamil, Jawad (1954–).

———. "All Windows Are Open for Your Eyes." *API*: 125.

Janabi, A. K. El- "Eight Poems." Trans. by the author? *Banipal* 1 (Feb. 1998): 38–39.

———. "Three Poems." Trans. and reworked by the author. *Banipal* 8 (Summer 2000): 52–53 [History Always Wants to Refer Me to You, André Breton, Willingly, the Light, Every Sea Has a Boat to Immobilize It].

Janabi, Hatif (1952–).

———. "The Abyss." Trans. Khaled Mattawa. *Indiana Review* 18 (2/Fall 1995): 49.

———. "An Initial Description." Trans. Khaled Mattawa. *Indiana Review* 18 (2/Fall 1995): 45.

———. "Kingdom of Dust." Trans. Khaled Mattawa. *A Crack in the Wall: New Arab Poetry*. Ed. Margaret Obank and Samuel Shimon. London: Saqi Books, 2001: 115–16.

———. "The Little Prince." Trans. Khaled Mattawa. *Tampa Review* 13 (Fall–Winter 1996): 66.

———. "The New World." Trans. Khaled Mattawa. *Warsaw Tales 2006: New Europe Writers' Ink*. Ed. and coauthored James G. Coon. Warsaw: Wydawnictwo Ksiažkowe IBIS, 2005, 14.

———. "Paradises, Soldiers, and Stags." Trans. Khaled Mattawa. *Kaleidoscope* 33 (Summer–Fall 1996): 26. Rpt. in *LFAN*: 108–09.

———. "Poems of the New Regions." Trans. Khaled Mattawa. *Indiana Review* 19 (2/Fall 1995): 46–48.

———. "Questions and their Retinue." Trans. Khaled Mattawa. *International Quarterly* (3/1994): 128–130. Rpt. in *Literatures of Asia, Africa and Latin America*. Ed. Willis Barnstone and Tony Barnstone. Upper Saddle River, NJ: Prentice Hall, 1999, 1211–14. See also *Questions and Their Retinue/Selected Poems* below.

———. *Questions and Their Retinue/Selected Poems*. Trans. Khaled Mattawa. Fayetteville: University of Arkansas Press, 1996 [Includes The Abyss; Autumn; The Chemistry of Knowledge; The Claws of Memory; Diary of an Angel; For Hope All the Eyes in the World; Heart of the Night; In Frost; Incantation; An Initial Description; The Little Prince; Moroccan Diary; The New World; Open Form; Paradises, Soldiers, and Stags; A Party; The Pickaxe of Childhood; Playing the Skull; Poems in a Manner of Speaking; Poems of the New Regions; Poems without a Shelter; Qassidas; Questions and Their Retinue; The Rule; The Sail; Savage Continents; The Search for My Grandmother; The Storm; To Where; Willis Barnstone's Masks; A Window Small as a Palm, Vast as Suffering; and The Yellow Face of Hunger].

———. "Savage Continents." Trans. Khaled Mattawa. *Artful Dodge* 28/29 (1995): 8–9.

———. "The Search for My Grandmother." Trans. Khaled Mattawa. *Kaleidoscope* 33 (Summer–Fall 1996): 30.

———. "The Search for My Grandmother." Trans. Khaled Mattawa. *BSOF*: 99.

———. "Six Poems." Trans. Khaled Mattawa. *Banipal* 4 (Spring 1999): 42–43 [Only five titles are given: Psalm at the End of the Night, The Poet, The Kingdom of Dust, You Do Not Know, and A Wish].

———. "To Where." Trans. Khaled Mattawa. *Artful Dodge* 28/29 (1995): 10–11.

———. "A Window Small as a Palm, Vast as Suffering." Trans. Khaled Mattawa. *Indiana Review* 18 (2/Fall 1995): 43–44.

———. "A Wish." Trans. Khaled Mattawa. *A Crack in the Wall: New Arab Poetry*. Ed. Margaret Obank and Samuel Shimon. London: Saqi Books, 2001, 118.

———. "The Yellow Face of Hunger." Trans. Khaled Mattawa. *Graham House Review* 19 (Winter 1995–1996): 57–58.

———. "You Do Not Know." Trans. Khaled Mattawa. *A Crack in the Wall: New Arab Poetry*. Ed. Margaret Obank and Samuel Shimon. London: Saqi Books, 2001, 116–18.

Janabi, Nabil. "Untitled." *Index on Censorship* 18:1 (1989): 41 [Part of an article entitled "Memoir of Terror: An Iraqi Poet Now Living in Exile in Britain Describes His Experience of Torture"].

———. "Those Words I Said." *Conscience Be My Guide: An Anthology of Prison Writings.* Ed. Geoffrey Bould. 2nd ed. London: Zed Books, 2005, 9–10.

Jasim, Aziz al-Sayyid. "Gratis-Love Elegy." Trans. George N. El-Hage. *JAL* 37.2 (2006): 269–71.

———. "The Martyr." Trans. George N. El-Hage. *JAL* 37.2 (2006): 271–76.

———. "Untitled" First of "'Munajayat al-sab'in' ('Orisons of the Seventies')." Trans. George N. El-Hage. *JAL* 37.2 (2006): 266–68.

Jasim, Saad (1960–).

———. "The Mirror of Fire . . . The Mirror of Memory." Trans. Sadek Mohammed. *IP*: 71. Rpt. in *FF*: 53.

Jawad, Ala' Madhloom. "Songs from the Mountain." Trans. Sahar Fahad. *TISP*: 39–40.

———. "Season of Sparrows and Rain." Trans. Sahar Fahad. *TISP*: 41–42.

Jawad, Kadhim [Kazim] (1929–1985).

———. "Baghdad in 1954." *FK*: 286.

———. "Walladah Bint el-Mustakfi." Trans. Kadhim Saadedin. *Iraq Today* (1–15 Mar. 1979): 27–28.

Jawahiri, Muhammad Mahdi al- (1899/1901/1903?–1997).

———.Come Down, Darkness." Trans. Christopher Tingley, Salma K. Jayyusi, and Christopher Middleton. *JM*: 79–80.

———. "Effeminate Youth." *API*: 29.

———. "Forlorn Letters from Afar." [An Extract] *SBL*: 211–13.

———. "A Good Tigris." *API*: 30.

———. "I Love People." Trans. Kadhim Saadedin. *Iraq Today* (1–15 Dec. 1978): 30–31.

———. "Lullaby for the Hungry." Trans. Issa Boullata and John Heath-Stubbs. *JM*: 80–81.

———. "A Lullaby for the Hungry." Trans. Terri DeYoung. *IPT*: 94–99.

———. "Lullaby for the Hungry." *API*: 27–28.

———. "O Insomnia." Trans. Kadhim Saadedin. *Iraq Today* (1–15 Dec. 1978): 31.

———. "Oh, Sleeplessness." *The Arab Review*, London. 2 (2/1993): 26–28.

———. "The Old Man and the Forest." Trans. Kadhim Saadedin. *Iraq Today* (1–15 Dec. 1978): 30.

———. "Pricks." *API*: 24–26.

———. "Qays, the Martyr" [Untitled excerpt on the death of the seventeen-year-old Qays al-Alusi killed during the revolt of 1948]. Trans. Safa Khulusi. *The Islamic Review* (Aug.–Sept. 1962): 17.

———. "A Story." *FK*: 84–85.

——. "Transplant of Conscience." *FH*: 80.
——. "Zorba." Trans. Kadhim Saadedin. *Iraq Today* (1–15 Dec. 1978): 31.
Jihad, Kadhim (1955–).
——. "South." Trans. Fady Joudah. *LFAN*: 371–73.
Jizani, Zahir al- (1948–).
——. "Fears of the Lady." *MIP*: 138–140.
Jubouri, Amal al- (1965–).
——. "Enheduanna." Trans. Hebert Mason. *Banipal* 8 (Summer 2000): 54.
——. "Enheduanna." Trans. Salih J. Altoma. *World Literature Today* 77.3 (Oct.–Dec. 2003): 40.
——. "Enheduanna and Goethe." Trans. Salih J. Altoma. *The Poetry of Arab Women*. Ed. Nathalie Handal. New York: Interlink Books, 2001, 134.
——. "Master of the White House," a poem by Amal al-Juburi. *WATA Journal of Languages and Translation* 3 Oct. (2007).
——. "Protest." Trans. Salih J. Altoma. *AlJadid* 26 (Winter 1999): 31. Rpt. in The *Poetry of Arab Women*. Ed. Nathalie Handal. New York: Interlink Books, 2001, 135.
——. "Reproach." Trans. Hebert Mason. *Banipal* 8 (Summer 2000): 54.
——. "The Stranger." Trans. Salih J. Altoma. *AlJadid* 26 (Winter 1999): 31.
——. "Veil of Religions." Trans. Seema Atalla. *Poetry International Web* 2007.
Jubouri, Abdul Jabbar al-. "The Last Prayer." Trans. Jwan Moosa. *TISP*: 43–44.
——. "Poems Not for the Time Being." Trans. Jwan Moosa. *TISP*: 45.
——. "A Violent Childbirth." Trans. Jwan Moosa. *TISP*: 46–47.
Jubouri, Ma'd al- (1947–).
——. "A Leaf of Time." *API*: 117–119.
——. "A Pause for the Summer." *MIP*: 129–130.
——. "A Pause for My Friend Abdul-Wahab." *MIP*: 130–137.
——. "Two Poems: Asian Ivory, Cage." Trans. Mohammed Darwish. *Gilgamesh* 2 (1989): 21–22.
Juburi, Amal al-. See Jubouri, Amal al-.
Jumá, Jamal (1956–).
——. "The Anchor's Song." Trans. Nathalie Khankan. *The Online International Library of Contemporary Poets*. 4 Jan. 2007.
——. *Book of the Book: Poems*. Trans. Nina Larissa Basset. New York: iUniverse, 2005.

———. "from Book of the Book." Trans. Nina Basset. Rpt. in Poetry *International* 10 (2006): 116–117.

———. "Books." Trans. Salam Yousif. *Jusoor* 9/10 (1997/1998): 514.

———. "From Letters to My Brother." Trans. Salaam Yousif (Emily Howard's Poetic Emendation). *IPT*: 101–104. [See Juma, Jamal, and Maycock, Robert regarding Michael Nyman's adaptation of this poem for his anti-war choral work *A Handshake in the Dark*].

Jum'ah, Jamal. See Jumá, Jamal.

Kabi, Haider al-. "Bombardment." Trans. Sadek Mohammed. *IP*: 34–35. Rpt. in *FF*: 7–8.

Kamal al-Din, Adib. See Kamal Ad-Deen, Adeeb.

Kamal Ad-Deen, Adeeb (1953–).

———. "An Attempt at Madness." Trans. Sadek Mohammed. *FF*: 62–65.

———. "An Attempt at Magic." Trans. Sadek Mohammed. *FF*: 59–61.

———. "An Attempt at Music." Trans. Sadek Mohammed. *IP*: 68–70. Rpt. in *FF*: 56–58.

———. "[Four Poems] Boredom; An Attempt at Isolation; Time Runs, Time Drowns; An Attempt at the Bullet." Trans. the author. *Gilgamesh: Journal of Iraqi Culture* 3 (2005): 21–24.

———. "Sleeplessness." *Meanjin*, Melbourne, Australia. 66.2 (2007) 212. Rpt. in *The Best Australian Poems 2007*. Melbourne, Australia: Black Ink, 2007, 50.

Kamali, Shafiq al- (1929–1984).

———. "As If I Were in Baghdad." *API*: 85–86.

———. "Blocked Are My Ways." *API*: 87.

———. "Coda." Trans. Sargon Boulus and Christopher Middleton. *JM*: 287–88. Rpt. in *BSOF*: 4.

———. "Disposition No. 1." Trans. Sargon Boulus and Christopher Middleton. *JM*: 286–87.

———. "The Emigrant Moon." Trans. Kadhim Saadedin. *Iraq Today* (1–16 Feb. 1977): 28–29.

———. "Farewell." *API*: 80–81.

———. "The Harvest." Trans. Sargon Boulus. *JM*: 288.

———. "Marwan's Cares and His Slender Sweetheart." *SICP*: 25–29. Rpt. in *Ur* (2/1980): 44–47.

———. "Sighs of the Arabian Prince." *SICP*: 31–36.

Kamaludin, Adeeb. See Kamal Ad-Deen, Adeeb.

Karim, Fawzi (1945–)

———. "Crumbled Papers for Future Poem." Trans. Saadi Simawe and Chuck Miller. *IPT*: 107.

———. "Dawn Is Imminent." *BR*: 100–1.

———. "15 Poems." Trans. Saadi Simawe and Melissa Brown. *Banipal* 19 (Spring 2004): 79–88 [A Reader in Darkness, A Soldier May Cross, At the Gardenia's Door, Do Not Make Promises to Yourself, Letters Keep Going, Malice, Painting Al-Husairy The Dissident Student, The Head Is the Bird's Refuge, The Invaders, The Last Gypsies, The Scent of Mulberry, The River, Who Among Us Yearns the Most?, Reading in Darkness.]

———. "Fools' Paradise." *API*: 113.

———. "I Stretch Out My Hand." *API*: 114.

———. "Malice." Trans. Saadi Simawe. *IPT*: 108.

———. "Robin." Trans. Saadi Simawe and Chuck Miller. *IPT*: 106–7.

———. "[Untitled]. Trans. Lily al-Tai. *Exile Writers Ink: Voices in a Strange Land Online*

———. "What Was My Choice?" Trans. Saadi Simawe and Chuck Miller. *IPT*: 105. Rpt. in *The Poker* 2 (Spring 2003): 53–54.

Kasid, Abd al-Karim (1946–).

———. "Croaking." Trans. Sadek Mohammed. *IP*: 70. Rpt. in *FF*: 66.

———. "Elegy for a Coffee Shop Waiter." Trans. Sadek Mohammed. *IP*: 65.

———. "Four Elegies. 1. Waters in the Depths of the City. 2. The Wolf. 3. Consolation. 4. Space." Trans. Soheil Najm. *Gilgamesh: Journal of Iraqi Culture* 1 (2005): 20–21.

———. "The Gravestone." Trans. Lena Jayyusi and Anthony Thwaite. *JM*: 289–90.

———. "The King and the Shoes." *BR*: 137–138.

———. "Lament for a Marketplace in Babylon. Trans. Salaam Yousif and Brenda Hillman. *Poetry International* 10 (2006): 142.

———. "Leaves." Trans. Saadi Simawe and Chuck Miller. *IPT*: 111–13.

———. "Ten Poems." Trans. the author, Sara Halub and revised by David Khurt. *Banipal* 18 (Autumn 2003): 48–51 [Café, Game, House of Poetry, In Wonderland, My Nephew, Shadows, The Shroud, That Death, The Underworld, and Twelve Epigrams].

———. "The Seer." Trans. Saadi Simawe and Chuck Miller. *IPT*: 111.

———. "The Suitcases." Trans. Lena Jayyusi and Anthony Thwaite. *JM*: 292–94.

———. "Tales about My Father." Trans. Lena Jayyusi and Anthony Thwaite. *JM*: 291–292.

———. "Trilogy of Travel." Trans. Saadi Simawe and Chuck Miller. *IPT*: 109–10.

———. "Untitled." *Exile Writers Ink: Voices in a Strange Land Online.*

———. "What the Shadow Said in the Presence of the Poem." Trans. Saadi Simawe and Chuck Miller. *IPT*: 110–11.

Kazimi, Abd al-Muhsin al- (1871–1935).

———. "Onward, Onward." *API:* 10–11.

el-Kawaz, Jebbar. See Kawwaz, Jabbar.

Kawwaz, Jabbar. "The Void Sign." Trans. Abdul-Settar Al-Assady. *GAP*: 524.

Keitan, Abdul Khaliq. See Kitan, Abd al-Khaliq.

Khattab, Sabah (1956–).

———. "More Than One, Less Than Two." Trans. Haider Al-Kabi. *IP*: 73. Rpt. In *FF*: 70–71.

Kharsani, Hassan Raheem el-. See Khurasani, Hasan Rahim al-.

Khatib, Maha al-. "Only for You." *GAP*: 319–20.

Khazraji, Atika Wahbi al- (1924–1996).

———. "College Farewell." *API*: 43.

———. "Farewell to Baghdad." Trans. Safa Khulusi. *Islamic Review* (1951).

———. "Love of the Fatherland." Trans. S. A. Khulusi. *JRAS* 3–4 (1950): 156–157.

———. "Meeting and Silence." *API*: 44.

———. "The Miserable Woman" [Excerpts]. Trans. Safa Khulusi. *JRAS* 3–4 (1950): 154–55.

———. "O' Palestine" [Excerpts]. Trans. Safa Khulusi. *JRAS* 3–4 (1950): 151–52.

———. "To Yathrib." Trans. Safa Khulusi. *Islamic Review* (1951).

———. "Untitled Poem." Trans. Safa Khulusi. *JRAS* 3–4 (1950): 153–154.

Khazraji, Khalid al-. "Beirut, My Love." *AWW*: 125–126.

———. "The Birds Are Dying of Thirst." *AWW*: 126–127.

———. "I Remembered" [An Extract]. Trans. Salih J. Altoma. *WATA Journal of Languages and Translation* 4 (Dec. 2007).

Khurasani, Hasan Rahim al-. "Baghdad the Subject of International Deliberation." Trans. Sami Khamou. *GAP*: 491.

Kitan, Abd al-Khaliq (1969–).

———. "The King of Sorrows." Trans. Sadek Mohammed. *IP*: 56–57. Rpt. in *FF*: 41–42 under the title "The Sultan of Sorrows."

Kubba, Rim Qays. "A Drop." Trans. Soheil Najm. *IP*: 48. Rpt. in *FF*: 21.

Laibi, Shakir. See Lu'aybi

Lu'aibi, Shakir. "A Butterfly Frozen in Stone." Trans. Saadi Simawe and Ralph Savarese. *IPT*: 115.

———. "My Days Pass with the Beads of Rosary." Trans. Saadi Simawe and Ralph Savarese. *IPT*: 114.

———. "Scorpions Are Relaxing in the Darkness of the Garden." Trans. Sadek Mohmmed. *FF*: 28.

———. "Six Poems: The Barefoot Ladies Went Walking, The Dove Quivered at My Face, My Cane Will Never Age, Light Flaps Its Wings on the Table, The Gazelle's Lips, Metaphors Fell on Her Eyelashes." Trans. Sinan Antoon. *Banipal* 24 (Autumn/Winter 2005): 104–9.

———. "The Soul of a Pebble on the Top of the Mountain." Trans. Saadi Simawe and Ralph Savarese. *IPT*: 114–15.

———. "The Stone of the Arabian Woman." Trans. Saadi Simawe and Ralph Savarese. *IPT*: 115–16.

———. "The Unshod Ladies Went on Foot." Trans. Sadek Mohammed. *FF*: 27.

Lutfi, Abd al-Majid (1905–1992).

———. "Rejuvenation of Words." Trans. Safa Khulusi. *JAL* 11 (1980): 66–67.

Maaly, Khalid al- (1956–).

———. "Five Poems." Trans. Sargon Boulus. *Banipal* 3 (Oct. 1980): 60–61 [Death by Thirst, Doubts, The Dream of Returning, The End of the Idea, and Let Me Arrive].

Mahdi, Sami (1939/1940–).

———. "Abel's Brothers." Trans. Ferial Ghazoul. *IPT*: 117–18.

———. "Abdul Ilah." Trans. Karam Helmy. *Gilgamesh* (1/1986): 18.

———. "The Accident." *MIP*: 99–101.

———. "The Accident." Trans. Mohammad Darweesh. *BO* (15 Dec. 1984): 6.

———. "Awakening." Trans. May Jayyusi. *JM*: 312–13. Rpt. in *BSOF*: 52.

———. "Beirut." *UM*: 120.

———. "Burden." Trans. Saadi Simawe and Ellen Dore Watson. Rpt. in *Poetry International* 10 (2006): 123.

———. "Cities; Lisbon; Rotterdam; Deauville." Trans. S. Marsden. *Ur* (2/1981): 53.

———. "Concession." Trans. Karam Helmy. *Gilgamesh* (1/1986): 21.

———. "Elegy." Trans. Karam Helmy. *Gilgamesh* (1/1986): 19.

———. "Engagements." Trans. Karam Helmy. *Gilgamesh* 1/1986): 22.

———. "Fear." Trans. Saadi Simawe and Brenda Hillman. *Poetry International* 10 (2006): 125.

———. "The Fire Tent." Trans. Salman D. Al-Wasiti. *Ten Iraqi Soldier-Poets: An Anthology.* Ed. Salman D. Al-Wasiti. Baghdad: Dar al-Mamun, 1988, 13.

———. "The Inheritance." Trans. May Jayyusi. *JM*: 313.

———. "The Killer." *MIP*: 98–99.

———. "The Mistake." Trans. May Jayyusi. *JM*: 314.

———. "My Father Gains Wisdom." *MIP*: 97–98.

———. "The Occult." Trans. Kadhim Sa'adedin. *Iraq Today* (1–15 May 1977): 24–25.

———. "On Details." Trans. May Jayyusi and Charles Doria. *JM*: 312.

———. *Poems*. Selected and intro. By Hatim al-Saqr. Trans. Mohammed Darweesh. Baghdad: Dar al-Ma'mun, 1988 [Includes: The Ants; Appointments; A Clear Sky; The Column; The Exit; A Fighter's Leave; The Golden Cloud; Halt, Friends Both, Let Us Weep; Land and Sea; The Mail of the Continents; The Man and the Dog; The Martyr Writes to His Woman; The Meeting; The Mystery; On Writing; The Sniper; A Story about the Flood; Trains; Transience; Ulysses's Happiness; A Village; What is Left for Me; What Is Left to Us; When We Learned the Names; and The Young Man and the Lady].

———. "The Sayyid." *MIP*: 97.

———. "The Shapers." Trans. Noel Abdulahad. *Jusoor* 4 (1994): 110–14.

———. "The Sound." *SBL*: 251–253.

———. "War's Diaries." Trans. Ferial Ghazoul. *IPT*: 117. Rpt. in *The Poker*. Cambridge, MA. No. 2 (Spring 2003): 52.

———. "What's in a Name." Trans. Saadi Simawe and Ellen Dore Watson. *Poetry International* 10 (2006): 124.

———. "World of Fancy." Trans. May Jayyusi. *JM*: 314.

Majedi, Abdul Rahman al- (1965–).

———. "Four Poems." Trans. Sargon Boulus. *Banipal* 18 (Autumn 2003): 52–53 [Escape, Graveyard, Most People Are Poets, and Shoes].

Majidi, Khaz'al al- (1951–).

———. "Branches." *MIP*: 141–144.

Mala'ikah, Nazik al- (1923–2007).

———. "Arrival." *MMAP*: 44.

———. "Between the Jaws of Death." *API*: 33–34.

———. "The Bottom of the Stairs." Trans. M. M. Badawi in his *A Critical Introduction to Modern Arabic Poetry*. Cambridge: Cambridge University Press, 1975, 230.

———. "Cholera." Trans. Husain Haddawy with Nathalie Handal. *The Poetry of Arab Women*. Ed. Nathalie Handal. New York: Interlink Books, 2001, 176–77.

———. "The Cholera." Trans. Kadhim Saadedin. *Iraq Today* (1–15 Apr. 1980): 31–32.

———. "The Cholera." *API*: 35–37.

———. "Denial." *Global Literature: One World, Many Voices.* Vol. II. Ed. Charles Duncan. Orlando, FL: Harcourt Brace, 1997.

———. "Elegy for a Woman of No Consequence." *FH*: 106.

———. "Elegy for a Woman of No Consequence." Trans. Anne Fairbairn. *Meanjin* (University of Melbourne, Australia), 50.1 (Autumn 1991): 4.

———. "Elegy for a Woman of No Importance." Trans. Chris Kniff and Muhammad Sadiq. *OB*: 153.

———. "Elegy on the Death of a Woman of No Importance." Trans. Rose Ghurayyib. *AGH*: 135.

———. "Enamoured River." *API*: 38–40.

———. "Escapists." *MMAP*: 45.

———. "Five Hymns to Pain." Trans. Husain Haddawy. *The Poetry of Arab Women* Ed. Nathalie Handal. New York: Interlink Books, 2001, 177–182.

———. "Five Songs to Pain." *BM*: 11–13.

———. "Five Songs to Suffering" [Stanzas 1, 2, and 5]. Trans. Rose Ghurayyib. *AGH*: 135–36.

———. "Four Poems: The Train Passed, To the New Year, The Arrival, Busy in Mar." Trans. Salman al-Wasiti. *Gilgamesh* 4 (1989): 19–26.

———. "The Ghosts' Prayer." *MIP*: 35–39.

———. "The Hijrah [Migration] to God." Trans. Saadi Simawe and Jenna Abdul Rahman. *IPT*: 126–28.

———. "I Am." *WB*: 22. Rpt. in Dalya Cohen-Mor. *A Matter of Fate: The Concept of Fate in the Arab World as Reflected in Modern Arabic Literature.* Oxford and New York: Oxford University Press, 2001, 137.

———. "I Am." Trans. B. M. Bennani. *MA* 7 (2/1974): 61. See also *Paintbrush* 28 (2001–2002): 182–83.

———. "Ice and Fire." See "My Silence."

———. "Insignificant Woman" *WB*: 18. Rpt. in *LFAN*: 96–97.

———. "Jamilah." *WB*: 22. Rpt. in AP 1 (4 July 1980): 46, and in *WP*: 101.

———. "Jamilah and US." Trans. Basima Bezirgan and Ibtisam S. Barakat. *IPT*: 119–120.

———. "Let Us Dream Together." *AWW*: 79–80.

———. "Lilies for the Prophet." Trans. Matthew Sorenson and Christopher Middleton. *JM*: 329–333.

———. "A Lily Called Jerusalem." Trans, Patricia Alamah Burns with the help of the editor Salma Jayyusi. *My Jerusalem: Essays, Reminiscences, and Poems.* Ed. Salma Khadra Jayyusi and Safar I Ansari. Northampton, MA: Olive Branch Press, 2005, 201–2.

———. "Love Song for Words." Trans. Matthew Sorenson and Christopher Middleton. *JM*: 334–36.

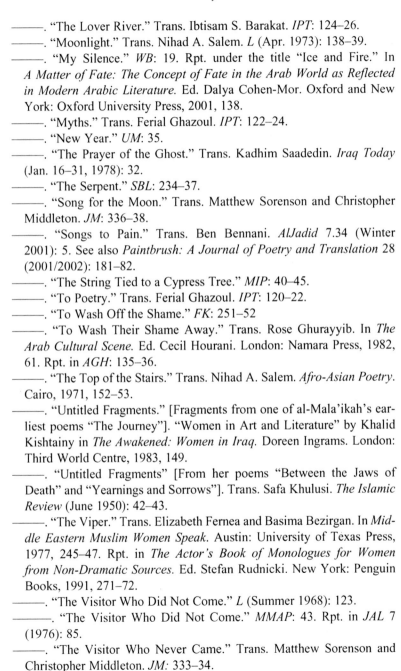

————. "The Lover River." Trans. Ibtisam S. Barakat. *IPT*: 124–26.

————. "Moonlight." Trans. Nihad A. Salem. *L* (Apr. 1973): 138–39.

————. "My Silence." *WB*: 19. Rpt. under the title "Ice and Fire." In *A Matter of Fate: The Concept of Fate in the Arab World as Reflected in Modern Arabic Literature*. Ed. Dalya Cohen-Mor. Oxford and New York: Oxford University Press, 2001, 138.

————. "Myths." Trans. Ferial Ghazoul. *IPT*: 122–24.

————. "New Year." *UM*: 35.

————. "The Prayer of the Ghost." Trans. Kadhim Saadedin. *Iraq Today* (Jan. 16–31, 1978): 32.

————. "The Serpent." *SBL*: 234–37.

————. "Song for the Moon." Trans. Matthew Sorenson and Christopher Middleton. *JM*: 336–38.

————. "Songs to Pain." Trans. Ben Bennani. *AlJadid* 7.34 (Winter 2001): 5. See also *Paintbrush: A Journal of Poetry and Translation* 28 (2001/2002): 181–82.

————. "The String Tied to a Cypress Tree." *MIP*: 40–45.

————. "To Poetry." Trans. Ferial Ghazoul. *IPT*: 120–22.

————. "To Wash Off the Shame." *FK*: 251–52

————. "To Wash Their Shame Away." Trans. Rose Ghurayyib. In *The Arab Cultural Scene*. Ed. Cecil Hourani. London: Namara Press, 1982, 61. Rpt. in *AGH*: 135–36.

————. "The Top of the Stairs." Trans. Nihad A. Salem. *Afro-Asian Poetry*. Cairo, 1971, 152–53.

————. "Untitled Fragments." [Fragments from one of al-Mala'ikah's earliest poems "The Journey"]. "Women in Art and Literature" by Khalid Kishtainy in *The Awakened: Women in Iraq*. Doreen Ingrams. London: Third World Centre, 1983, 149.

————. "Untitled Fragments" [From her poems "Between the Jaws of Death" and "Yearnings and Sorrows"]. Trans. Safa Khulusi. *The Islamic Review* (June 1950): 42–43.

————. "The Viper." Trans. Elizabeth Fernea and Basima Bezirgan. In *Middle Eastern Muslim Women Speak*. Austin: University of Texas Press, 1977, 245–47. Rpt. in *The Actor's Book of Monologues for Women from Non-Dramatic Sources*. Ed. Stefan Rudnicki. New York: Penguin Books, 1991, 271–72.

————. "The Visitor Who Did Not Come." *L* (Summer 1968): 123.

————. "The Visitor Who Did Not Come." *MMAP*: 43. Rpt. in *JAL* 7 (1976): 85.

————. "The Visitor Who Never Came." Trans. Matthew Sorenson and Christopher Middleton. *JM:* 333–34.

———. "The Visitor Who Never Came." Trans. Rose Ghurayyib. *AGH*: 132–33.

———. "Washing Off Disgrace." *WB*: 20–21. Rpt. in *AP* 1 (4 July 1980): 45. Rpt. in "Women in Art and Literature" by Khalid Kishtainy, *The Awakened: Women in Iraq*. Doreen Ingrams. London: Third World Centre, 1983, 149–51 and Dalya Cohen-Mor. *A Matter of Fate: The Concept of Fate in the Arab World as Reflected in Modern Arabic Literature*. Oxford and New York: Oxford University Press, 2001, 139–140.

———. "The Way Back." Trans. Rose Ghurayyib. *AGH*: 132.

———. "When I Killed My Love." *AWW*: 78–79.

———. "When I Killed My Love." [Stanza 4]. Trans. Rose Ghurayyib. *AGH*: 129.

———. "Who Am I?" *AK*: 79–81. Rpt. in *Middle Eastern Muslim Women Speak*. Ed. Elizabeth Fernea and Basima Q. Bezirgan. Austin: University of Texas Press, 1977, 244.

Mala'ikah, Salma al- (1909–1953).

———. "Untitled Fragments." [From the poetry of Nazik's mother concerning Jamil Sidqi al-Zahawi and Palestine]. Trans. Safa Khulusi. *Islamic Review* (June 1950): 41–42.

Maliki, Mujbilal-. "Iraq's PalmTree." Trans. Salih J. Altoma. *WATA Journal of Languages and Translation* 4 (Dec. 2007).

Mardan, Husayn (1927–1972).

———. "Glass." *MIP*: 65.

———. "Man of the Fog." *API*: 73–74.

———. "Spring and Hunger." Trans. Muhammad Darweesh. *BO* (24 Nov. 1984): 6.

Matar, Ahmad (1950–).

———. "A Pen." *FF*: 112.

———. "A Plan." Trans. Abdul Settar Al-Assady. *GAP*: 536.

———. "The Riddle." Trans. Abdul Settar Al-Assady. *GAP*: 537.

Meraiby, Bassem al-. See Mur'ibi, Basim al-.

Mijbil, Ajwad. See Mujbil, Ajwad.

Mikhail, Dunya (1965–).

———. "Bags of Bones." Trans. Sadek Mohammed. *IP*: 30–31. Rpt. in *FF*: 5–6.

———. "America." Trans. Liz Winslow. *IPT*: 132–37. See also *World Beat: International Poetry Now*. Ed. Eliot Weinberger. New York: New Directions, 2006, 17–32.

———. "The Chaldean Ruins." Trans. Samira Kawar. *The Poetry of Arab Women*. Ed. Nathalie Handal. New York: Interlink Books, 2001, 211–13.

———. "Christmas." Trans. Liz Winslow. *IPT*: 130. Rpt. in *Poetry International* 10 (2006): 114–27.

———. "The Dawn Fairy." Trans. Samira Kawar. In *The Poetry of Arab Women*. Ed. Nathalie Handal. New York: Interlink Books, 2001, 210–11.

———. *Diary of a Wave Outside the Sea*. Trans. the author and ed. Louise I. Hartung. Cairo: Ishtar Publishing House, 1999.

———. "The Foreigner." Trans. Elizabeth Winslow. *Mizna* 3.2 (2000): 24.

———. "The Jewel." Trans. Salaam Yousif. *IPT*: 129.

———. "Non-Military Statements." Elizabeth Winslow. In *World Beat: International Poetry Now*. Ed. Eliot Weinberger. New York: New Directions, 2006, 23–24.

———. "The Prisoner." Trans. Liz Winslow. *IPT*: 131–32. Rpt. in Poetry *International* 10 (2006): 126.

———. "Rain." Trans. Samira Kawar with Nathalie Handal. In *The Poetry of Arab Women*. Ed. Nathalie Handal. New York: Interlink Books, 2001, 208–10.

———. "Santa Claus." Trans. Salaam Yousif. *IPT*: 129. Rpt. in *The Poker* 2 (Spring 2003): 50 and *Poetry International* 10 (2006): 128.

———. "Snow Storm." Trans. Liz Winslow. *IPT*: 130–31.

———. "Three Poems." Trans. the author. *Banipal* 3 (Oct. 1998) 51–52 [The Cup, Pronouns, and The War Works Hard]. Rpt. in A *Crack in the Wall: New Arab Poetry*. Ed. Margaret Obank and Samuel Shimon. London: Saqi Books, 2001, 165–68.

———. "An Urgent Call." Trans. Elizabeth Winslow. In *World Beat: International Poetry Now*. Ed. Eliot Weinberger. New York: New Directions, 2006, 15–16.

———. "The War Works Hard." Trans. Elizabeth Winslow. *World Beat: International Poetry Now*. Ed. Eliot Weinberger. New York: New Directions, 2006, 14–15.

———. "The War Works Diligently." Trans. Salih J. Altoma. *WATA Journal of Languages and Translation* 4 (Dec. 2007).

Mikhail, Murad (1906–1986).

———. "The Voice of Conscience." Trans. Sadok Masliyah and Christina Coyle. *Poetry International* 10 (2006): 114–15.

Mousawi, Sajida al-. See Musawi, Sajidah.

Mohammed, Hayat J. See Muhammad, Hayat J.

Mohammed, Sadek (1964–).

———. "Assumptions." Trans. the author. *FF*: 89–91.

Mu'alla, Abd al-Amir al- (1942–1997).

———. "Arise!" *MIP*: 120–124.

———. "Two Nights." *MIP*: 119–20.

Mudhaffar, May/Mai. See Muzaffar, May.

Muhammad, Hayat Jasim (1936–).

———. "A Baghdad Love Song." Trans. the author. *Kalimat* 9 (Mar. 2002): 102–3.

Muhammad, Jalal Qadir. "The Big Wedding." Trans. Arwa Fu'ad. *TISP*: 49.

———. "The Shawl and the Rifle." Trans. Arwa Fu'ad. *TISP*: 50.

———. "The Martyr." Trans. Arwa Fu'ad. *TISP*: 51.

Muhammad, Muwaffaq. "The House of the Poet." Trans. Ayid Matar. *Gilgamesh* 4 (2006): 55–56.

Muhammad, Salman Dawud (1957–).

———. "Unarmed Morning." Trans. Sadek Mohammed. *FF*: 69.

Mujbil, Ajwad. "A Swing for Absence." *SBL*: 68–69.

Mur'ibi, Basim al- (1960–).

———. "Seven Poems." Trans. Khaled Mattawa. *Banipal* 4 (Spring 1999): 46–47 [Only five titles are given: Blind Ink, A Capricorn Chronicle, I Hear the Axe, A Land Woven by Pirates, and My Father]. See also *A Crack in the Wall: New Arab Poetry*. Ed. Margaret Obank and Samuel Shimon. London: Saqi Books, 2001, 162–64.

———. "The Mouth of Every Beautiful Woman Owes Me a Kiss." Trans. Nicolas Suescún. *PROMOTEO: Revisita Latinoamericana de Poesia* 74–75 (June 2008).

Musawi, Majid al-. "Forlornness." Trans. Abdul-Settar Al-Assady. *GAP*: 525.

———. "A Poem." Trans. Dunia Khalil? *Gilgamesh: Journal of Iraqi Culture* 7 (2008): 22.

Musawi, Sajidah (1950–).

———. "Four Beats of the Heart." Trans. Basima Bezirgan and Elizabeth Fernea. *IPT*: 146–47.

———. "The Hero." *MIP*: 150.

———. "My Road to You." *MIP*: 148.

———. "The Wounded." *MIP*: 148–49.

Mushatat, Raad [a pseudonym]. "Many Dresses." Trans. Shirley Eber. *Index on Censorship* (2/1986): 30.

———. "Three Iraqi Women 1979." Trans. Shirley Eber. *Index on Censorship* (2/1986): 31.

Mustafa, Jamal. "The Black Box." Trans. Haider Al-Kabi. *IP*: 75.

———. "A Present." Trans. Haider Al-Kabi. *IP*: 26. Rpt. in *FF*: 1.

Mustafa, Khalid Ali. "Basra-Haifa." Trans. Kadhim Saadedin. *Iraq Today.* (1–15 Nov. 1978): 31.

————. "Basra-Haifa." *MIP*: 112–18.

————. "Exiles." Trans. Muhammad Darweesh. *BO* (7 July 1985): 6.

————. "Private Cases of a Palestinian Lover." Trans. Salim K. Hassan. *Iraq Today* (1–30 Apr. 1979): 39.

————. "The Voice of the Wounded." Trans. Nihad A. Salem. *L* (Apr. 1970), 149–50.

Mutashar, Ra'ad. See Mutashshar, Ra'd.

Mutashshar, Ra'd. "That Is It." Trans. Soheil Najm. *Gilgamesh* 3 (2005): 20.

Muttalibi, Abdulwahab el-. See Muttalibi, Abd al-Wahhab al-.

Muttalibi, Abd al-Wahhab. "The Sonata of the Unfamiliar Seagull." Trans. Khaloud al-Muttalibi. *GAP*: 504–5.

Muttalibi, Khaloud al-. "A Poet's Reverie." *GAP*: 496.

————. "The Tiresome Journey." *GAP*: 497.

Muttalibi, Malik al- (1942–).

————. "Multiple Fall." *MIP*: 124–25.

Muzaffar, May (1940–).

————. "A Calm Moment." Trans. Pauline Kaldas. *International Quarterly* 1 (3/1994): 156.

————. "A Man and a Woman." Trans. Pauline Kaldas. *International Quarterly* 1 (3/1994): 157.

————. "A Man and a Woman." Trans. Samira Kawar. *Banipal* 1 (Feb. 1998): 23.

————. "The Message." Trans. Samira Kawar. *Banipal* 1 (Feb. 1998): 23.

————. "Snapshots." Trans. Peter Philips. Haifa Zangana. In *City of Widows: An Iraqi Woman's Account of War and Resistance.* New York: Seven Stories Press, 2007, 143.

————. "[Six Poems]." Trans. Tahia Abdel Nasser. In *The Poetry of Arab Women.* Ed. Nathalie Handal. New York: Interlink Books, 2001, 233–35 [Includes The Absent, A Flash, Friends, Reticence, Spinning, and The Voice].

————. "A Woman." Trans. Samira Kawar. *Banipal* 1 (Feb. 1998): 23.

Najafi, Ahmad al-Safi al- (1897–1977).

————. "Apprehensions." *API*: 19–21.

————. "The Flower Seller." *AK*: 77–79.

————. "Garments of the Soul." *FH*: 114.

————. "God and Mind." *API*: 22–23.

————. "Immortal Liberty." Trans. M. A. Khouri and H. Algar. *JAL* 1 (1970): 75–76. Rpt. in *AK*: 75–77.

————. "The Moth." Trans. Issa Boullata and John Heath-Stubbs. *JM*: 87–88.

———. "The Pleasures of Darkness." Trans. Issa Boullata and Salma Khadra Jayyusi. *JM:* 86–87.

———. "The Ship of Life." Trans. Salma Khadra Jayyusi and John Heath-Stubbs. *JM*: 87.

———. "To a Clock." *AM*: 5–6. Rpt. in *AW* 9 (July–Aug. 1963): 13.

———. "Where Is the Guard?" Trans. Sharif Elmusa and Thomas G. Ezzy. *JM*: 85–86.

Naji, Hilal (1929–).

———. "Untitled Poem." *FK*: 253.

Najim, Suhail. See Najm, Soheil.

Najm, Soheil "The Map of the Soul." Trans. Abdul Settar Al-Assady. *GAP* 534–35.

———. "Seven Attempts to Portray Mr. President." Trans. Haider Al-Kabi. *IP*: 36–37. Rpt. in *FF*: 12–13.

Nasir, Awad. "A Moment of Love." Trans. Saadi Simawe and Ralph Savarese. *Poetry International* 10 (2006): 131.

———. "Parade." Trans. Saadi Simawe and Ralph Savarese. *Poetry International* 10 (2006): 130.

———. "A Poem's Fate." Trans. Saadi Simawe and Ralph Savarese. Rpt. in *Poetry International* 10 (2006): 133.

———. "A Poet's Fate." Trans. Saadi Simawe and Ralph Savarese. *IPT*: 150. Rpt. in *Poetry International* 10 (2006):132.

———. "Three Poems." Trans. Saadi Simawe and Ralph Savarese. *IPT*: 148–49.

———. "Trilogy of the Man in Black." Trans. Saadi Simawe and Ralph Savarese. *IPT*: 149.

Nassar, Hanadi al-. "The Execution of an Executioner." Trans. Sadek Mo-hammed. *IP*: 38–39. Rpt. in *FF*: 14–15.

Nassar, Mohammed al-. See Nassar, Muhammad al-.

Nassar, Muhammad al-. "When Will I Awaken from This Life?" Trans. Soheil Najm with poetic editing by Susan Bright. http://earthfamilyalpha.blogspot.com/2008/01/iraqi-poet-mohammed-al-nassar.html.

Nassar, Za'im al- (1957–).

———. "No Way." Trans. Soheil Najm. *FF*: 72–73.

———. "A White Window." Trans. Soheil Najm. *FF*: 32–33.

Nawwab, Muzaffar. al- (1936–).

———. "Bridge of Old Wonders." Transcribed and trans. Carol Bardenstein and Saadi Simawe. *IPT*: 151–85.

———. "Five Poems from the Dialect of the Iraqi Marsh Arabs by Mudha-fer Al Nawab." Trans. Tony Curtis and Mustafa Hadi. In Curtis's *Taken for Pearls*. Bridgend, Mid Glam: Poetry Wales Press, 1993, 41–50 [Includes Knocked Flat; A Liar; The Summer-rain Is Coming; To the Train and Hammad [sic], and Twice Robbed].

———. "From 'Tel al-Zaatar'." *Index on Censorship* 10 (3 June 1981): 48.

———. "Jerusalem." Trans. Michael Beard and Andy Tenner. *Nimrod* 24.2 (Spring–Summer 1981): 134–38.

———. "Night-Strings." (Excerpts) Trans. Adnan Haydar and Michael Beard. *Minnesota Review* 26 (Spring 1986): 44–55.

———. "Poem." [Extracts from his Arabic collection *Night Tunes or Night Strings*]. *Index on Censorship* (2/1986): 31–32.

———. "Wine and Grief." Trans. Sinan Antoon. *Al-Ahram Weekly Online*, (17–23 Apr. 2003.

Niyazi, Salah (1935–).

———. "The Abode." Trans. the Author. *Poetry Review*. London. 82.2 (Summer 1992).

———. "Back from War." Trans. the author. *Exiled Ink* 8 (Winter 2007/ 2008): 22.

———. "Canned Neighing." *API*: 110–11.

———. "The Circle." *API*: 107–9.

———. "Four Poems." Trans. by the author with thanks to John Heath-Stubbs. *Banipal* 8 (Summer 2000): 46–47 [Back from the War, Flat-Hunting, An Iraqi in Marbella, The Vikings]. Rpt. in [with the exception of "An Iraqi in Marbella"] in *Gilgamesh: Journal of Iraqi Culture* 5 (2007): 35–37.

———. "From The Thinker." *UM*: 115.

———. "Hameed." Trans. Lena Jayyusi and Charles Doria. *JM*: 365–66.

———. "The Muslim." *API*: 112.

———. "The Return of the Veil." *UM*: 116.

———. "The Runaway President." [Extract] Trans. the author with thanks to Sian Williams. *Banipal* 17 (Summer 2003): 60–61.

———. "Selected Poems." A twelve-page mimeographed text, part of a program of readings at Kufa Gallery, London, Aug. 20, 1988 [Includes the three poems published in *UM* and "The Harems and the Walls of Mirrors"; "Horses on Tape" translated by Jareer Abu Haidar, and "Nightmare" translated by J. Masri].

———. "The Thinker between the Bronze Shield and the Human Flesh." Trans. Saadi Simawe and Melissa Brown. *IPT*: 186–91.

———. "Third World." *UM*: 116.

———. "Um Hakeem." Trans. Lena Jayyusi and Charles Doria. *JM*: 366–67.

———. "The Wind." Trans. Jareer Abu Haidar. *Banipal* 1 (Feb. 1998): 24–25. Rpt. in *A Crack in the Wall: New Arab Poetry*. Ed. Margaret Obank and Samuel Shimon. London: Saqi Books, 2001, 204–6.

Nouri, Golala. See Nuri, Kulalah

Nuri, Kulalah (1969–).

———. "Three Poems: Stone Mummy, Optimism, Blackness." Trans. Khaled Mattawa. *Banipal* 19 (Spring 2004): 100.

Qasim, Hamid. "True Nature." Trans. Soheil Najm. *Gilgamesh* 7 (2008): 20.

Qassim, Hamid. See Qasim, Hamid.

Rahim, Abd al-Rahim Salih al- (1950–).

———. "Every day." Trans. Saadi Simawe and Ralph Savarese. *IPT*: 194. Rpt. in *Poetry International* 10 (2006): 137.

———. "My Heart." Trans. Saadi Simawe and Daniel Weissbort. *IPT*: 195–196. Rpt. in *Poetry International* 10 (2006): 139.

———. "Poisonous Illusion." Trans. Saadi Simawe and Daniel Weissbort. *IPT*: 194. Rpt. in *Poetry International* 10 (2006): 136.

———. "The Road." Trans. Saadi Simawe and Daniel Weissbort. *IPT*: 195. Rpt. in *Poetry International* 10 (2006): 135.

———. "A Shadow." Trans. Saadi Simawe and Ralph Savarese. *IPT*: 196.

———. "The Train of the Stars." Trans. Adil Salih Abid. *SBOF*: 37.

———. "Wailing." Trans. Saadi Simawe and Daniel Weissbort. *IPT*: 195. Rpt. in *Poetry International* 10 (2006): 138.

———. "Who?" Trans. Saadi Simawe and Daniel Weissbort. *IPT*: 197. Rpt. in *Poetry International* 10 (2006): 141.

———. "Who Are You?" Trans. Saadi Simawe and Daniel Weissbort. *IPT*: 196–197. Rpt. in *Poetry International* 10 (2006): 140.

Rahman, Ali Khamees. "The Face of Water." Trans. Sura Bahjat. *TISP*: 59–60.

———. "Among Them." Trans. Sura Bahjat. *TISP*: 61–62.

Ramli, Muhsin al- (1967–).

———. "No to Liberating Iraq from Me." Trans. Alycia M. Rivard. *PRO-MOTEO: Revisita Latinoamericana de Poesia* 74–75 (June 2006).

Rawi, Mouayed al- (1939–).

———. "The Illusion of Place." Trans. Noel Abdulahad. *AlJadid* no. 49 (Fall 2004): 8.

———. "Nearness of Illusion."*Tigris* 1 [See note regarding Tigris under Boulus, Sargon].

———. "The Procession of March." Trans. Sargon Boulus. *Banipal* 18 (Autumn 2003): 58–59.

———. "Second Continuation." *Tigris* 1.

———. "Three Poems." Trans. Sargon Boulus. *Banipal* 12 (Autumn 2001): 32–34 [Interpretation of Place, The Wolf, and Words about Things].

Riadh, Dalia. See Riyad, Daliya.

Riyad, Daliya (1970–). "Two Poems" [Maybe, Please]. Trans. Sharif El-musa. *Banipal* 8 (Summer 2000): 59.

Rubai, Sharif. See Rubay'i, Sharif al-.

Rubaiee, Abdul Razaq al-. See Rubay'i, Abd al-Razzaq al-.

Rubay'i, Abd al-Razzaq al- (1961–).

———. "The Grandchildren of Sinbad." Trans. Salaam Yousif and Brenda Hillman. *Poetry International* 10 (2006): 142. Rpt. in *Poetry International* 10 (2006): 142.

———. The Statute." Trans. Mohammed Sadek. *IP*: 32–33. Rpt. in *FF*: 9–11.

———. "Tomorrow the War Will Have a Picnic." Trans. Mohammed Sadek. *IP*: 41–43. Rpt. in *FF*: 16–19.

———. "Wrinkles on the Face of the Country." Trans. Salaam Yousif and Brenda Hillman. *Poetry International* 10 (2006): 143.

Rubay'i, Sharif al- (1943–1997).

———. "The Ashes of Intimacy." Trans. S. B [Sargon Boulus]. *Banipal* 3 (Oct. 1998): 59. Rpt. in *A Crack in the Wall: New Arab Poetry*. Ed. Margaret Obank and Samuel Shimon. London: Saqi Books, 2001, 228–30.

Rusafi, Ma'ruf al- (1875–1945).

———. "The Abyss of Death." Trans. Issa Boullata and Christopher Middleton. *JM*: 96.

———. "Complaint to al-Raihani." *API*: 14–15.

———. "Fairest." *AM*: 4–5.

———. "At a Game of Football." Trans. John A. Haywood in his *Modern Arabic Literature: 1800–1970*. London: Lund Humphries, 1971, 113–14.

———. "O My People." *API*: 12–13

———. "The Negative Truth about Me." Trans. John A. Haywood in his *Modern Arabic Literature: 1800–1970*. London: Lund Humphries, 1971, 112–13.

———. "The Past and Us." *FK*: 245.

———. "Poem to al-Raihani." Trans. Issa Boullata and Christopher Middleton. *JM*: 95–96.

———. "Sleepers, Wake!" *AM*: 3–4. Rpt. in *Modern Islamic Literature*. Ed. James Kritzeck. New York: Holt, Rinehart, 1970, 158.

———. "To the Fairest." Trans. Najib Ullah. *Islamic Literature*. New York: Washington Square Press, 1963, 191.

————. "Untitled Poem." [Urging the Arabs to Rise]. *AA*: 164–68.

Sabti, Kamal (1958– 2006).

————. "Poems from Jungles." Trans. Lena Jayyusi and Naomi S. Nye. *JM*: 394–97.

Sadoun, Abdulhadi. See Sa 'dun, Abd al-Hadi.

Sa'dun, Abd al-Hadi (1968–).

————. "The Hotel Borges." Trans. Lenni Friedman [from the Arabic and Spanish]. *Banipal* 17 (Summer 2003): 66.

————. "Tank Carpets." *9th Poetry Africa Festival* (10–15 Oct. 2005). Centre for Creative Arts, University of KwaZulu-Natal.

————. "Dead Fish." *PROMOTEO: Revisita Latinoamericana de Poesia* 74–75 (June 2004).

Saggar, Muhammad Sa'id al-. See al-Sakkar. Muhammad Sa'id.

Sa'di, Arif al-. "Here I Come." *SBL*: 89–91.

Sa'id, Amjad Muhammad (1947–).

————. "Every Day." *MIP*: 134–135.

————. "Forty Days and Mowsil Is the Horizon." *API*: 120–122.

Sa'id, Hamid. "Captain Jalal." *MIP*: 108–111.

————. "Daily Delights." Trans. Lena Jayyusi and Naomi Shihab Nye. *JM*: 399–401.

————. "Daily Pleasures." Trans. Kadhim Saadedin. *Iraq Today* (16–30 Nov. 1977): 32.

————. "Dying at the Edge of Death." Trans. Diana Der Hovanessian and Lena Jayyusi. *JM*: 398–99.

————. "Emanations." Trans. Lena Jayyusi and Naomi Shihab Nye. *JM*: 401–5.

————. "The Fires of al-Hudur." Trans. G. Masri. *Ur* (4/1980): 40–43.

————. "The First Path Shortened." *SICP*: 69–73.

————. "The Great Mulberry." Trans. Karam Helmy. *Gilgamesh* (1/1986): 21.

————. "The Last Painting" [Dedicated to Layla al-Attar]. Trans. Noel Abdulahad. *Jusoor* 4 (1994): 139–43.

————. "The Last Painting." Trans. Salih J. Altoma. *The Literary Review* 45.3 (2002): 578–79 [Preceded by the translator's "Introductory Remarks," 576–77].

————. "Love and Death." Trans. Mohammed Darweesh. *BO* (15 Jan. 1985): 6.

————. "Luminosities." Trans. K. Saadedin. *Iraq Today* 2 (43/15–30 July 1977): 30–31.

————. "Mansour." *Iraq* (15 Dec. 1984): 42.

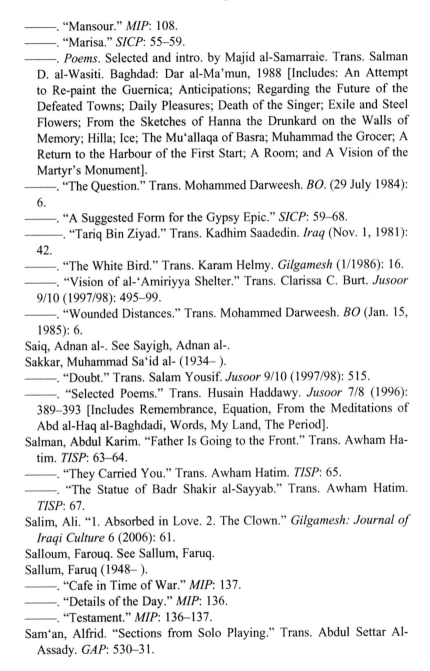

———. "Mansour." *MIP*: 108.

———. "Marisa." *SICP*: 55–59.

———. *Poems*. Selected and intro. by Majid al-Samarraie. Trans. Salman D. al-Wasiti. Baghdad: Dar al-Ma'mun, 1988 [Includes: An Attempt to Re-paint the Guernica; Anticipations; Regarding the Future of the Defeated Towns; Daily Pleasures; Death of the Singer; Exile and Steel Flowers; From the Sketches of Hanna the Drunkard on the Walls of Memory; Hilla; Ice; The Mu'allaqa of Basra; Muhammad the Grocer; A Return to the Harbour of the First Start; A Room; and A Vision of the Martyr's Monument].

———. "The Question." Trans. Mohammed Darweesh. *BO*. (29 July 1984): 6.

———. "A Suggested Form for the Gypsy Epic." *SICP*: 59–68.

———. "Tariq Bin Ziyad." Trans. Kadhim Saadedin. *Iraq* (Nov. 1, 1981): 42.

———. "The White Bird." Trans. Karam Helmy. *Gilgamesh* (1/1986): 16.

———. "Vision of al-'Amiriyya Shelter." Trans. Clarissa C. Burt. *Jusoor* 9/10 (1997/98): 495–99.

———. "Wounded Distances." Trans. Mohammed Darweesh. *BO* (Jan. 15, 1985): 6.

Saiq, Adnan al-. See Sayigh, Adnan al-.

Sakkar, Muhammad Sa'id al- (1934–).

———. "Doubt." Trans. Salam Yousif. *Jusoor* 9/10 (1997/98): 515.

———. "Selected Poems." Trans. Husain Haddawy. *Jusoor* 7/8 (1996): 389–393 [Includes Remembrance, Equation, From the Meditations of Abd al-Haq al-Baghdadi, Words, My Land, The Period].

Salman, Abdul Karim. "Father Is Going to the Front." Trans. Awham Hatim. *TISP*: 63–64.

———. "They Carried You." Trans. Awham Hatim. *TISP*: 65.

———. "The Statue of Badr Shakir al-Sayyab." Trans. Awham Hatim. *TISP*: 67.

Salim, Ali. "1. Absorbed in Love. 2. The Clown." *Gilgamesh: Journal of Iraqi Culture* 6 (2006): 61.

Salloum, Farouq. See Sallum, Faruq.

Sallum, Faruq (1948–).

———. "Cafe in Time of War." *MIP*: 137.

———. "Details of the Day." *MIP*: 136.

———. "Testament." *MIP*: 136–137.

Sam'an, Alfrid. "Sections from Solo Playing." Trans. Abdul Settar Al-Assady. *GAP*: 530–31.

Samawi, Aziz al-. "Iraqi Sorrows." Trans. Alex Bellem. *IPT*: 204–5.
———. "Mountain of Dreams." Trans. Alex Bellem. *IPT*: 205–7.
———. "Neighing of the Fingers." Trans. Alex Bellem. *IPT*: 207–11.
———. "Suns in the Night of the Massacre." Trans. Alex Bellem. *IPT*: 211–15.
Samawi, Shakir al-. "The Dream of A Snow Flower." Trans. Saadi Simawe and Chuck Miller. *IPT*: 216–17.
———. "Quartets of Inner Whispering." Trans. Saadi Simawe and Chuck Miller. *IPT*: 216.
———. "Solo for the Lone Intuition." Trans. Saadi Simawe and Chuck Miller. *IPT*: 217–18.
Samawi, Yahya al- (1949–).
———. "My Love Humiliated Me." Trans. Salih J. Altoma. *World Literature Today* 77.3 (Oct.–Dec. 2003): 40.
———. *Two Banks with No Bridge.* Trans. Eva Sallis. Warner Bay, N.S.W., Australia: Picaro Press, 2005.
———. "The Last Poem" Trans. Salih J. Altoma. *Famous Reporter* 33 (July 2006). Rpt. in alhadaf althaqafi. Dec. 1, 2006. http://www.tahayati .com/the-last-poem.htm.
Sarhan, Salam. "Fingers of Eternity." Trans. the author. *Banipal* 2 (June 1998): 49.
Sa'igh, Yousif al-. See Sayigh, Yusuf al-.
Sawad, Muwaffaq al- (1971–).
———. "Three Poems: Ashes; A Script for a Tiny Dream; I Am the transient, It Is the City." Trans. Sinan Antoon. *Banipal* 23 (Summer 2005): 69–71.
Saygh, Sadiq. See Sayigh, Sadiq al-.
Sayigh, Adnan al- (1955–).
———. "God's Money." Trans. Soheil Najm. *IP*: 28. Rpt. in *FF*: 20.
———. "Night's Prayer." Trans. Soheil Najm. *IP*: 29. Rpt. in *FF*: 4.
———. "Passage to Exile." Trans. Abbas S. Kadhim. *PROMOTEO: Revisita Latinoamericana de Poesia* 74–75 (June 2005); Rpt. in *GAP*: 572.
———. "from 'Slightly Quarrelsome Texts. Doors. Perplexity. Iraq." Trans. Soheil Najm. *IP*: 74. Rpt. in *FF*: 76–78.
———. "Ulysses." Trans. Salih J. Altoma. *World Literature Today* 77.3 (Oct.–Dec. 2003): 41.
———. "Whiteness." Trans. Abdul Settar Al-Assady. *GAP*: 539.
Sayigh, Sadiq al- (1936–).
———. "The Day You Gave Away Your Life." Trans. the author. *Banipal* 8 (Summer 2000): 51.

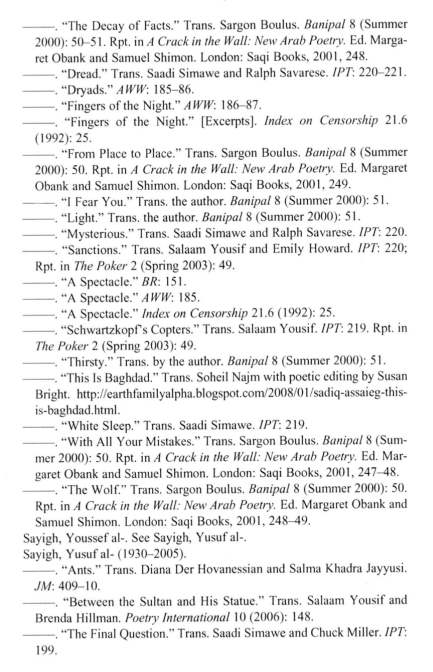

———. "The Decay of Facts." Trans. Sargon Boulus. *Banipal* 8 (Summer 2000): 50–51. Rpt. in *A Crack in the Wall: New Arab Poetry*. Ed. Margaret Obank and Samuel Shimon. London: Saqi Books, 2001, 248.

———. "Dread." Trans. Saadi Simawe and Ralph Savarese. *IPT*: 220–221.

———. "Dryads." *AWW*: 185–86.

———. "Fingers of the Night." *AWW*: 186–87.

———. "Fingers of the Night." [Excerpts]. *Index on Censorship* 21.6 (1992): 25.

———. "From Place to Place." Trans. Sargon Boulus. *Banipal* 8 (Summer 2000): 50. Rpt. in *A Crack in the Wall: New Arab Poetry*. Ed. Margaret Obank and Samuel Shimon. London: Saqi Books, 2001, 249.

———. "I Fear You." Trans. the author. *Banipal* 8 (Summer 2000): 51.

———. "Light." Trans. the author. *Banipal* 8 (Summer 2000): 51.

———. "Mysterious." Trans. Saadi Simawe and Ralph Savarese. *IPT*: 220.

———. "Sanctions." Trans. Salaam Yousif and Emily Howard. *IPT*: 220; Rpt. in *The Poker* 2 (Spring 2003): 49.

———. "A Spectacle." *BR*: 151.

———. "A Spectacle." *AWW*: 185.

———. "A Spectacle." *Index on Censorship* 21.6 (1992): 25.

———. "Schwartzkopf's Copters." Trans. Salaam Yousif. *IPT*: 219. Rpt. in *The Poker* 2 (Spring 2003): 49.

———. "Thirsty." Trans. by the author. *Banipal* 8 (Summer 2000): 51.

———. "This Is Baghdad." Trans. Soheil Najm with poetic editing by Susan Bright. http://earthfamilyalpha.blogspot.com/2008/01/sadiq-assaieg-this-is-baghdad.html.

———. "White Sleep." Trans. Saadi Simawe. *IPT*: 219.

———. "With All Your Mistakes." Trans. Sargon Boulus. *Banipal* 8 (Summer 2000): 50. Rpt. in *A Crack in the Wall: New Arab Poetry*. Ed. Margaret Obank and Samuel Shimon. London: Saqi Books, 2001, 247–48.

———. "The Wolf." Trans. Sargon Boulus. *Banipal* 8 (Summer 2000): 50. Rpt. in *A Crack in the Wall: New Arab Poetry*. Ed. Margaret Obank and Samuel Shimon. London: Saqi Books, 2001, 248–49.

Sayigh, Youssef al-. See Sayigh, Yusuf al-.

Sayigh, Yusuf al- (1930–2005).

———. "Ants." Trans. Diana Der Hovanessian and Salma Khadra Jayyusi. *JM*: 409–10.

———. "Between the Sultan and His Statue." Trans. Salaam Yousif and Brenda Hillman. *Poetry International* 10 (2006): 148.

———. "The Final Question." Trans. Saadi Simawe and Chuck Miller. *IPT*: 199.

———. "Habitude." Trans. Saadi Simawe and Chuck Miller. *IPT*: 198. Rpt. in *Poetry International* 10 (2006): 149.

———. "Hair." Trans. Diana Der Hovanessian and Salma Khadra Jayyusi. *JM*: 410.

———. "Intermittent." Trans. Saadi Simawe and Chuck Miller. *IPT*: 199. Rpt. in *Poetry International* 10 (2006): 147.

———. "An Iraqi Evening." Trans. Saadi Simawe, Ralph Savarese, and Chuck Miller. *IPT*: 198. Rpt. in *The Poker* 2 (Spring 2003): 51. Rpt. in *Poetry International* 10 (2006):150.

———. "Is This All That Remains from Love?" Trans. Diana Der Hovanessian and Salma Khadra Jayyusi. *JM*: 407–08.

———. "Is This, Then, All That's Left?" *SBL*: 277–78.

———. "Lady of the Marches." Trans. Mohammed Darweesh. *BO* (27 Mar. 1985): 6.

———. "Memoirs of a Very Ordinary Hero." Trans. Salman al-Wasiti. *Gilgamesh* (2/1986): 28–31.

———. "Memoirs of a Very Ordinary Hero." *MIP*: 82–86.

———. "Odour of Rains." Trans. Husain Haddawi. *Ur* (1/1984): 48–49.

———. "Reflections of a Very Ordinary Hero." *Iraq* (15 Dec. 1984): 42.

———. "Reincarnation." Trans. A. W. Lu'lu'a. *Gilgamesh* (2/1986): 27.

———. "The Slain Date-Palm." Trans. Salman al-Wasiti. *Gilgamesh* (2/1986): 28.

———. "Sound." *FH*: 166.

———. "A Story." Trans. Diana Der Hovanessian and Salma Khadra Jayyusi. *JM*: 408.

———. "Supper." Trans. Saadi Simawe. *IPT*: 199. Rpt. in *Poetry International* 10 (2006): 146.

———. "Thread." Trans. Saadi Simawe and Chuck Miller. *IPT*: 200.

———. "The Tune." Trans. Saadi Simawe. *IPT*: 199. Rpt. in *Poetry International* 10 (2006): 145.

———. "Turtle." Trans. Saadi Simawe and Chuck Miller. *IPT*: 200–1. Rpt. in Poetry *International* 10 (2006): 144.

———. "Wake Up, Yousif." Trans. Saadi Simawe and Ralph Savarese. *IPT*: 200–3.

———. "Westwards . . . Till Mount Olive." *API*: 96–100.

———. "Wet." Trans. Diana Der Hovanessian and Salma Khadra Jayyusi. *JM*: 409.

———. "Why." Trans. Diana Der Hovanessian and Salma Khadra Jayyusi. *JM*: 408–9.

———. "Words That Did Not Smile." *API*: 101.

Sayyab, Badr Shakir al- (1926–1964).

———. "An Ancient Song." Trans. Adel Salama. *JAL* 3 (1972): 118–19.

———. "Before the Gate of God." Trans. M. A. Khouri and H. Algar. *JAL* 1 (1970): 119–21. Rpt. in *AK*: 83–87.

———. "The Book of Job." Trans. Desmond O'Grady. *Ten Modern Arab Poets: Selected Versions.* Dublin: The Dedalus Press, 1992, 57–58. Rpt. in his *Trawling Tradition: Translations 1954–1994.* Salzburg: University of Salzburg, 1994, 207–8.

———. "from 'The Book of Job.'" Trans. Saadi Simawe and Brenda Hillman. *Poetry International* 10 (2006): 151.

———. "Burning." Trans. M. A. Khouri and H. Algar. *JAL* 1 (1970): 122. Rpt. in *AK*: 87–89; *HN* 86; and *AP*: 1 (4 July 1980): 41.

———. "Burning." *FH*: 168.

———. "The Call of Death." *SSP*: 43–44.

———. "The Caravan of the Refugees." *APR* 4 (12 Dec. 1972): 50–52.

———. "Christ after Crucifixion." Trans. Basima Bezirgan and Elizabeth Fernea. *Ur* (Jan.–Feb. 1979): 41–43.

———. "Christ after Crucifixion." *AWW*: 140–42.

———. "Christ after Crucifixion." Trans. Pierre Cachia. *An Overview of Modern Arabic Literature.* Edinburgh: Edinburgh University Press, 1990, 198–99 [About half the poem].

———. See also "The Messiah after Crucifixion."

———. "City of Mirage." Trans. Robert Bringhurst. *Quarry* 2 (Fall 1972): 37–38.

———. "City of Sinbad." *BHM*: 17–21.

———. "City of Sindbad." Trans. M. A. Khouri and H. Algar. *JAL* 1 (1970): 124–28. Rpt. in *AK*: 93–103 and in *Divine Inspiration: The Life of Jesus in World Poetry.* Ed. Robert Atwan et al. New York: Oxford University Press, 1998, 177–180.

———. "City of Sindbad." Trans. Ben Bennani. *Paintbrush* 28 (2001–2002): 203–7.

———. "A City without Rain." *BM*: 3–5.

———. "The Cry of the Mallard." Trans. Robert Bringhurst. *Gazelle Review* 7 (1980): 3.

———. "Day Has Gone." Trans. Adnan Haydar and Michael Beard. *Banipal* 5 (Summer 1999): 10–11.

———. "Death and the River." *SSP*: 29–31.

———. "Death and the River." Trans. Lena Jayyusi and Christopher Middleton. *JM*: 435–36.

———. "Eram [Iram] of the Pillars." Trans. Kadhim Saadedin. *Iraq* (1 June 1981): 42–43.

———. "For I Am a Stranger." Trans. M. A. Khouri and H. Algar. *JAL* 1 (1970): 121–22. Rpt. in *AK*: 89–91; *HN*: 85–86; and *AP* 1 (4 July 1980): 41.

———. "The Fox of Death." *SSP*: 36–37.

———. "Fragrance." *API*: 45–46.

———. "From Return to Jaikour." Trans. Jabra I. Jabra. *Middle East Forum* 43 (1967): 25–26. Rpt. in *Critical Perspectives on Modern Arabic Literature.* Ed. Issa J. Boullata, 1980, 197–98.

———. "From 'The Book of Job'." *AWW*: 144–145.

———. "Garcia Lorca." *SSP*: 35.

———. "Garcia Lorca." Trans. Ben. M. Bennani. *International Poetry Review* 3 (1/1977): 10. See also *BHM*: 22. See also *Paintbrush* 28 (2001–2002): 207–8.

———. "Garcia Lorca". Trans. Rasheed el-Enany. *Third World Quarterly* 10.4 (1989): 252.

———. "Hymn of the Rain." Trans. T. DeYoung. *JAL* (1993): 59–61.

———. "Hymn to Rain." Trans. Adel Salama. *JAL* 3 (1972): 119–22.

———. "In the Arab Maghreb." Trans. Lena Jayyusi and Christopher Middleton. *JM*: 437–42.

———. "In the Arab Maghrib." Trans. Hussein Kadhim. *JAL* 30 (1999): 138–42 [Included in his article "Rewriting the Waste Land and Badr Shakir al-Sayyab's 'Fi al-Maghrib al-Arabi'," 128–65].

———. "In the Arab West" [Excerpts] Trans. Pieter Smoor. *Centennial Hauntings: Pope, Byron and Eliot in the Year 88.* Ed. C. C. Barefoot and Theo D'haen. Amsterdam; Atlanta, GA: Rodopi, 1990, 348.

———. "The Informer." *SSP*: 49–52.

———. "In Front of the Gate of Allah." *L* (Mar. 1967): 68–69. Rpt. in *Afro-Asian Poetry.* Ed. Edward el-Kharrat and Nihad Salem. Cairo: Atlas Press, 1971, 144–46.

———. "In the Hospital." *API*: 56–57.

———. "Jaikur and the Trees of the City." *SSP*: 38–39.

———. "Jaikur and the City." Trans. Lena Jayyusi and Christopher Middleton. *JM*: 432–35.

———. "Jaykur and the City." [Excerpts] Trans. Arieh Loya. *The Muslim World* 61 (1971): 193–95.

———. "The Last Night." Trans. Tahia Khaled Abdel Nasser. *Jusoor* 4 (Winter–Spring 1994): 82–83.

———. "Love Me." Trans. Mustafa Kamal and Ralph Savarese. *IPT*: 223–26.

———. "A Message from the Grave." *SSP*: 40–42.

———. "The Messiah after the Crucifixion." Trans. B. M. Bennani. *Agni* 5/6 (1976): 125. Rpt. in *BHM*: 23–25. See also *Paintbrush* 28 (2001–2002): 208–10.

———. "The Messiah after the Crucifixion" Trans. M. M. Badawi. *JAL* 6 (1975): 136–38. Rpt. in *Divine Inspiration: The Life of Jesus in World Poetry.* Ed. Robert Atwan et al. New York: Oxford University Press, 1998, 505–07.

———. "Mirage City." Trans. S. Boulus. *MA* 10 (1/1977): 62–63.

———. "Myths." [Extract] Trans. Terri DeYoung. *Edebiyât* 5 (1994): 232–34.

———. "O Estrangement of the Spirit." Trans. Tahia Khaled Abdel Nasser. *Jusoor* 4 (Winter–Spring 1994): 78–79.

———. "Ode to the Rain." Trans. Kadhim Saadedin. *Iraq Today* (1–15 Oct. 1977): 32–33.

———. "An Ode to Revolutionary Iraq." *AK*: 92–93.

———. "Rain Song." Trans. Desmond O'Grady. *Ten Modern Arab Poets: Selected Versions.* Dublin: The Dedalus Press, 1992, 54–56. Rpt. in his *Trawling Tradition: Translations 1954–1994.* Salzburg: University of Salzburg, 1994, 205–7.

———. "Rain Song." *UM*: 29–32.

———. "Rain Song." Trans. Lena Jayyusi and Christopher Middleton. *JM*: 427–30, Rpt. in *Global Voices: Contemporary Literature from the Non-Western World.* Ed. Arthur W. Biddle, Gloria Been, et al. Englewood Cliffs, NJ: Prentice Hall, 1995, 458–61; *Qasida Poetry in Islamic Asia and Africa.* Ed. Stefan Sperl and Christopher Shackle. Vol. 2. Leiden: Brill, 1996, 132–39 [Text in Arabic and English].

———. "Rain Song." Trans. Noel Abdulahad. *AlJadid* 32 (Summer 2000): 29 [Described in a footnote as "an interpretive translation"].

———. "Return to Jaykur." Trans. Adnan Haydar and Michael Beard. *Banipal* 5 (Summer 1999): 9–10.

———. "The River and Death." *UM*: 32–34. Rpt. in *Poems for the Millennium.* Vol. II. Ed. Jerome Rothenberg and Pierre Joris. Berkeley: University of California Press, 1998, 185–86.

———. "The River and Death." *The Arab Review* 1.4 (1993): 35–37.

———. "The River and Death." Trans. M. A. Khouri and H. Algar. *JAL* 1 (1970): 123–24. Rpt. in *AK*: 105–07; *Edebiyât* 1 (1976): 140–41 and in

Critical Perspectives on Modern Arabic Literature. Ed. Issa J. Boullata (1980): 294–95.

———. "River and Death." Trans. Nazeer el-Azma. *JAOS* 88 (1968): 675. Rpt. in Critical *Perspectives on Modern Arabic Literature.* Ed. Issa J. Boullata (1980): 224–25.

———. "River of Death." *AWW*: 139–40.

———. *Selected Poems.* Trans. Nadia Bishai. Beirut: Arab Institute for Research and Publishing and London: Third World Centre for Research and Publishing, 1986 [Includes: The Song of the Rain; Death and the River; Garcia Lorca; Take Me; The Fox of Death; Jaikur and the Trees of the City; A Message from the Grave; The Call of Death; Christ after the Crucifixion; The Informer; and The Wind Is Knocking at the Door].

———. "Shadows of Jaikur." Trans. Abdullah al-Udhari. In *Arab Rebirth: Pain and Ecstasy.* Jacques Berque. London: AL SAQI Book, 1983. Rpt. in *UM*: 34.

———. "The Sindbad City." Trans. Mohammed Shaheen. *The Modern Arabic Short Story.* Basingstoke; New York: Palgrave Macmillan, 2002, 191–96.

———. "Sinbad's Town." *FK:* 254.

———. "The Singer Has Aged." Trans. Ibtisam S. Barakat. *IPT*: 222–23.

———. "Song in August." Trans. Lena Jayyusi and Christopher Middleton. *JM*: 430–32. Rpt. in *Global Voices: Contemporary Literature from the Non-Western World.* Ed. Arthur W. Biddle, Gloria Bien, et al. Englewood Cliffs, NJ: Prentice Hall, 1995, 461–63.

———. "The Song of Rain." Trans. Issa J. Boullata. *MA* 9: 1 (1976): 66. Rpt. in *BM*: 7–10 and *AP* 1 (4 July 1980): 42–43.

———. "The Song of Rain." Trans. Bassam Frangieh. *Banipal* 17 (Summer 2003): 29–31.

———. "The Song of the Rain." *SSP*: 24–28.

———. "A Song of the Rain." *AWW*: 142–44.

———. "Song of the Rain." Trans. Basima Bezirgan and Elizabeth Fernea. *CE*: 264–268. Rpt. in *Ur* (Jan.–Feb. 1979): 36–40.

———. "The Song of Rain." *Azure* 4 (1979): 53–55.

———. "Song of the Rain." *API*: 47–452.

———. "Stranger at the Gulf." Trans. Tahia Khaled Abdel Nasser. *Jusoor* 4 (Winter–Spring 1994): 73–77.

———. "from 'A Stranger at the Gulf.'" Trans. Saadi Simawe and Ellen Dore Watson. *Poetry International* 10 (2006): 152.

———. "Take Me." *SSP*: 32–34.

———. "Town without Rain." *MIP*: 31–34.

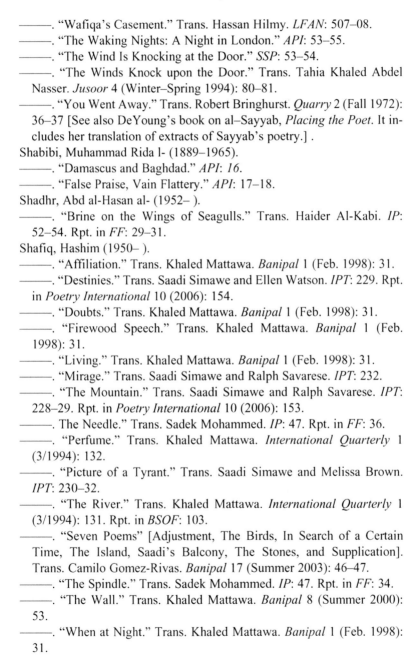

———. "Wafiqa's Casement." Trans. Hassan Hilmy. *LFAN*: 507–08.

———. "The Waking Nights: A Night in London." *API*: 53–55.

———. "The Wind Is Knocking at the Door." *SSP*: 53–54.

———. "The Winds Knock upon the Door." Trans. Tahia Khaled Abdel Nasser. *Jusoor* 4 (Winter–Spring 1994): 80–81.

———. "You Went Away." Trans. Robert Bringhurst. *Quarry* 2 (Fall 1972): 36–37 [See also DeYoung's book on al–Sayyab, *Placing the Poet*. It includes her translation of extracts of Sayyab's poetry.] .

Shabibi, Muhammad Rida l- (1889–1965).

———. "Damascus and Baghdad." *API*: *16*.

———. "False Praise, Vain Flattery." *API*: 17–18.

Shadhr, Abd al-Hasan al- (1952–).

———. "Brine on the Wings of Seagulls." Trans. Haider Al-Kabi. *IP*: 52–54. Rpt. in *FF*: 29–31.

Shafiq, Hashim (1950–).

———. "Affiliation." Trans. Khaled Mattawa. *Banipal* 1 (Feb. 1998): 31.

———. "Destinies." Trans. Saadi Simawe and Ellen Watson. *IPT*: 229. Rpt. in *Poetry International* 10 (2006): 154.

———. "Doubts." Trans. Khaled Mattawa. *Banipal* 1 (Feb. 1998): 31.

———. "Firewood Speech." Trans. Khaled Mattawa. *Banipal* 1 (Feb. 1998): 31.

———. "Living." Trans. Khaled Mattawa. *Banipal* 1 (Feb. 1998): 31.

———. "Mirage." Trans. Saadi Simawe and Ralph Savarese. *IPT*: 232.

———. "The Mountain." Trans. Saadi Simawe and Ralph Savarese. *IPT*: 228–29. Rpt. in *Poetry International* 10 (2006): 153.

———. The Needle." Trans. Sadek Mohammed. *IP*: 47. Rpt. in *FF*: 36.

———. "Perfume." Trans. Khaled Mattawa. *International Quarterly* 1 (3/1994): 132.

———. "Picture of a Tyrant." Trans. Saadi Simawe and Melissa Brown. *IPT*: 230–32.

———. "The River." Trans. Khaled Mattawa. *International Quarterly* 1 (3/1994): 131. Rpt. in *BSOF*: 103.

———. "Seven Poems" [Adjustment, The Birds, In Search of a Certain Time, The Island, Saadi's Balcony, The Stones, and Supplication]. Trans. Camilo Gomez-Rivas. *Banipal* 17 (Summer 2003): 46–47.

———. "The Spindle." Trans. Sadek Mohammed. *IP*: 47. Rpt. in *FF*: 34.

———. "The Wall." Trans. Khaled Mattawa. *Banipal* 8 (Summer 2000): 53.

———. "When at Night." Trans. Khaled Mattawa. *Banipal* 1 (Feb. 1998): 31.

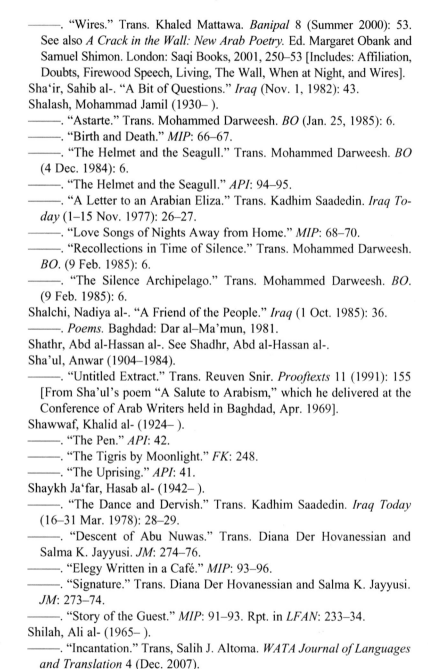

————. "Wires." Trans. Khaled Mattawa. *Banipal* 8 (Summer 2000): 53. See also *A Crack in the Wall: New Arab Poetry*. Ed. Margaret Obank and Samuel Shimon. London: Saqi Books, 2001, 250–53 [Includes: Affiliation, Doubts, Firewood Speech, Living, The Wall, When at Night, and Wires].

Sha'ir, Sahib al-. "A Bit of Questions." *Iraq* (Nov. 1, 1982): 43.

Shalash, Mohammad Jamil (1930–).

————. "Astarte." Trans. Mohammed Darweesh. *BO* (Jan. 25, 1985): 6.

————. "Birth and Death." *MIP*: 66–67.

————. "The Helmet and the Seagull." Trans. Mohammed Darweesh. *BO* (4 Dec. 1984): 6.

————. "The Helmet and the Seagull." *API*: 94–95.

————. "A Letter to an Arabian Eliza." Trans. Kadhim Saadedin. *Iraq Today* (1–15 Nov. 1977): 26–27.

————. "Love Songs of Nights Away from Home." *MIP*: 68–70.

————. "Recollections in Time of Silence." Trans. Mohammed Darweesh. *BO*. (9 Feb. 1985): 6.

————. "The Silence Archipelago." Trans. Mohammed Darweesh. *BO*. (9 Feb. 1985): 6.

Shalchi, Nadiya al-. "A Friend of the People." *Iraq* (1 Oct. 1985): 36.

————. *Poems*. Baghdad: Dar al-Ma'mun, 1981.

Shathr, Abd al-Hassan al-. See Shadhr, Abd al-Hassan al-.

Sha'ul, Anwar (1904–1984).

————. "Untitled Extract." Trans. Reuven Snir. *Prooftexts* 11 (1991): 155 [From Sha'ul's poem "A Salute to Arabism," which he delivered at the Conference of Arab Writers held in Baghdad, Apr. 1969].

Shawwaf, Khalid al- (1924–).

————. "The Pen." *API*: 42.

————. "The Tigris by Moonlight." *FK*: 248.

————. "The Uprising." *API*: 41.

Shaykh Ja'far, Hasab al- (1942–).

————. "The Dance and Dervish." Trans. Kadhim Saadedin. *Iraq Today* (16–31 Mar. 1978): 28–29.

————. "Descent of Abu Nuwas." Trans. Diana Der Hovanessian and Salma K. Jayyusi. *JM*: 274–76.

————. "Elegy Written in a Café." *MIP*: 93–96.

————. "Signature." Trans. Diana Der Hovanessian and Salma K. Jayyusi. *JM*: 273–74.

————. "Story of the Guest." *MIP*: 91–93. Rpt. in *LFAN*: 233–34.

Shilah, Ali al- (1965–).

————. "Incantation." Trans, Salih J. Altoma. *WATA Journal of Languages and Translation* 4 (Dec. 2007).

———. "Amulet." Trans. Rudiger Fischer. *International Poetry Festival of Medellin Magazine.* 2005. Online.

Shimon, Samuel (1956–).

———. "Fifteen Poems." Trans. James Kirkup and Samia Akl Boustani. *Banipal* 15/16 (Autumn 2002/Spring 2003): 16–17 [Translation from French and Arabic].

———. "Five Poems." Trans. James Kirkup. *Banipal* 17 (Summer 2003): 41 [Translation from French and Arabic].

———. "Two Poems: To Queen Elizabeth—To Luc Besson." Trans. James Kirkup and Samia Akl Boustani. *Banipal* 19 (2004): 117.

Shugaidil or Shgeidel, Kareem. See Shughaydil, Karim.

Shughaydil, Karim. "At the End of the Last Year before the Birth." Trans. Siham Abd al-Karim. *Gilgamesh: Journal of Iraqi Culture* 1 (2005): 19.

———. Flour Below Zero." Trans. Sadek Mohammed. *IP*: 59–61. Rpt. in *FF*: 44–47.

———. "Wheat Seed." Trans. Sadek Mohammed. *IP*: 62–63. Rpt. in *FF*: 48–49.

Slioa, Vivian (1976–).

———. Clay Tablets." Trans. Sinan Antoon. *Banipal* 18 (Autumn 2003): 45.

———. "Dust." Trans. Sinan Antoon. *Banipal* 18 (Autumn 2003): 45.

Sultani, Fadhil al- (1948–).

———. "Incomplete Anthem." Trans. the author with thanks to Richard McKean. *IPT*: 20–22

———. "Morning." Trans. Raghid Nahhas. *IPT*: 19–20.

———. "That Thing." Trans. Raghid Nahhas. *IPT*: 19.

———. "Three Poems." Trans. the author. *Banipal* 8 (Summer 2000): 58–59. [Ama=ar=gi, Dream, The Statue]. Rpt. in *A Crack in the Wall: New Arab Poetry.* Ed. Margaret Obank and Samuel Shimon. London: Saqi Books, 2001, 254–56.

———. "A Tree." Trans. Saadi Simawe. *IPT*: 18. Rpt. in *Poetry International* 10 (2006): 105.

———. "[Two Poems] My Mother, in Memoriam and RS Thomas." Trans. Saadi Simawe and Melissa Brown. *IPT*: 22–23.

———. "Van Gogh." Trans. Raghid Nahhas. *IPT*: 18–19. Rpt. in *Poetry International* 10 (2006): 106.

———. "What Shall I Do with This War? What Shall I Do with This Tyrant?" Trans. the author. *Banipal* 17 (Summer 2003): 38.

Sundooq, Laith al-. "The Bullet." Trans. Salman Al-Wasiti. *TISP*: 69–70.

———. "Poems on the War." Trans. Salman Al-Wasiti. *TISP*: 70–72.

———. "From the Iraq of Crescents." Trans. Tariq Sahib. *TISP*: 73.

———. "From the Unknown Soldier." Trans. Tariq Sahib. *TISP*: 75–76.

Ta'i, Fawzi al-. "The Fighting Time." Trans. Rayya Hashim. *TISP*: 77–78.

———. "Transformations." Trans. Rayya Hashim. *TISP*: 79–80.

———. "A Night at the Eastern Border." Rayya Hashim *TISP*: 81–82.

Tahmazi, Abd al-Rahman al-. "A Domestic Poem Elegy, The Green Man, An Open Book." Trans. Mohammed Darwish. *Gilgamesh* 2 (1989): 19–20.

Taqah, Shadhil (1926–1974).

———. "And the Man Returned." Trans. Nihad Salem. *Afro-Asian Poetry.* Cairo: 1971, 154–56.

———. "The One-Eyed Liar." *AWW*: 91–92.

———. "Sindbad Songs." *MIP*: 58–61.

Ubaydi, Sayyid Habib al-. "Outcry of Heaven and Echo of Heart." Trans. Leslie Tramontini. *Al-Abhath* 50/51 (2002–2003): 177–78.

———. "They Stayed Up While We Slept." Trans. Leslie Tramontini. *Al-Abhath* 50/51 (2002–2003): 183–84.

Witri, Akram al- (1930–).

———. "I Passed on the Bridge." *MIP*: 75–76.

———. "I Passed on the Bridge." *API*: 90–91.

———. "Sad Baghdad." *MIP*: 76–77.

———. "Sad Baghdad." *API*: 92.

———. "Ungrateful Cord." *API*: 93.

Yaqoob, Jawad. See Ya'qub, Jawad.

Ya'qub, Jawad. "The Only Choice." Trans. Saadi Simawe and Chuck Miller. *IPT*: 237–38.

———. "The Resurrection of Layla al-Attar." Trans. Saadi Simawe and Chuck Miller. *IPT*: 238–39. Rpt. in *The Poker* 2 (Spring 2003): 48.

Yaseen, Rasheed (1929/1931–).

———. "The Ears of Corn." *MIP*: 71.

Yasin, Hadi. "In Vain." *API*: 126.

Yasin, Rashid. See Yaseen, Rasheed.

Yasiri, Isa al- (1942–).

———. "Empty Chairs." Trans. Anne Fairbairn. *Voices: The Quarterly Journal of the National Library of Australia* 3 (2/1993): 24.

———. "For the Sake of Things I Like." Trans. Abdul Wahid Mohammed. *Gilgamesh: Journal of Iraqi Culture* 4 (2006): 59.

———. "Awakening." Trans. Soheil Najm. *Gilgamesh: Journal of Iraqi Culture* 4 (2006): 60.

———. "Tonight We Wake You with Roses." *FH*: 208.

Yassiri, Issa, al-. See al-Yasiri, Isa.al-.

Yousif, Khalid Jabir. "My Blood Flowers in the Flames." Trans. Luna Agoab. *TISP*: 83–85.

———. "The Bells of Noble Departure." Trans. Amal Kadim. *TISP*: 87–88.

———. "Diaries." Trans. Ahmad A. Abdul Karim. *TISP*: 89–92.

Yousuf, Sa'di. See Yusuf, Sa'di.

Youssef, Saadi. See Yusuf, Sa'di.

Yusuf, Faruq (1955–).

———. "Fish." *MIP*: 145.

———. "On Genius." *MIP*: 145.

Yusuf, Sa'di (1934–).

———. "Abdallah Samarah." Trans. Khaled Mattawa [=KM]. *The Chattahoochee Review* (Georgia Perimeter College) 19.2 (Winter 1999): 40 [KM].

———. "Abduction." *API*: 106.

———. "Abu Dahab." *The Chattahoochee Review* 19.2 (Winter 1999): 39–40 [KM].

———. "Algerian Glances." *Modern Poetry in Translation* 13 (1998): 115–16 [KM].

———. "America, America." Trans. Salih J. Altoma. *AlJadid* 21 (Fall 1997): 17.

———. "America, America.". *Banipal* 7 (Spring 2000): 3, 5 [KM]. Rpt. in *A Crack in the Wall: New Arab Poetry*. Ed. Margaret Obank and Samuel Shimon. London: Saqi Books, 2001, 265–69. Rpt. in *LFAN*: 197–201.

———. "April Chatter." *Chelsea* 67 (1999): 90 [KM].

———. "Artillery." *Atlanta Review* 6.2 (Spring–Summer 2000): 6 [KM].

———. "The Attempt." *Literary Review* 44.3 (2001): 542 [KM].

———. "Attention." *SBOF*: 32.

———. "Attention." *Paris Review* 42.154 (Spring 2000): 415.

———. "Blue." *UM*: 121.

———. "Cavafy's House." *Quarterly West* (Autumn–Winter 1998–1999): 64 [KM].

———. "Cavafy's Residence." Trans. Ferial Ghazoul. *Jusoor* 1–2 (1993): 106–07.

———. "The Chalets Bar." *Another Chicago Magazine* 35 (1999): 186 [KM].

———. "Chemical Weapons." Trans. Mohammed B. Alwan. *AlJadid* 4.22 (Winter 1998): 9.

———. "A City of the First Century." Trans. Anton Shammas. *Mediterraneans* (2–3/1991): 78–81 [Arabic and English].

————. "Climbing Plant." *AWW*: 124.

————. "The Collapse of the Two-Rivers Hotel." *Kenyon Review* 22.2 (2000): 45–46 [KM].

————. "Daily Chores" [Poems written during the siege of Beirut, 1982]. *Atlanta Review* 6.2 (Spring 2000): 4–6 [KM].

————. Days of June." *Jusoor* 9/10 (1997/1998): 492–94.

————. "Departure of '82." Trans. Lena Jayyusi and Naomi Shihab Nye. *JM*: 481.

————. "Details." *API*: 102–3.

————. "Drunk." *River Styx* 58/59 (2000–2001): 5 [KM].

————. "Elaboration." *SBL*: 242–43.

————. "Electricity." *UM*: 122–23.

————. "Electricity." *Atlanta Review* 6.2 (Spring–Summer 2000): 5 [KM].

————. "Elegy." *MIP*: 79–81.

————. "Elsinore, Hamlet's Castle." Trans. Sargon Boulus. *Banipal* 15/16 (Autumn 2002/Spring 2003): 11.

————. "Endings." *Banipal* 2 (June 1998): 6 [KM].

————. "The Ends of the African North." *Banipal* 2 (June 1998): 4–5 [KM].

————. "Enemies." Trans. Khaled Mattawa. *IPT*: 241–45.

————. "Evacuation." *AWW*: 124.

————. "Evening in Late November." *API*: 104–05.

————. "Exhaustion." *UM*: 121.

————. "Exhaustion." *Paris Review* 42: 154 (Spring 2000): 415 [KM].

————. "The Fence." *AWW*: 123.

————. "The Fence." *AGNI* 48 (1998): 203 [KM].

————. "A Fighting Position." *UM*: 121.

————. "First Snow." *Crab Orchard Review* (University of Southern Illinois) 5: 1 (1999): 219 [KM].

————. "Five Crosses." Trans. Khaled Mattawa. *Literature from the "Axis of Evil": Writings from Iran, Iraq, North Korea, and Other Enemy Nations.* Ed. editors of *Words without Borders.* New York; London: The New Press, 2006, 75–76.

————. "The Five Crosses." Trans. Sargon Boulus. *MA* 10 (1/1977): 67.

————. "Flying." *UM*: 121.

————. "For Jamal Jumaa." *Artful Dodge* 28–29 (1995): 12 [KM].

————. "The Forests" *River City* (University of Memphis) 19: 2 (1999): 112 [KM].

————. "Freedom."*SBOF*: 87 [KM].

————. "A Friendship." *Jusoor* 9/10 (1997/1998): 478–79 [KM].

———. "The Gardener." *Third Coast* (Fall 1999): 31 [KM].

———. "Good Morning, Fakhani." Trans. Khaled Mattawa. *IPT*: 240. Rpt. in *Poetry International* 10 (2006): 158.

———. "Guns." *UM*: 123.

———. "Hamlet's Balcony." Trans. Sargon Boulus. *Banipal* 15/16 (Autumn 2002/Spring 2003): 11.

———. "Hammond's Death." *The Chattahoochee Review* 19.2 (Winter 1999): 39 [KM].

———. "Hamra Night." *UM*: 124.

———. "Hand in Hand." *Chelsea* 67 (1999): 89 [KM].

———. "Happiness." *Iowa Review* 29.2 (1999): 59 [KM].

———. "Hawk Island." *AlJadid* 4.25 (Fall 1998): 12 [KM].

———. "The Hermit." *Banipal* 7 (Spring 2000): 5–7 [KM]. Rpt. in A *Crack in the Wall: New Arab Poetry*. Ed. Margaret Obank and Samuel Shimon. London: Saqi Books, 2001, 270–72.

———. "Hoarding." *Modern Poetry in Translation* 13 (1998): 114–15 [KM].

———. "A Hot Evening." Trans. Lena Jayyusi and Naomi Shihab Nye. *JM*: 484.

———. "A House of Mirth." *Banipal* 2 (June 1998): 7 [KM].

———. "How L'Akhdar Ben Youssef Wrote His Last Poem." Trans. Khaled Mattawa. *IPT*: 245–47.

———. "In Search of Khan Ayub in Hayel Maidan, Damascus." *Iraq* (1–15 Nov. 1978): 32.

———. "Insistence." Trans. Saadi A. Simawe. *Arab Studies Quarterly* 19: 4 (1997): 177–78.

———. "In Their Hands." *Jusoor* 9/10 (1997/1998): 497 [KM].

———. "In Those Days." Trans. Saadi A. Simawe. *Arab Studies Quarterly* 19: 4 (1997): 181–82.

———. "In Those Days." *Jusoor* 9/10 (1997/1998): 490–91 [KM].

———. "Ithaca Trees." Trans. Ferial Ghazoul. *Jusoor* 1–2 (1993): 109–31.

———. "Koofa." *Jusoor* 9/10 (1997/1998): 483 [KM].

———. "The Lost Letter." *Chelsea* no. 67 (1999): 91 [KM].

———. "Martyrdom." *AlJadid* no. 25 (Fall 1998): 12 [KM].

———. "Meeting a Man." *Jusoor* 9/10 (1997/1998): 485 [KM].

———. "The Moment." *Third Coast* (Fall 1999): 33 [KM].

———. "The Mouse." *International Quarterly* 1 (3/1994): 133 [KM].

———. "The Murdered Walk at Night." *Jusoor* 9/10 (1997/1998): 489 [KM].

———. "The New Baghdad." *Banipal* 2 (June 1998): 7 [KM].

———. "New Orleans." Trans. by the Author. *Wasafiri* 22.2 (July 2007): 63–64.

———. "Night Fugitive." *Jusoor* 9/10 (1997/1998): 486 [KM].

———. "Night in Hamdan." *International Quarterly* 1 (3/1994): 134. Rpt. in *SBOF*: 43 [KM].

———. "The Night of Hamra." Trans. Ferial Ghazoul. *Arab Studies Quarterly* 8 (1986): 113–14.

———. "Nightmare." Trans. Shafik Megally. *L* (Oct. 1973): 80–81.

———. "Nocturnal." *Crab Orchard Review* 5: 1 (1999): 220 [KM].

———. "Noontime." *Kenyon Review* 22: 2 (2000): 46 [KM].

———. "Nursery Song." Trans. Saadi A. Simawe. *Arab Studies Quarterly* 19: 4 (1997): 175–76.

———. "Occupation 1943." Trans. Khaled Mattawa. *Poetry* 188. 1 (2006): 14–15.

———. "Old Pictures from Kout El-Zain." *Crab Orchard Review* 5: 1 (1999): 222 [KM].

———. "The Oleander Tree." Trans. Ferial Ghazoul. *Arab Studies Quarterly* 8 (1986): 115.

———. "Oleander Tree." *Meridian* (Fall 2000): 105 [KM].

———. "On L'Akhdar Again." *Meridian* (Fall 2000): 102–4 [KM].

———. "On the Red Sea." *Willow Springs* 36 (June 1995): 104 [KM].

———. "The Other Person." *The Chattahoochee Review* 19.2 (Winter 1999): 41 [KM].

———. "A Personal Song." Trans. Sinan Antoon. *Al-Ahram Weekly Online* 17–23 Apr. 2003.

———. "The Piano of Condoleezza Rice." Trans. Salaam Yousif and Brenda Hillman. *Poetry International* 10 (2006): 157.

———. "Poetry." Trans. Khaled Mattawa. *IPT*: 248.

———. "The Porcupine." *AGNI* 48 (1998): 202 [KM].

———. "Position." *Mississippi Review* 28.3 (Spring 2000): 94 [KM].

———. "A Pungent Evening." *Quarterly West* (Autumn–Winter 1989–1999): 65 [KM].

———. "Radio." *Atlanta Review* 6.2 (Spring–Summer 2000): 5 [KM].

———. "A Raid." *Atlanta Review* 6.2 (Spring–Summer 2000): 4 [KM].

———. "That Rainy Day." Trans. the author. *Banipal* 12 (Autumn 2001): 15. Rpt. in *Index on Censorship* 31.3 (2002) 128–29. Rpt. in Peter Money and Saadi Yousef. *Today Minutes Only: That Rainy Day.* Brownsville, VT: Goates and Compass, 2004 [Unpaginated in an edition of 300].

———. "Rainy October Afternoon." *Jusoor* 9/10 (1997/1998): 481 [KM].

———. "Rations." *Atlanta Review* 6.2 (Spring–Summer 2000): 6 [KM].

———. "Reception." *Banipal* 7 (Spring 2000): 8 [KM]. Rpt. in *A Crack in the Wall: New Arab Poetry*. Ed. Margaret Obank and Samuel Shimon. London: Saqi Books, 2001, 264–65.

———. "Resurrection." *UM*: 123.

———. "The River." *The Chattahoochee Review* 19.2 (Winter 1999): 42–43 [KM].

———. "The Road." *Iowa Review* 29.2 (1999): 58 [KM].

———. A Room." *UM*: 122.

———. "A Room." *Atlanta Review* 6.2 (Spring–Summer 2000): 4 [KM].

———. "A Secret," *The Chattahoochee Review* 19.2 (Winter 1999): 37 [KM].

———. "Selected Poems." *Jusoor* 9/10 (1997/1998): 478–94 [Includes: Days of June; A Friendship; In Their Hands; In Those Days; Koofa; The Murdered Walk at Night; Meeting a Man; Night Fugitive; 1989; Rainy October Afternoon; To Socialism; Tower; and Trying to Flee] [KM].

———. "Selected Poems." Trans. Raghid Nahhas. *Kalimat* 23 (Mar. 2006): 26.

———. "Sentiment." Trans. Lena Jayyusi and Naomi Shihab Nye. *JM*: 481–82.

———. "Shatt al-Arab." *MIP*: 78–79.

———. "Six Poems." *AWW*: 122–123 [1–6, no titles].

———. "Six Poems." *The Chattahoochee Review* (Georgia Perimeter College) 19: 2 (1999): 35–45. [Includes: The Other Person, The River, A Secret, Spanish Plaza, Three Stories from Kuwait, and Whims] [KM].

———. "Snow." Trans. Ferial Ghazoul. *Arab Studies Quarterly* 8 (1986): 115.

———. "Snow May Fall." *River Styx* 58/59 (2000–2001): 57–60 [KM].

———. "The Solitary One Awakens." *Another Chicago Magazine* 35 (1999): 187 [KM].

———. "Solitude." *Banipal* 2 (June 1998): 7 [KM].

———. "Solos on the Oud." Trans. Khaled Mattawa. *Paintbrush* 28 (2001–2002): 214–15; Al-*Ahram Weekly Online*, 17–29 Apr. 2003. See also Sa'di's *Without an Alphabet, Without a Face* listed below: 38–39.

———. "Spanish Plaza." *The Chattahoochee Review* 19.2 (Winter 1999): 44–45 [KM].

———. "The Spring." *Indiana Review* 22.1 (2000): 57–60 [KM].

———. "Spring Showers." Trans. the author. *Banipal* 17 (Summer 2003): 31.

———. "A State of Fever." Trans. Lena Jayyusi and Naomi S. Nye. *JM*: 484.

————. "A Stone." Trans. Sargon Boulus. *MA* 10 (1/1977): 68. Rpt. in *MA*: 12–13 (1980–81): 31.

————. "To Socialism." *Jusoor* 9/10 (1997/1998): 488 [KM].

————. "Three Dispositions Regarding One Woman." Trans. Sargon Boulus and Naomi Shihab Nye. *JM*: 482–83.

————. "Three Bridges." Trans. Khaled Mattawa. *IPT*: 254–55.

————. "Three Stories from Kuwait." *The Chattahoochee Review* 19.2 (Winter 1999): 39–40 [KM].

————. "The Tormented of Heaven" Trans. Salih J. Altoma. *Blackmail Press* Issue 12 (2005). http://nzpoetsonline.homestead.com/index12 .htm [On Abu Ghraib's Episode]. Rpt. in Across *Borders: An International Literary Journal* Premiere Issue (2005): 52.

————. "Tower." *Jusoor* 9/10 (1997/1998): 480 [KM].

————. "The Trees of Ithaca." Trans. Khaled Mattawa. *IPT*: 248–54.

————. "Trying to Flee." *Jusoor* 9/10 (1997/1998): 484 [KM].

————. "A Vision." Trans. *AlJadid* 25 (Fall 1998): 12 [KM].

————. "A Vision." Trans. Salih J. Altoma. *Free Verse: A Journal of Contemporary Poetry and Poetics* [A bi-annual electronic journal] (Winter 2002). Rpt. in *World Literature Today* 77.3 (Oct.–Dec. 2003): 41.

————. "A Vision." *Los Angeles Times*, 12 Jan. 2003.

————. "Water." *UM*: 123.

————. "Where." *Atlanta Review* 6.2 (Spring–Summer 2000): 5 [KM].

————. "Whims." *The Chattahoochee Review* 19.2 (Winter 1999): 38 [KM].

————. "The Whole of Night." Trans. Sargon Boulus. *MA* 10 (1/1977): 68.

————. "Winds." *Paris Review* 42.154 (Spring 2000): 416 [KM].

————. *Without an Alphabet, Without a Face: Selected Poems by Saadi Youssef.* Trans. Khaled Mattawa. Saint Paul, Minnesota: Graywolf Press, 2002 [Includes all the poems in the entries marked by KM in addition to the following: Abduction, About That Lizard, About This Night, L'Akhdar Ben Youssef and His Concerns, The Attempt, Autumn, Chemical Weapon, A Cloud, The Cold, Crawling Plant, From "Daily Chores," Drowsiness, A Fever, The Flags, Immersion, Inheritance, The Kurdish Quarter, Lines, Mariam Comes, A Moment, A Naïve Song to a Wounded Smuggler, 989, The Orchard, Scene, Snow May Fall, Solos on the Oud, Sparrows, Summer, Thank You Imru ul-Qais, Trying to Flee, The Village, and The Visit].

————. "A Woman." Trans. Lena Jayyusi and Naomi Shihab Nye. *JM*: 483–84.

———. "A Woman." Trans. the author. *Banipal* 7 (Spring 2000): 8 [A slightly different version from Jayyusi's and Nye's translation]. Rpt. in *A Crack in the Wall: New Arab Poetry.* Ed. Margaret Obank and Samuel Shimon. London: Saqi Books, 2001, 272.

———. "The Woods." Trans. Lena Jayyusi and Naomi Shihab Nye. *JM*: 480–81.

Zahawi, Jamil Sidqi al- (1863–1936).

———. "Both Strangers." Trans. Issa Boullata and Christopher Middleton. *JM*: 109.

———. "Go Unveiled." [Extract] Trans. Sadok Masliyah. *Middle Eastern Studies* 32: 3 (1996): 168. [See Masliyah's article "Zahawi: A Muslim Pioneer of Women's Liberation." *Ibid.* 161–71].

———. "Heralds of Change." *API*: 8–9.

———. "In Iraq." *API*: 5.

———. "The Sky of Iraq." Trans. Najib Ullah. In *Islamic Literature.* New York: Washington Square Press, 1963, 190–91.

———. "Song of the Drowned." *API*: 6–7.

———. "To My Wife." Trans. Najib Ullah. In *Islamic Literature.* New York: Washington Square Press, 1963, 190.

———. "Untitled." Trans. John A. Haywood in his *Modern Arabic Literature: 1800–1970.* London: Lund Humphries, 1971, 108–09.

Zaidan, Ibrahim. "The Graveyard." Trans. Selwa Adnan. *TISP*: 93–96.

———. "The Prophet: That Splendid One." Trans. Rafah Abdul Ilah. *TISP*: 97–98.

———. "The Star." Trans. Yusra Abdul Qadir. *TISP*: 99.

Zair, Rasmiah. See Zayir, Rasmiyyah.

Zayir, Rasmiyyah (1955/56–).

———. "Short Poems. Window, Morning, Dawn, The Fog, Flower, My Mother, Rain." Trans. Salaam Yousif and Brenda Hillman. *Poetry International* 10 (2006): 159–50.

———. "Strange and Lonely Child Sitting in a Dark Garden, This Is My Heart." Trans. Soheil Najm. *IP*: 76–77. Rpt. in *FF*: 74–75.

A

Iraqi Writers and Poets in Western Countries

[This list includes only writers whose works have appeared in English translation]

Abd al-Amir, Ali (USA)
Abd Allah, Najat (New Zealand)
Abd al-Ilah. Lu'ay (UK)
Abd al-Jabbar, Adil (UK/Lebanon)
Abd al-Razzaq, Wafa' (UK)
Abed, Kareem (UK)
Ahmad, Ibrahim (Sweden)
Alfaker, Muniam (Denmark)
Amarah, Lami'ah Abbas (USA)
Anbari, Shakir (Denmark)
Antoon, Sinan (USA)
Asadi, Salam (USA)
Ataymish, Abd al-Latif (UK)
Ayyub, Dhu'l-Nun (Austria)
Azzawi, Fadhil (Germany)
Baghdadi, Tajia (UK)
Bazzaz, Ali (Netherlands)
Blasim, Hassan (Finland)
Boulus, Sargon (USA/Germany)
Dawway, Salam (Australia)
Faiq, Salah (UK/Philippines)
Farman, Gha'ib Tu'mah (Russia)

Furat, Basim (New Zealand/Japan)
Ghali, Duna (Denmark)
Ghassani, Anwar (Costa Rica)
Harbi, Tariq (Norway)
Hariri, Ibrahim (Canada)
Hasan, Salah (Netherlands)
Haydar, Jalil (Sweden)
Haydari, Buland (UK)
Hillawi, Janan Jassim (Sweden)
Hilli, Khalid (Australia)
Hussin, Jabbar Yassin (France)
Iqabi, Hamid (Denmark)
Isknader, Gareeb (UK)
Jaafar, Abid (UK)
Jabbar, Emad (New Zealand)
Jabir, Zaki (USA)
Jabr, Fadel K. (USA)
El-Janabi, A. K. (France)
Janabi, Hatif (Poland)
Janabi, Nabil (UK)
Jasim, Saad (Netherlands)
Jaza'iri, Zuhayr (Uk/Iraq)
Jihad, Kadhim (France)
Jizani, Zahir (USA)
Jubouri, Amal (Germany)
Jumá, Jamal (Denmark)
Kabi, Haider al- (USA)
Kachachi, Inaam (France)
Kamal Ad-Deen, Adeeb (Australia)
Karim, Fawzi (UK/ Iraq)
Kasid, Abd al-Karim (UK)
Khatib, Burhan (Sweden)
Khattab, Sabah (Australia)
Lu'aibi, Shakir (Switzerland/Tunisia)
Maaly, Khalid (Germany)
Majedi, Abdul Rahman (Netherlands)
Majidi, Khaz 'al (Netherlands)

Mamdouh, Alia (France)
Mana [al-Mani'], Samira (UK)
Mardan, Nasrat (Austria)
Matar, Salim (Switzerland)
Mikhail, Dunya (USA)
Mirza, Fu'ad (USA)
Mozany, Hussain (Germany)
Muhammad, Hayat Jasim (USA)
Mur'ibi, Basim (Sweden)
Mustafa, Jamal (Denmark)
Mustafa, Najm (Germany)
Mutashahr, Ra'd (UL/UAE)
Nasir, Awad (UK)
Nawwab, Muzaffar (UK/Syria)
Niyazi, Salah (UK)
Qazwini, Iqbal (Germany)
Ramli, Muhsin (Spain)
Rawi, Mouayed (Germany)
Rubay 'I, Sharif (UK)
Sa'dun, Abd al-Hadi (Spain)
Sabti, Kamal (Netherlands)
Saeed, Mahmoud (USA)
Sakkar, Muhammad Sa'id (France)
Salih, Salimah (Germany)
Samawi, Aziz (UK)
Samawi, Shakir (Sweden)
Samawi, Yahya (Australia)
Sarhan, Salam (UK)
Sawad, Muwaffaq (Netherlands)
Sayigh, Adnan (Sweden/UK)
Sayigh, Sadiq (UK)
Shafiq, Hashim (UK)
Shilah, Ali (Switzerland)
Shimon, Samuel (UK)
Simawe, Saadi (USA)
Slioa, Vivian (UK)
Sultani, Fadhil (UK)

Wali, Najem (Germany)
Yasiri, Isa (Canada)
Yaseen, Rasheed (USA)
Yusuf, Faruq (Sweden)
Yusuf, Sa'di (UK)
Zangana, Haifa (UK)

B

Women Writers Listed under Studies, Autobiographical Essays, Drama, Fiction, and Poetry

STUDIES

Abulaali, Wafa [Wafa A. Zeanal' Abidin]
Amarah, Lami'ah Abbas
Amir, Daisy al-
Dulaymi, Lutfiyah al-
Ghazoul, Ferial J.
Juburi, Amal al-
Kachachi, Inaam
Khedairi, Betool
Mala'ikah, Nazik al-
Mamdouh, Alia
Muhsin, Fatimah
Mana, Samira al-
Nasiri, Buthaynah al-
Radi, Nuha al-
Riverbend
Zangana, Haifa

AUTOBIOGRAPHICAL ESSAYS

Amarah, Lami 'ah
Amir, Daisy al-
Mal'ikah, Nazik al-
Mana (=Mani'), Samira al-

DRAMA

Mana (=Mani'), Samira al-

FICTION

Abdallah, Ibtisam
Amir, Daisy al-
Dulaymi, Lutifyah al-
Hadi, Maysalun
Juburi, Irada
Kachachi, Inaam
Khedairi, Betool
Mala'ikah, Nazik al-
Mamdouh, Alia
Mana, Samira al-
Muzaffar, May
Nasiri, Buthaynah al-
Qazwini, Iqbal
Sadr, Aminah Haydar al-
Salih, Salimah
Talib, Aliya
Zangana, Haifa

POETRY

Abd Allah, Najat
Abd al-Razzaq, Wafa'
Amarah, Lami'ah Abbas
Baghdadi, Tajia al-
Bustani, Bushra al-
Dixon, Zuhur
Hasan, Faliha
Jabbar, Siham
Juburi, Amal al-

Khazraji, Atika
Kubba, Rim Qays
Mala'ikah, Nazik al-
Mikhail, Dunya
Musawi, Sajidah
Muzaffar, May
Nuri, Kulalah
Riyad, Daliya
Shalchi, Nadia al-
Zayir, Rasmiyyah

For more information on Iraqi women writers see *Arab Women Writers: A Critical Reference Guide 1873–1999*. Ed. Radwa Ashour, Ferial Ghazoul, and Hasna Reda-Mekdashi. Trans. Mandy McClure. Cairo: The American University in Cairo Press, 2008. See pp. 333–520. This guide provides bio-bibliographical notes for Iraqi women writers including brief entries on more than 70 Iraqi women who have published books (in Arabic) representing different genres: poetry, fiction, drama, memoirs, and biographies.

Author Index

Abbadi, Ghazi al-, 43
Abbas, Adnan, 1
Abbas, Lu'ay Hamza, 43
Abd al-Amir, Ali, 66, 131
Abd al-Amir, Khudayyir, 43–44
Abd al-Aziz, Talib, 66
Abd al-Halim, M. A. S., 1
Abd al-Hurr, Mundhir, 66
Abd al-Husayn, Ahmad, 66
Abd al-Ilah, Lu'ay, 44, 131
Abd al-Jabbar, Adil, 44, 131
Abd Allah, Adil, 66
Abdallah, Ibtisam, 43, 136
Abd Allah, Najat, 66, 131, 136
Abd al-Latif, Husayn, 66
Abd al-Latif, Nu'man Thabit, 67
Abd al-Latif, Salah, 44
Abd al-Majid, Muhammad, 44
Abd al-Qadir, Abd al-Ilah, 44
Abd al-Qadir, Ra'd, 67
Abd al-Razzaq, Abd al-Ilah, 44
Abd al-Razzaq, Wafa', 67, 131, 136
Abd al-Wahhab, Mahmud, 44
Abd al-Wahid, Abd al-Razzaq, 63,
    67
Abdel Wahab, Mahmoud. *See* Abd
    al-Wahhab, Mahmud
Abd, Karim. *See* Abed, Kareem

Abdoullatif, Hussien. *See* Abd al-
    Latif, Husayn
Abdrabou, Abdelrahman, 1
Abdul-ameer, Ali. *See* Abd al-Amir,
    Ali
Abdul-Hur, Munthir. *See* Abd al-
    Hurr, Mundhir
Abdulhussein, Ahmed. *See* Abd al-
    Husayn, Ahmad
Abdulilah, Luay. *See* Abd al-Ilah,
    Lu'ay
Abdulqadir, Ra'ad. *See* Abd al-
    Qadir, Ra'd
Abdul Rahman, Kamal, 68
Abdul Razak, Wafaa. *See* Abd al-
    Razzaq, Wafa'
Abdul Wahhab, Mahmood. *See* Abd
    al-Wahhab, Mahmud
Abed al-Razzaq, Wafaa. *See* Abd al-
    Razzaq, Wafa'
Abed, Kareem, 44, 68, 131
Abu Haidar, Farida, 1
Abu Haidar, Jareer, 1
Abulaali, Wafa, 1, 135
Addam, Majid, 68
Ahmad, Ibrahim, 44, 131
Ahmady, Kazim.al-, 44
Ajami, Fouad, 1

Yaseen, Rasheed, 122, 134
Yasin, Faraj, 60
Yasin, Hadi, 122
Yasin, Najman, 60
Yasin, Rashid. *See* Yaseen, Rasheed
Yasiri, Isa al-, 122, 134
Yassiri, Issa, al-. *See* Yasiri, Isa al-
Yazici, Huseyin, 30
Yousif, Khalid Jabir, 123
Yousif, Salaam, 30
Youssef, Saadi. *See* Yusuf, Sa'di
Yousuf, Sa'di. *See* Yusuf, Sa'di

Yusuf, Faruq, 123, 134
Yusuf, Sa'di, iv, 30–31, 37, 60, 66,
    123–29, 134

Zahawi, Jamil Sidqi al-, 129
Zaidan, Ibrahim, 129
Zair, Rasmiah. *See* Zayir, Rasmiyyah
Zangana, Haifa, 31, 43, 60–61, 134,
    135, 136
Zayir, Rasmiyyah, 129, 137
Zeidan, Joseph T., 31
Zubaida, Sami, 31

Translator Index

Abbas, A. M. al-, 64, 82
Abd al-Jabbar, Adil, 43
Abdulahad, Noel, 74, 77, 81, 90, 99, 108, 110
Abdulhadi, Nibras, 28
Abid, Adil Salih, 108
Abu Haidar, Farida, 40, 45, 53, 59, 60
Abulaali, Wafaa, 1, 81
Abulahad, Noel, 117
Adhami, Mundher al-, 61
Adnan, Selwa, 129
Aghajan, Hrant, 43
Agoab, Luna, 123
Ahmed, Shihab, 80, 83
Algar, H., 75, 105, 115, 116, 117
Ali, Batool, 50
Ali, M. T., 73
Ali, Su'ad, 25, 49
Allam, Thoraya Mahdi, 90
Alland, Sonia, 84
Altoma, Salih J., 67, 69, 70, 71, 74, 76, 77, 78, 85, 86, 87, 88, 89, 90, 94, 97, 102, 103, 110, 112, 120, 123, 128
Alwan, M. Bakir, 63, 75, 78, 85, 86, 87, 88, 123
Amara, Lamea Abbas, 69

Amin, Abd al-Hakim, 86
Antoon, Sinan, 3, 70, 85, 98, 107, 112, 121, 126
Assady, Abdul Settar al-, 81, 82, 84, 85, 91, 97, 102, 104, 106, 111
Assaf, Muhieddein, 64, 65
Atallah, Yania S., 43, 47, 51, 52, 56
Atalla, Seema, 94
Azeriah, Ali, 50
Azma, Nazeer el-, 118
Azouqa, Aida, 74, 75
Azzawi, F. al-, 72

Badawi, M. M., 73, 76, 87, 99, 117
Bahjat, Sura, 108
Bamia, Aida, 41, 49
Barakat, Ibtisam S., 100, 101, 118
Bardenstein, Carol, 106
Basset, Nina Larissa, 94, 95
Batchachi, Maysoon, 21
Beard, Michael, 64, 79, 107, 115, 117
Beckman, Joshua, 48
Bellem, Alex, 112
Bennani, Ben, 87, 101, 115, 116, 117
Bennani, B. M., 100
Bezirgan, Basima, 69, 79, 100, 102, 104, 115, 118

About the Author

Salih J. Altoma is professor emeritus of Arabic and Comparative Literature at Indiana University since 1964. He has served as director of the Middle Eastern Studies Program (1986–1991) and chair of Near Eastern Languages and Cultures Department (1985–1991). His publications include *The Problem of Diglossia in Arabic: A Comparative Study of Classical and Iraqi Arabic* (Harvard, 1969), *Modern Arabic Literature: A Bibliography of Articles, Books, Dissertations, and Translation in English* (Indiana University Asian Studies Research Institute, 1975), *Modern Arabic Poetry in English Translation: A Bibliography* (Tangier: King Fahd School of Translation, 1993), and *Modern Arabic Literature in Translation: A Companion* (London: Saqi, 2005). He served as guest editor of the 2000 volume of *The Yearbook of Comparative and General Literature*, which was dedicated to *Arabic-Western Literary Relations*. Altoma is a recipient of several fellowships including Harvard Research Fellowship, 1963–1964, Indiana University Ford International Program Fellowship, 1967–1968, National Endowment for the Humanities, 1971–1972, American Research Center in Egypt Fellowship, 1972, and Fulbright Fellowship, Fall, 1991 and Summer, 1992. In addition to his works in English, Altoma has published extensively in Arabic.

Breinigsville, PA USA
05 October 2010
246690BV00002B/4/P